The MERCURY
Diaries

A memoir of
healing and hope

Daniel Forsyth

Capsule Press, Beacon, NY

The information provided in this book is intended solely to educate, and should not be taken as medical advice. Please consult a trained medical professional if you have any questions about your health.

Published by Capsule Press, Beacon, NY
www.capsulepress.com

ISBN: 9780983781813

The MERCURY
Diaries

All truth passes through three stages. First, it is ridiculed. Second, it is violently opposed. Third it is accepted as being self-evident.

Arthur Schopenhauer. Philosopher (1788-1860)

CONTENTS

Part I: My Story

1. To mercury hell and back again   3
2. In the beginning   5
3. Jack and the Beanstalk   11
4. May the force be with you   13
5. Giving it all up. Hallelujah!   16
6. Ignorance sure hurts like hell   18
7. Hello, Sunshine   20
8. Universal Reactor   22
9. You may feel a little prick   23
10. Salad, salad, salad   27
11. Nail in the coffin of my ex-life   33
12. The missing link   36
13. "Insane in the membrane"   39
14. Nine months of hell   41
15. Chelation starts here   44
16. Star Wars Episode IV: A New Hope   57
17. The Great Raw Cat Food Experiment and Me   60
18. Power Rangers   61
19. That feeling of healing   62
20. A New Life   64
21. Wrong?   65
22. Aliens   67
23. Juicy   69
24. The lady with the pearl necklace   71
25. Auto-printout BS   78
26. Steak and kidney pie   85
27. No sex please, we're British   89

28. Muggles & I wish I had cancer   90

29. Village idiot   92

30. Oil   94

31. What the funk is that black gunk?   99

32. The Holy Grail   101

33. Understanding   108

34. First things first   109

35. Aliens II   112

36. "Life in all its fullness is mother nature obeyed."   115

37. Sleeping on toxic slag   119

38. Me, myself and my hormones   124

39. Doctors for the last and final time   127

40. Incurable, my arse!   131

41. White Gold   133

42. Ace, Ace baby!   135

43. Crushed up thyroid glands   140

44. "Wax on, wax off. "   148

45. Rub-A-Dub-Dub   150

46. Sole bath fantastic   154

47. Warm and fuzzy   155

48. Lung Cleanse, June 2008: I didn't expect that!   156

49. No Dumping Please   159

50. Who's the Daddy!   160

51. Trouble at t'mill after introducing ALA   167

52. Armour   169

53. Armour II   177

54. "Well, here's another fine mess..."   184

55. Cold Turkey   189

56. The Curious Incident of the Dog...   194

57. The Big Wake-up Call   201

58. "I have one speed: Go."   205

Part II: What I Learned on my Travels

59. Voodoo People   227
60. Good plan, Batman   232
61. If the herbs are so good, why do I have to keep taking them? 236
62. To supplement or not to supplement, that is the question   239
63. Meet the Fockers   243
64. Breakfast at Sunshine's   247
65. Raw Milk   250
66. "There's no such thing as a free lunch."   253
67. Choose life   262
68. Deprived? Cheated?   264
69. Why did I get so sick?   269
70. "The path of the righteous man..."   273
71. "Doctor, doctor..."   276
72. Textbook mercury poisoning   280
73. To friends and relations   284
74. Live for today, chelate for tomorrow   286
75. So long and thanks for all the fish   289

Part III: Some final bits'n'bobs

76. Send cash now!   295
77. Books that sparkled and inspired me   298
78. Mercury Attack Check-List   306
79. Summary of what I did   307
80. About this book   308
81. Thanks   312
Epilogue: "It's A Long Way To The Top"   315

Part I
My Story

1. To mercury hell and back again

No way in a million years could I have believed that I would get poisoned by mercury and that my once-beautiful life would be flushed away in a torrent of ill-health. In this day and age it's pretty far-fetched to think normal people get mercury poisoned and that it's such a big deal. It's difficult to comprehend that modern medical doctors so rarely understand or believe, that diagnosing it is so tricky and that even if they do, they are more likely to do harm than to help.

Not many people get better from mercury poisoning. I am very much in the minority to have recovered. The problems it causes are numerous and ghastly, made all the more difficult by our western medical profession that is blind to it.

Five years ago, back in 2007, all hell broke loose, I was wildly ill and my health and my life collapsed due to mercury that leaked out of my amalgam fillings.

I was just a typical London businessman. I wore a pinstripe suit to work every day for the first ten years of my career. The next twelve years have been a bit more relaxed and I wear smart casual these days. I spent my days on the phone negotiating deals. I did a lot of lunches, dinners and lundinnies. I worked long hours, but no longer than anyone else. I was just getting on with life like everyone else. Just another city bloke. I knew nothing about medical matters.

I had a good life before all this started. First and foremost a fabulous wife, we have been happily together 24 years now, since we were 18. I also had cool friends, a great family and a steady well-paid job that I was good at and loved. I was into all the normal things that normal people are into: football, cricket, rugby, good food, good company, drinking, cars, PlayStations and holidaying anywhere hot. I worked hard and played hard too.

Weekdays were spent working at my desk on the trading floor. By night I could be found unwinding down the pub with the lads. Friday nights became eagerly awaited for the trip to a club for hours of dancing to the wildest and loudest music in town, staggering home exhausted and bleary-eyed at sunrise.

I was a typical white-collar party animal, out all the time, drinking, smoking, partying, clubbing; everything to excess and generally having the time of my life. I am a product of Maggie Thatcher's 1980s chemical generation of young dog-eat-dog city blokes living it up large, totally wrapped up in my own little world of work and play. Life was good and I made sure I enjoyed myself.

My full-on exciting lifestyle came with a blatant disregard for my health. I was never that healthy in the first place; I always seemed to have a cold and was overly skinny as a kid. Slowly but surely, my health was slipping and sliding downwards. Once the hectic lifestyle started to bite, I toned things down a little, worked out down the gym, changed my diet a little, but nothing stopped the health-crash that came.

Anyway, I did get better, I kept my job, my life, my family, my friends, and today I lead a normal life again, but it was an uphill struggle and for a long time it looked like I was never going to make it. I changed too; I went from an ignorant party-animal, to an educated ex-party-animal.

This is my story of what happened to me and how I managed to get back to the land of the living. It's written in chronological order; I didn't know anything in the beginning. As I struggled along I figured stuff out, discovered what meant what. I explain things when I understood them, which is not necessarily when they happened.

Everything in here happened to me and I didn't discover anything new. Everything I did, someone else discovered before me, I just read about it somewhere, either in a book or online, and then tried it myself. If you want to check out and verify the things I did, to read, review and research an idea, just Google it or read some of the books I recommend; the knowledge is not far away.

My story is written for regular people who are sick and want to get better. I was just a normal bloke whose life was almost wasted by a poison.

I use friendly words like 'stuff' and 'gunk' and 'funk' because big long medical words mean nothing to me. This is just the story of how I got better; if you want a reference book full of long incomprehensible words, there are many out there to satisfy those needs.

2. In the beginning

Back in the 1990s when I was in my twenties, I was down the pub daily. I had a regular hangover and was smoking 40 a day. After a while something had to give, so I decided to give up smoking. I used the eat-as-much-junk-food-sugar-and-cakes-and-heavy-drinking-method to give up. Even after everything else that's happened, after everything that you will read about in here, giving up smoking remains the most difficult thing I have ever done in my life. However this is not the story of how I gave up smoking, so I will spare you the details, but it involved a lot of gritted teeth and mental agony.

I succeeded eventually after three torturous years but ballooned in weight to a whopping 202 pounds (92kg) which mostly sat on my beer belly. At the tender age of 26 my waist-line looked like Coco the Clown's and my teeth rotted from all the beer and junk food I'd scoffed while I was giving up smoking.

In early 1995, when I was 26 years old, I went to the dentist to be told my teeth were full of holes.

"What do you want son, white or metal?"

"What's the difference?"

"White costs money and you need eight. Silvers are free, courtesy of Her Majesty's Government."

"Great, I'll have the free metal fillings please."

The dentist gave me four new fillings and four others he drilled out and renewed. I now had eight amalgam fillings.

This was not a stand-out moment in life. This was just another day. I didn't think anything of it, and why would I? Why would I think this almost random decision to have metal fillings rather than white would have such a dramatic effect on my life? I didn't know what I'd done, and I didn't think about it for another 11 years.

A couple of months later I went on my annual ski holiday and at the top of the mountain, on a black run, for no apparent reason, my back gave out and that was the end of that holiday and any future skiing holidays.

Up until that point in life my spine had been just like any other city boy's back, it ached from time to time, but was mostly fine. I spent an agonising week unable to move, lying in bed.

My back healed up just enough so that I could walk about. But from then onwards I had a very painful and very weak back. It got progressively worse over the years with repeated injuries from the most innocent of challenges. I have put my back out brushing my teeth, getting out of the bath, getting out of bed, getting in the car and out of the car, in the gym, rowing, walking, running, swimming, biking, hiking, lifting, shagging and even flying my kite.

My back was so weak and feeble I had to be oh so careful; it was like walking on eggshells all the time. Eleven years later by the end of 2007 (when I was 37) my back and neck hurt 24 hours a day. I could not carry anything heavy, no suitcases, no shopping bags. I could not lift my young daughter whatsoever, I could not put her in the car, or highchair, or her cot, nor could I even bend down to cuddle her. Sitting on the train I could not read a book or newspaper as the neck pain would be staggering from such a simple taken-for-granted activity. I had to sit on the train to the office and focus solely on my posture for the whole journey. Standing on the train was completely out of the question.

All the muscles in my back, neck and legs were stiff as boards. I had massages once a week for years to keep the pain down and was on loads of painkillers.

"Wow, feels like you have bags of rocks in your shoulders," one osteopath memorably said. My muscles seemed unable to unwind or relax.

The massages hurt like crazy, but they did give good, limited relief in the short term. I mean, they helped, but I still had to go back again the next week.

My digestion got progressively worse and worse over the years and I had to stop drinking booze completely in my early thirties. I was teetotal for two years, and the four years before that, my alcohol consumption was sporadic due to the nasty after-effects that lasted weeks from a single sip of beer.

I had heartburn, bloating and digestive pains 24 hours a day for years. After each meal I had to go for a 20-minute walk otherwise the heartburn would be excruciating for two to four days thereafter, no matter what I did. Rain or shine I had to go for those walks, after breakfast, lunch and dinner, wandering around in the pissing rain feeling sorry for myself. Why was this happening, what was wrong, why me, how could I get better, why could no one help? Why, why, why?

• • •

Everyone knows if you have a health problem you should get some exercise. I tried working out in the gym, tried rowing, running, swimming and weight training but I always got injured no matter how careful I was. I was focused too. I don't do things by half measures, I worked out five to seven times a week, every week.

I was fit from all the exercise I did, but I somehow still got constantly injured. I would row for 30 minutes, everything would be cool as a cucumber, and as I stood up to get off the machine, my neck would crick and I'd be off games for a couple of weeks. Why? No idea, but it happened monthly and towards the end, weekly. Eventually, after five years the gym was out of bounds totally as I kept getting hurt and recovery took longer and longer.

Much to my amazement (I'm a broker in the city for heaven's sake!) I discovered Ashtanga Yoga, also called Power Yoga, and that was marvellous. It's the kind of yoga that's full-on and sweaty, a real workout. I loved it and it stopped some of the pain, loosened me up and kept me nice 'n' supple.

But even so, I continued to get constantly injured. For three years I worked out five to seven times a week in the morning before work. I would get up at 5am and practice for an hour and a half almost every day and I continued to get injured repeatedly, mostly back and neck muscles and it was usually from the most innocent of mistakes or slips.

Each injury forced me to stop practicing for a week or two. During this downtime it felt like my body was seizing up, like an engine run out of oil. After three years, my daily yoga practice was impossible. I could no longer do any postures because my back was so weak.

Yoga is supposed to make you agile, strong, flexible and fit. Practised with the frequency that I was practising, it should have purified my body and mind. However it was as if I was driving with the handbrake on. I was on a downwards spiral. Nothing I did seemed to help. Something was badly wrong and I had no idea why. I thought exercise would make me better, especially exercise five to seven times per week, but it didn't, no matter how hard I tried, no matter how hard I wished.

It felt like the bones in my spine were a jigsaw puzzle put back together in the wrong order, any false move and it would knock out of shape. I complained to my doctors periodically and they told me there was nothing neither they, nor I, could do and I was told to "learn to live with the pain".

• • •

With the yoga gone, I was now in chronic and constant pain 24 hours a day, with no way to help myself. I hurt standing up. I hurt sitting down. The muscles in my back and neck were giving me major and chronic grief. I was aggressive, moody, grumpy and miserable most of the time; chronic pain does that.

Losing the ability to practise yoga was when I started to panic. Not being able to do any exercise was a serious problem; it was the only thing that had helped relieve the pain over the years of my dwindling health.

I was now scared for myself. The doctors were no help. Exercise was no longer an option, what now? For a while I just wished my pain away and sat on my hands doing nothing but I was beyond the point of no return now. I hurt all the time. Doing nothing was no longer an option, so what next?

My posture was terrible, I was skinny and had a sunken, caved-in chest, I realised the more I slouched, the more sunken my chest, the worse the digestive troubles got. Seems my ribs were digging into my internal organs causing me massive heartburn and acid indigestion.

I work in an office sitting in a chair all day, hunched over my keyboard. My back hurt all the time and I was intentionally tightening/gripping my back muscles to stop my back and chest from collapsing. This is a very poor postural habit and created even more problems as the muscles in my back and legs were perpetually locked rock-hard tight; after a couple of years I could not un-lock them. I could not sit on a sofa as the relaxed posture caused major digestive troubles and constant back pain.

I didn't understand why, but it was straight-back chairs only. I couldn't sit on the floor, even for a minute otherwise the heartburn would go into overdrive. This was constant, nightmare, 24/7, nagging, perpetual, unfathomable and chronic heartburn that ruined my every moment and was all somehow made worse by my posture.

So I thought I had a problem with posture. (I did, but it was a symptom, not a cause). I discovered the 'Alexander Technique.' This strange system helps to identify and prevent harmful postural habits— of which I had many—that aggravate, stress and cause pain. You learn how to sit, walk, move, breathe, and relax your body and mind. It is a subtle and thoughtful discipline. It works through re-establishing the natural relationship between the head, neck and spine. It is rather like a re-education of how the mind and body interact together.

My first Alexander Technique lesson was pretty wild.

"Hello. I am Fumiaki-san. You take coat and shoes off. You stand there."

"I'm here about my back."

"OK. Stand here please."

"My back really…"

"OK. Stand still here please."

"Do you want me to do anyth…"

"No, no, stand here for minute please. We talk soon."

The Japanese chap walked around me, looking at my body, checking me out from the back, front and side. After a couple minutes of fidgety standing still he stood behind me and just gently made some subtle adjustments to my neck, almost a caress. His touch to my neck was as calm a holding a telephone. Instantly I could feel my stiff body start to relax.

"In a minute, I ask you walk across room. I hold you neck. You relax. You let me hold you neck. I walk with you. OK?"

"OK."

"OK, you walk across room now. I hold neck."

And all the pain from my tight and tensed muscles dropped away. He walked me across the room holding my neck a softly as you'd hold a kitten and it was like magic; all the pain evaporated. Spooky, startling and absolutely fabulous.

He took his hand away, my body slumped and the pain returned, but I'd had a glimpse of what this amazing technique could give me. A pain free life again. I was instantly hooked.

It's an amazing experience to be in pain 24/7 for years and years and for some bloke that you met five minutes ago to pick you up by the neck, oh so gently, and for the pain to disappear. He didn't even ask me any questions about what was wrong. At last, I thought, this is it. This is the answer to all my problems. Hooray!

Practice involved laying down on the floor with a book under my head, with my knees up and feet on the floor. You lie like this for 10 or 20 minutes and think of nothing, just being aware of your surroundings, your body and just letting go.

OK, it's a bit more complicated than that, but, essentially you are lying on the floor, with a book under your head, wishing the pain away. This is one of the most comfortable, stress-free positions your body can take and it is very restful. Muscles relax and go back to their natural pain-free position automatically. Eventually.

I spent the next three years (yes, three years!) furiously practising the Alexander Technique in an effort to get better. I had lessons two or three times per week for those three long years. I practised three times a day on my own too: first thing in the morning, when I got back home from work and just before bed. If I missed a day I would suffer with even more low-grade, persistent, chronic, frustrating, infuriating, degrading, unending pain.

That's a huge effort to make, practising every day, going to the lessons every week, not to mention the money, all of which came out of my pocket. It worked well, but well in a very limited way, it allowed me to continue working and keeping the semblance of having a normal life. Looking back now I can see that spending an hour a day lying down trying to wish my pain away was, well, wishful thinking in the extreme.

Don't get me wrong, I am a much better man for those three years of Alexander Technique. It is awesome when you get good at it. It made me totally body aware, it was great for calming my whizzing mind and my depression was gone. I am much calmer and more controlled now, but this was not the solution to my problems because after three years of daily practice, I was still in chronic and constant pain.

I didn't know any better. I didn't know anything else. I didn't know any other way. My doctors could not help. None of my friends knew what to do, or my work colleagues, or my family. I had never heard of alternative or holistic healthcare. I never thought I could learn about my body, educate myself about what was wrong and then take actions myself.

Today I struggle to understand how or why I never even realised that alternative healthcare even existed. It's amazing that not one person I knew at that time ever suggested alternative health to me. My friends are friends; if they knew how to help, they would have. They didn't know, just like me, ignorant, and ignorance sure hurts like hell.

3. Jack and the Beanstalk

Up to this point I had been seeing the regular doctors in the UK (NHS) and private doctors on my medical insurance (BUPA) and looking back, now that I understand what happened, I can't see any advice, any drugs, anything whatsoever that was even remotely correct for me and my problems. I would say that applies to all the many times I saw a doctor in my whole life, going back to when I was a kid, even.

All their advice was either completely wrong or led me down the garden path—the wrong garden path. Certainly all the drugs I took didn't work, and made things worse. My briefcase was like a drug store, people would come to me in the office when they were hungover because they knew I'd have something for them.

One day, a doctor stuffed a camera down my throat and had a look about (and yes that hurts like hell too). This specialist said I had Gastroesophageal Reflux Disease (GERD) and to take these magic beans every day.

For three months I took the magic beans (proton pump inhibitors) and then I went back to the doctor and said they didn't work very well, so he gave me the most powerful magic beans available for heartburn and digestive troubles.

For three more months I took the super-strong magic beans, and again I went back and said to the doctor that they worked OK-ish in a limited I'm-still-ill-kinda-way and when can I stop taking them? I remember the oily look on his face as he said,

"No, no, no, you don't understand, Sunshine. Some people have to take these pills for the rest of their lives. Some people are just unlucky. You must learn to live with the pain."

He looked at me like I was a fool. Obviously I was a fool for seeing that arsehole. In that little comment, from that dumbarse doctor, something snapped, something said, No more! This is bull$hit, it's just not right that I will have to live in chronic and constant pain for the rest of my life. My digestion and back in chronic pain forever. Oh no! What a 'mare! Why me? What had I done to deserve this? I was no different from the next man in the street. I was only 36 years old for heaven's sake! All my friends had similar lifestyles to me and they were fine. Why me? I couldn't believe I would be like this forever. No way.

From that day forward, I started to take responsibility for my own health. I opened my eyes and looked beyond my immediate world. I ventured into the unknown and tried to find a solution to my diet and back problems. I was forced into a fundamental change of perspective. I switched from trusting the doctors to not trusting them, to doubting their every word. I switched from a sheep to a hunter. Now I had to hunt for solutions.

I always thought we had to trust doctors. It was strange to lose faith in something that I believed in since I was a kid. Until that moment I didn't realise doctors could be wrong.

I had no idea what to do, or how to solve my troubles, but from then on, I made a concerted effort. I no longer just followed orders. I would find someone that could help. I knew there must be a way somehow. Someone must know. Being in pain for the rest of my life was just not an option.

4. May the force be with you

I quietly started asking around if anyone had any experience in chronic back pain and heartburn. Did anyone know anyone with similar problems? My circle of friends and clients seemed as clueless as me, but I kept gently probing, asking as many people as I naturally came in contact with. Did anyone have any ideas?

A client recommended a superb new back specialist to me. This 'wonderful specialist' tied me in knots, then used his considerable weight to crack my bones. Maybe that's fine with other people, but my tired and gaunt skeleton hated every second of bone-crunching pain.

I kept hunting and eventually, Katie my osteopath recommended someone to check out. I travelled out of London and went to see him in his office in the countryside. I told him of my troubles and he looked me up and down like he was inspecting a horse. He opened my mouth and peered in.

"I see you have a mouth full of metal."

"Yeah."

"That's not very good."

"Why not?"

"Those metal fillings are 50 percent mercury. Sometimes they cause health problems."

"Really? Never heard of that." And I thought to myself: what a load of bull$hit.

He reached in and started fiddling with my teeth. He kept pressing down on the fillings and making me push my arm away from my body. Very odd.

"Yup, these bad boys are giving you some serious grief. The big one on the top right is a beast. You might want to consider getting it removed."

"OK, I will think about it."

But honestly I had no intention of thinking about it. Sounded mental and I quickly changed the subject.

"Do you have any ideas what to do about my digestion? I am struggling badly here. I have chronic 24/7 hassles and it's making my life hell."

"Have you ever changed your diet?"

"Yeah sure, I had to give up booze because it's so bad!"

He gave me a really funny look. A look of disbelief. He looked at me like I was a fool.

"Errr OK, Sunshine. Did you know that some common foods can cause digestive problems?"

"Errr, not really. Like what?"

"Well, some food can cause the digestive problems you have. Like dairy, or wheat allergies."

"Really?" I looked at him blankly. I thought to myself: what a load of bull$hit.

"Errr OK. Well next time you come and see me, bring a sample of all the different foods you eat. Not a lot, just a mouthful so I can test them on you. That way we can see if anything in your diet is giving you troubles."

Next appointment I brought in Cornflakes, Rice Krispies, pasta, pizza, eggs, tomatoes, white rice, white bread, cheese, sausages, bacon, salt and vinegar crisps, Hula Hoops, and low-fat margarine. All the normal food I ate. All the normal food everyone eats.

One at a time he put a little bit of food on my tongue so I could taste it. Then he got me to push up on my arm. He seemed to be testing how strong my arm was with the food in my mouth. Very odd. This guy certainly did things in his own special way!

After we had tested all the different foods he sat back in his chair and said,

"Well, you are intolerant to everything."

"What?"

"Yes, everything. Every food I tested, you reacted badly to them all. Every food you eat, your body is rejecting."

"What? Are you mad! Everything?"

What was he on about? How could that be?

"Everything?"

"Everything. You are pretty far gone, probably pre-diabetic too."

What was this guy talking about? How could I be intolerant to all my diet. That was just mental. Had to be bull$hit.

The look of disbelief on my slack face was obvious, so he proceeded to test me again, but this time he tested me so that I could feel the difference myself.

He had me stand up and hold a heavy-ish dumbbell in my right hand, just dangling by my thigh. He asked me to lift the weight out to my side, keeping my arm straight all the time. The dumbbell was heavy but I easily lifted it out to my side. Next he popped a little bit of bread in my mouth and asked me to lift the weight again.

And the strangest thing happened: I couldn't lift the weight. Five seconds earlier I had easily lifted it, but now with the bread on my tongue I couldn't. So strange! Energy drained out of my body and I couldn't lift the weight.

"What the funk is this? What's going on?"

I spat the bread out and again I could lift the weight.

I put some more bread in and again I was unable to lift the weight.

I tried all the food I'd brought. Every single bit made me weak and

I was incapable of lifting the dumbbell.

I was stunned.

"What…is…this…weirdness?"

"It's called muscle testing or Applied Kinesiology. It's a way of seeing what stresses your body. The things in your diet are harmful to you and your body goes weak when you eat them. We are just reading the signs your body is giving."

My initial reaction was similar to Luke Skywalker dropping by and asking if I knew the way to Betelgeuse in the Omega System! Shocked disbelief, but I could not deny what I felt, nor what I saw, nor the reaction I'd had. This wasn't me just reading a strange story in some book; this was me experiencing it first-hand. This muscle testing strangeness clearly showed that my body was rejecting some foods.

I'm used to muscle testing now, but back then it was like The Force from the Star Wars movies. It is freaky weird. It's an amazing skill if it's done correctly and so the person can feel it. It is far away from my old world view and was very very strange to experience this oddness for the first time.

I was in chronic pain, I was desperate, so I decided to give these strange discoveries a test. I gave up the food I reacted to.

5. Giving it all up. Hallelujah!

I gave up dairy products, wheat, processed foods and sugar for two weeks. I had already given up some sugar because that didn't agree, but now I gave it up properly. I read all the labels and avoided all these foods utterly.

You have to totally avoid the food you give up, even one mouthful will ruin the experiment and stop you getting better. Your body gets accustomed to the things it doesn't like, learns to cope as best as possible with the daily toxins. Just avoiding something that does not agree for a day or two is not enough, takes one or two weeks of total avoidance before the body says,

'Ah, cool, don't have to worry about that $hit no more,' and then starts getting a bit better.

After two weeks, 95 percent of my heartburn disappeared.

It's worth saying that again: After two weeks, 95 percent of my heartburn disappeared.

So, ten years of digestive troubles, taking every antacid known to man, cameras down me throat, super-strong magic beans, pain 24 hours a day for years and years, 20-minute walks after every meal, doctor after doctor after doctor fobbing me off as 'unlucky', 'it's the dust mites' and having to 'learn to live with the chronic pain', ten years of pain and suffering. Ten long hard years…and two weeks avoiding a few foods and 95 percent of my digestive problems disappeared.

Boy oh boy was I happy. Mega happy! Overjoyed! Hooray!

Angry too, very angry at all the doctors who didn't know their arse from their elbow, but wow, all that pain gone. Halle-bloody-lujah!

I was not cured, no no no, for if I ate some dairy, wheat or sugar my symptoms returned, but avoiding those foods stopped me having the digestive problems and allowed me some normality and gave my body a chance to recover. It is important to understand that: not cured, just avoiding the problematic foods. But still, this success was awesome. I was feeling oh so proud to have discovered this secret, but it was to be short-lived.

The muscle tester dude also told me that some people need more acid in their digestive tract to get their digestion working correctly and that some people need less acid. The digestive tract is a naturally acidic environment and in order to digest all the lovely food I ate, it needed to be acidic in order to work correctly.

All the magic beans I had been taking reduced the acid on the assumption that I had too much acid and that too much acid was giving me acid reflux, GERD. Acid reflux = acid = reduce the acid. That made perfect sense, didn't it! Or did it?

• • •

One lunchtime I drank some soup that had a dash of milk in it. I was dairy intolerant so a little heartburn paid me a visit. I decided to put the muscle tester dude's theory to the test. I wanted to know if I needed more acid or less acid. So I drank a tablespoon of apple cider vinegar (ACV) mixed up with a little bit of water. If I needed less acid, I would get much worse and it would hurt a lot more, and if I needed more acid I would get better.

Yes, it's a bit iffy, a bit dodgy, drinking vinegar, but I'd had heartburn 24/7 for years and it was much better now and I was keen to know what I needed.

I forced down the ACV, (be warned it has quite a kick!) and within ten minutes my heartburn completely disappeared. Crazy, eh! No wonder the magic beans didn't work: they did exactly the opposite of what I needed. Thanks, doc!

This kind of misdiagnosis and mistreatment of digestive problems is frequent and I am but one of millions that suffered for years in ignorance. Now, when I have digestive hassles I don't have any magic beans, instead I reach for the ACV and I have no more digestive hassles. (Apple cider vinegar (ACV) must be un-pasteurised and 'with mother'.)

Wow, I thought, this muscle tester guy really knows his stuff! Maybe he is right about the teeth thing? Amalgams? So I rushed out and got my biggest amalgam filling removed. Was cheap too, just round the corner from the office.

Drilled it out good and proper too.

DDDDDDDZZZZZZZZZIT.

Beautiful.

Not.

6. Ignorance sure hurts like hell

I don't have many regrets in life; in fact I only have one. And that's just that: rushing out in my eagerness to get better and getting my amalgam drilled out by a regular dentist with no safety precautions.

Oh no! What a mistake! What a fool. One thing's for sure, ignorance sure hurts like hell. I didn't know I should have used a specialist dentist. The muscle tester dude who told me about amalgams didn't know either. I didn't know a regular dentist might hurt me. Oh buggeration.

All hell broke loose after that. The pain got massively worse, food intolerances went haywire and life spiralled completely out of control. Brain fog, mega food intolerances, mega muscle pain, mega tired, no energy, and head totally in the clouds, like swimming with the fairies.

I ran out of breath walking up stairs, my muscles ached just pulling myself out of my bed, my head was fluffy like a teenager in love, except I was brain-fogged like a druggie wandering around in a zombie state.

The diet I'd found avoiding wheat, dairy and sugar stopped working and now all food seemed to make my digestive troubles worse. It was easier to not eat anything, but I was starving all the time.

At this point, I was still totally ignorant and didn't have a clue what I'd done to myself. But now, something was very very wrong and I was much much worse. It didn't happen overnight so I didn't connect my failing health with the amalgam removal, but in the space of one month my already critical health nose-dived.

Looking back, now that I know and understand so many things, now it is obvious amalgam removal caused this, but at the time I had absolutely no idea; not one iota. I was supposed to get better after amalgam removal, not worse. Took a lot of hard work to figure that out when I was so wildly ill.

Now that the alternative health door had been shown to me, now that I had discovered another way rather than to follow advice from my useless doctors, I dived in and read about alternative health in every spare moment and proceeded to try and figure out how to get better in the midst of a blizzard of mercury rampaging through my system. I became very obsessive and somehow managed to divert all of that obsessiveness into learning about my dire situation. My life and my job were going down the drain fast. No one, me included, knew what was going on.

7. Hello, Sunshine

Turns out there are lots of sick people in this world searching for cures. Now that the internet is everywhere, some of these people hang out together online and compare notes about what's wrong, what's working for them and what's not. Amazing, eh! I didn't know that in 2006, and the majority of the world's population still don't know it. Some of these forums are so big they attract 40,000 to 100,000 visitors a day. There are a lot of sick people out there, all searching for answers.

I started reading the health forums and quickly needed to ask questions. To do that I needed to register and choose a nickname. It had to be cheerful, nothing gloomy like 'Sosick' or 'Jinx'. I was wearing my favourite t-shirt which had 'Sunshine' blazoned across the front. I was in a hurry to reply to a message, and so without a moment's hesitation I became 'Sunshine'.

Note to my American readers: Calling someone 'Sunshine' in England is an affectionate way to address someone that you greatly like or admire. It is usually a greeting, "Hello, Sunshine", and applies to both sexes.

I remember telling my wife my nickname and she laughed out loud, for I was far from sunny in those dark, dismal days. People tell me I have grown into the name just fine now, but back then I was a miserable, grumpy, gloomy late-thirties city bloke whose life was fried. No one calls me Sunshine in the flesh; it's just my online name.

And another thing, Forsyth is not my real name either, that's my grandfather's name, my mother's maiden name. I am publishing with a pen-name because my life is back on track and I don't want my clients or competitors reading about the troubles I endured. If you think I'm hiding something or it detracts from the story, just imagine I didn't tell you. I just don't want my name in lights.

Actually, using a pen-name allows me to be truthful with you: I can include the parts of my journey that I would never admit to in the flesh. Anyway, my real name is irrelevant; it's what I did that counts.

It must be said, the forums are a bit of a madhouse, with people from all walks of life, with all manner of problems, all shouting about what they are doing. At first I had no idea where to turn, with every-which-way shouting to be considered. I discovered there are many different health-regaining activities you can do at home on your own, without the need of a doctor.

However, most people say that their solution is the answer to all the problems. How can everyone have the cure that I crave, and yet everyone have different solutions?

The liver flushers all say flushing the liver is the answer, bowel cleaners say bowel cleansing is the answer, the parasite people say you just need to kill the bugs, the thyroid people say it's the hormones and they can cure everything, and on and on and on. How on earth does anyone know which options to choose?

All this stuff was completely new to me. I was starting from scratch. Up until then I had never heard of any of these things.

I went to see a natural practitioner. She seemed to know all about mercury problems. She made it sound easy to solve:

"Start detoxing the mercury straight away. You don't have to wait until you are amalgam free. Take some NAC," whatever that was.

I found out later NAC is something called N-Acetyl-Cysteine, and cysteine is a sulphur supplement. Garlic and onions are full of sulphur too. Mercury and sulphur attract like lovers do. Some people are fine on it, and some people not so fine. I took three pills in one and a half days and lost another couple of months of my life as a fresh wave of nightmare symptoms washed over me, further wrecking my life. At that time I had no idea why, it just seemed like another idiot kicking me in the balls.

It hurt like hell that, a major set-back, really taught me a lesson too, taught me to trust no one. These bloody Natural Practitioners seemed to know just enough to hurt me even more!

Only then did I fully realise that I had to research everything myself, to make myself understand and then choose for myself if I wanted to try something. The majority of the advice I was receiving was hurting me real bad and I was so ill I could no longer afford to take any more risks; I could not afford to trust anyone. It's the reason I had to read up about everything I tried before I tried it. I read a lot of health books thereafter.

This understanding, that I needed to take care of my health and not rely on others, was a giant leap for me. Once I realised that my health was my responsibility, I guess you can say that was the beginning of the beginning. I have talked to many sick people on my travels these last few years and the people who realise that they are responsible for their own health, they are the ones who make it.

It's a giant leap because you must ignore the conventional wisdom that's been drummed into our heads since we were little kids, which is: 'If you get sick, go to the doctor and take what he says. Full stop'. To overcome that brainwashing from such a young age takes real courage, and a whole lot 'a' pain.

I have learnt that, as a general rule, people find one or two potential solutions to their problem(s) and then focus intensely on those one or two things, and that's it. That's all they do. I met people who had done 50 liver flushes (with olive oil and grapefruit juice) and were still ill and didn't think to try something else. Liver flushes are very heavy-duty things to do, and yet they kept on flushing away when it was most obviously not the solution to their problems.

I was the same. I did yoga exclusively for three years. I then did Alexander Technique exclusively for another three years. Only when I was at death's door, my life slipping away, was I forced to try other ideas.

8. Universal Reactor

I tried liver flushing, maybe that was my problem? So I did ten of them to see if it was. Very powerful things, liver flushes. Not for the fainthearted. People rave about how effective they are, how strong and empowering they can be, but it is also very much about taking control of your own health. Doing something yourself, on your own, it's about being brave. I did eight of them when I was ultra-sick. God knows how I survived them because it's a serious course of action.

I'd reserve a weekend for the flush because it takes a couple of days to do. You eat no food on Saturday, only drinking some Epsom salts mixed with water. At the end of the day you glug down a mixture of olive oil and grapefruit juice, then go to bed and listen to your tummy gurgle like crazy. Sunday is spent on the toilet as all hell breaks loose from your rear-end.

Strange but true, this procedure flushes the liver and gallbladder of any congested gallstones/gunk. Or I should say, it flushes some of the gunk out, which is why you have to keep repeating the damn things.

I got out about 700 gallstones in those ten flushes, mostly about the size of your little finger nail, many tiddlers ¼ cm across, but I also had a few almost as big as golf balls! My eyes almost fell out of me head to see those monsters in the toilet bowl, it is staggering to see such brutes waving up at you.

It's a sure thing they are better out than in, but however better I briefly felt after the flushes, and I did temporarily feel GREAT after-wards, I still felt like I'd been run over by a truck 99 percent of the time. On top of that, the recovery time after the flushes was getting silly: 10 to 14 days!

There are other less stressful and much more civilised ways to clean the liver which I discovered (and will talk about later). For mercury tox-ic people liver flushes are too powerful. In my opinion and experience they should be avoided. I survived the flushes when I was wildly sick, so you should be fine if you try them, but you have been warned, OK? That's Andy Cutler's advice too. And if anyone knows about mercury problems, Dr. Cutler is The Man. We have too many things wrong and it puts great stress on an already greatly stressed body.

Ten flushes and I was still ill, so time to move on. What next?

9. You may feel a little prick

I was reading a lot of health books by now; my health was well and truly taking over my life. I was online researching ideas daily. One of them was kidney issues. I'd had kidney problems in the past. Twelve years previously, back in 1995, my doctor had found blood in my urine and I was referred to a kidney specialist:

"It means your kidneys have a hole in them and they are leaking blood. You have an IgA disease, which is a type of Glomerulonephritis condition."

"Oh, that's not good. What can I do about it?"

"First we need to get a definite diagnosis, just to be 100 percent sure."

"OK."

"We need to do a biopsy. Then we'll know exactly what to do."

"What's a biopsy?"

"A biopsy is when we take a little sample of tissue. In this case we use a special needle to go into your lower back. The needle goes in and using ultrasound, we locate the kidneys and we nip out a little sample."

"And this needs doing?"

"Oh yes, we need to be sure."

"OK."

"Do you have health insurance? Good. Let me start the paper work."

• • •

Two weeks later…

"Just lie down here sir. You may feel a little prick."

"Thank goodness I don't have to go under. Will it hurt?"

"No, no, not really, just a little prick, sir."

"OK, but why are you strapping me down?"

"Think nothing of that, it's just in case, sir."

"Oh?"

"Here, pop this in your mouth, sir. You can bite on this, just in case."

Not sure if you remember that scene in Pulp Fiction where John Travolta has to puncture Uma Thurman's breast plate with an adrenaline shot because she was ODing?

THUMP went the needle into my lower back!

"AAHHHHHHHHHHHHHH FUNK!"

"Only take a moment sir, hold still."

"Ahhhhhhhhhhhhhhhhhhhhh."

"Only take a moment, hold still sir..."

"Ooofffffffff."

"Only a moment. Everything's fine. You are a brave, brave boy."

"Hofff."

"Only a moment sir, just, got, to, get, it, in, a, little, more."

"Ahhh."

"We're losing him! We're losing him!"

• • •

Two weeks later...

"Good to see you again, Sunshine."

"Ummmm."

"Yes, I understand you found the procedure a little painful?"

"The last thing I remember was hearing the nurse shout, 'We're losing him!' Then I blacked out."

"Yes, it can smart a little. Anyway, moving on, moving on. Unfortunately the biopsy failed to recover any kidney tissue. But the good news is the ultrasound did pick up a cyst in the right kidney. Here look, you can see it clearly here, and here, and here."

"The biopsy was a failure?"

"Yes, most unfortunate. I gather you are not keen on repeating the procedure? OK, well that's fine, that's fine. I think we can be pretty sure, yes most definitely sure; you do have IgA disease, which is a type of Glomerulonephritis condition."

"Eh?"

"Yes, we would not want to put you through that ordeal again would we? No. OK, in that case we can proceed with the knowledge that you have an IgA disease and a cyst."

"OK, so what's the cure for that?"

"Cure? There is no cure."

"No cure? What's the treatment then?"

"Treatment? There is no treatment."

"Are you a bloody retard? You put me through all that crap, cost the insurance company a small fortune and now you tell me there is no treatment, no cure. And I obviously didn't need the biopsy in the first place because you knew what was wrong and there is no cure, and there is no treatment!"

I wish I'd said that. What I actually said was,

"OK."

"Yes, no cure and no treatment for you. But, there are some things you can do to stop it progressing."

"What happens if it progresses?"

"Kidney failure. Nasty. Wired up to tubes and whatnot: dialysis. Nasty. Anyway, what I want you to do is take it easy on the drinking. Don't go too wild. You probably picked this up on your travels to South Korea. All those drinking games you told me about. That amount of whiskey is probably what caused this. And get down the gym occasionally. Take it easy; don't run yourself into the ground. Use your common sense and you'll probably be fine."

• • •

That's typical of the modern medicine way. No cure: go away. That experience always troubled me. I always thought the doc was just after the insurance money from the biopsy. Unsurprisingly, I never went back to see him again; I didn't trust him. I consider myself extremely lucky he didn't open me up and have a serious poke about, but the biopsy was bad enough.

So, yeah, I knew I had kidney issues, but I was told there was no cure and no treatment. Now after a little research I found lots of information, and lots of herbs that could help.

I read that crystals build up inside the kidneys from a poor diet, alcohol, and accumulated toxins. Sand and grit also get stuck, gumming up the works. I discovered that some herbs help dissolve the crystals, and some others help flush out the grime. I was chuffed I'd found a treatment and a cure to try out.

I read a book called *Timeless Secrets of Health and Rejuvenation* by Andreas Moritz. His book had the best explanation and was easiest to understand, so I used his herbs. A collection of ten different herbs to make into a herbal tea. This involved brewing up a pint in the morning and taking a couple of mouthfuls six to eight times per day, every day for a month.

That sounded great. What an incredibly British way to get better, eh!

"Here, drink this tea and you'll be right as rain in no time. Tally-ho."

I drank the incredibly bitter tea daily as instructed and it was all really rather eventful. I quickly had to reduce to a quarter dose strength because I had a multitude of side-effects bombarding me on all sides; rashes all over my legs, feet and torso. Swelling ankles. Weird spots/pimples all over my back, hips and legs. And wicked take-your-breath-away-minimal-sleep-at-night-heartburn. All of which lasted for the entire duration of the 30 days.

I did feel slightly better afterwards, but only minimally. Mostly I just felt thankful that the side effects had retreated.

It was obvious my kidneys were heavily congested with crystals and crud, that's what all the side effects meant, but I was still deathly ill at the end of it all. Kidneys were obviously a problem, but not the only problem. So what to try next?

Further reading for kidney issues: *Timeless Secrets of Health and Rejuvenation* by Andreas Moritz

10. Salad, salad, salad

Next I was diagnosed by a naturopath with Small Intestine Bacterial Overgrowth, commonly known as SIBO. What is SIBO? It's when you have an overgrowth of bacteria in your small intestines that will not go away. Think old man's big bushy beard that has not had a trim in a couple of years. Think that thicket of beard living inside your tummy. Nice! This stops you from digesting the food you eat. The bacteria literally steals the food right out of your digestive tract, where it lives.

The doc told me he gets one person per year with hydrogen breath test results through the roof, and that was me. Yeah great, I was in a terrible state.

The hydrogen breath test for SIBO involved drinking some Coke Zero and some milk. Ouch! And then testing me to see how I reacted. It of course made me sick as a dog for ten days.

Never again will I take a test that I know will hurt me. The Coke Zero was the worst and I felt symptoms galloping towards me almost immediately. I don't care what anyone says: doing tests that hurt you is utter bull$hit. And that includes stopping supplements to get a clear reading and hence getting sick again.

There are many other pain-free ways to understand what's going on. You may have to search around a bit, but there are many ways to figure things out before you must resort to hurting yourself. As I said, BS and never again.

The cure for SIBO was antibiotics or diet. I don't just follow doctor's orders anymore, so I read up and researched antibiotics and discovered the incredibly bad press these so-called wonder-pills had been getting. It was shocking to read such bad things about them. I thought they were mankind's knight in shining armour? Seems not anymore!

I had done at least 15 courses of antibiotics in my life and I was sick as a dog now. I needed to play it safe, so they were out of the question for me. I was happy I did avoid them because I have since met loads of people who got totally screwed from taking antibiotics when they were sick; made them much worse. (Cipro rings a bell. Nasty stuff.)

Antibiotics kill all life wherever they go, bad bacteria and good bacteria. This can initially be good news, but when the course is finished there are no good guys to replace the bad guys. The bad guys then have no competition and when the bad bacteria takes over completely, you will be completely screwed.

If you do take antibiotics, make sure you diligently take probiotics afterwards to replenish the good bacteria inside your digestive tract. Better still, spend an hour Googling and make up your own mind. Who do you believe? Will you take the chance?

If you know to ask the question, the choice can be yours.

• • •

So I embarked on the magical-special-diet to cure my SIBO.

"I assure you, Sunshine, the special diet I am recommending will definitely work and will definitely cure you. Ninety seven percent of my patients get completely cured. I know exactly what I'm doing. You are in safe hands here."

"Great, I look forward to being completely cured. Thank you. Can I ask another question?"

"Fire away, son. What is it?"

"Why have I got SIBO in the first place? Why has this happened to me? What have I done wrong? What's so broken that these bacteria have taken over inside me?"

He shrugged his shoulders, showed me his palms and said,

"That's a good question, son, but we don't know. That's just life."

I found that answer frustrating and astonishing. What an odd thing to say. He was a very highly-regarded specialist in this field, had been on TV, had a practice in Harley Street and he couldn't even guess why I might have had SIBO?

Don't know what you think about that, but I think it's a bit strange he couldn't even guess. What was he a specialist in if he couldn't even guess at the cause of the problem? Surely he must think about his work? Think about all the patients he sees? Or maybe he just didn't have the energy or patience to explain it?

I changed my diet radically. I really had no choice anyway because everything made me sick after I got that amalgam removed with no protection. At this point I still didn't realise unsafe/unprotected amalgam removal was what caused everything to go haywire.

I started all these special rotation diets and exclusion diets in the quest to cure my health. If you have ever done this type of diet, rotation diets, you will know they are hard labour. You have to exclude lots of different foods, and only eat specific foods on specific days. You must follow the program really carefully, rotating particular foods in and out every other day, keeping lists of what you ate and when. I did them daily for about eight months.

Took me a couple of months to figure out, but anything other than salad made me sick, so that's all I could eat. I rotated all the foods that made me sick out of my diet and all that was left was salad. I ate a packed lunch every day in the office, all handmade by me, which was salad.

Salad. Salad. Salad. Every day salad. Every meal salad. Breakfast, lunch and dinner was salad. That was March to August 2007, six months of salad only.

And I'm not talking about crispy croutons, or Caesar dressing, or blue cheese sauce, or grilled goat's cheese, or diced tuna, or roasted chicken, or ham, or pickle, or any fancy pants stuff. I'm talking about basic raw vegetable salad: lettuce, cucumber, carrots, beetroot and celery. The only dressing I could handle was lemon, apple cider vinegar and extra virgin olive oil.

That only takes up a few sentences in this story, but that was hardcore difficult, hardcore commitment to do that, and dull as dishwater. In that time I had zero cheats, not one, not once. I made occasional mistakes, because I didn't always realise what was in the food I ate, but seriously I was way, way too ill to have any cheats.

I spent much time measuring my pH on pH strips, which is a way to see how acidic or alkaline you are. The more acidic, the sicker you are. I was always acidic, no matter what I did, no matter how healthy my diet was, even when I had juice-only days, I could not get the pH strips to change. It's interesting to follow the pH values for a while, but it's just a test and this super-strict diet regime was not working for me.

If I made a mistake somehow, I got worse. If I ate the wrong food, I got worse. Anything outside of salad, I got worse. All this hard work in following the diets was not curing me of my troubles, more like treading water. I knew if I stopped treading water I was going to sink.

I was big into healthy diets at this point (you would be too if you did eight months of rotation diets!) and I was reading lots of health-regaining diet books. There are many to choose from and I read seven on the bounce. The solutions in each said diet alone would cure me, that a healthy diet will cure anyone of anything…but alas for me, diet alone didn't cure me. The diet stopped me from drowning, but I was still in deep water with no land in sight.

It's pretty soul-destroying having all that diet effort, liver flushes, kidney tea, all that life change, all that hope, all of it crushed, lead to nothing and no change. My symptoms continued, my food intolerances continued and my life continued to dump. I just could not understand why this ultra-strict diet was not having the desired effect? Why didn't the liver flushes work? Why didn't the kidney herbs work? Oh man, what a nightmare.

In the year 1999 I weighed in at 202 pounds (92kg). Now in 2007 I was down to 123 pounds (56kg). I was six foot one inch tall and I was all skin and bone. My waist size went from 40 inches to 27. I struggled to buy trousers to fit my scrawny, curled-up body.

Most food made me sick and the food that did stay in me was obviously not touching the sides because my weight had plummeted. I was intolerant to all dairy, wheat, grains, gluten, soya, sugar, fruit, alcohol, meat, sulphur foods, the nightshade family including tomatoes and tobacco.

I couldn't eat anything that was processed in any way whatsoever. That included things like white rice, because white rice has been refined from brown rice. Everything and anything that was refined caused me trouble that was real and immediate and did not go away quickly.

If you go to the supermarket the vast majority of food is processed and packaged. There are aisles and lanes, row after row of processed food that I could not eat. From the list of foods I had to avoid, there was not much left that I could eat without any trouble: only salad. When I went shopping I bought three bags of carrots, two cucumbers, some lemons and a couple of bunches of celery. That was it!

When I say sick, what happened after I had eaten a food that I was intolerant to: my back and/or neck would spasm and hurt like hell. Real deep-seated, inside throbbing, continuous, low grade, grinding pain would hit me. I was not bed-bound, just tiptoeing around pained, miserable and hurting 24/7.

Haemorrhoids (piles) became a way of life as the digestive problems went crazy. I had major acid bouncing up my gullet, and bouncing down causing bloating, abdominal pains and bleeding piles. I became even more tired and lacking in energy than before. All this hassle lasted for seven to ten days. Yes, seven to ten days from one mouthful of something; say, cream in a soup (dairy allergy).

For the rotation diets, I was writing a food diary, making a note of all the food I ate throughout each day. Although a right drag to remember, it's an interesting task to do and this enabled me to understand that I did not get an immediate intolerance reaction to a food. I discovered my reaction to a dodgy food was 22 hours after I'd eaten it. This was the reason it was so difficult to figure out what food was causing me trouble. (Note: my reactions came 22 hours after eating a problem food, but each person is different in when and if and how they react.) Understanding there was a delayed reaction of 22 hours enabled me to quickly find the offending food, assuming I'd kept my food diary, which enabled me to then avoid it.

I still find it amazing that a food that I ate, directly, caused me so much back pain. Never imagined that, crazy, eh! All those years of back pain caused by my diet? Odd, eh!

I had symptoms on top of symptoms and I learned that I was what is called a 'Universal Reactor.'

Quite a cool name that, very me, very sci-fi: 'Universal Reactor'. But the cool name was the only thing that was cool about it. It meant I rejected and reacted to everything I ate and came in contact with. It's not a very good thing to happen if you want to live happily ever after.

The special diets did not cure me. I still felt like my life was slipping away. The nightshade allergy was particularly horrible; it meant I could not tolerate tomatoes, peppers and cayenne. Tomatoes are so tricky to avoid as they are in many foods. It also meant I reacted to cigarette smoke too, so I had a passive smoking allergy on top of everything else too. Discovering this stopped all socialising, all business lunches and dinners, all of which I was expected to do weekly. I was a happy man when the smoking ban came into force, but I was still a wreck.

Life was bloody tough but the last thing I wanted to do was admit defeat. It is not in my nature to give up. I knew that if I jacked in the job, if I slunk off somewhere to lick my wounds and recover, I knew I'd never go back. You might think I should have, but I loved my job and the money was rock 'n' roll good.

The city is a dog-eat-dog world and once something like that happened, once someone had to stop because it was all getting too much, from what I saw, they were never the same again and I didn't want that happening to me. I wanted to get back to normal, not retreat.

I was too scared to jack it in, but I wished every day that I could.

11. Nail in the coffin of my ex-life

Somehow I was allergic to metals touching my skin, I had to remove my gold neck chain and signet ring as these were somehow adding to my neck and back pain. I had tennis elbow. My arms and legs were numb and tingly most of the time.

My short-term memory was playing major tricks with me now too. I couldn't remember simple everyday words in the middle of a sentence, like bus, or drain, or you know, thingy, yeah, at the end of the garden, like a house but made of wood, has a door, keep pots in it. Yes, thanks, words like shed.

My spelling was even worse than before, unbelievably bad, simple common words that I spelt everyday were completely gone. If I wanted to remember anything I had to write it down and I really did have to write everything down. My work, which was on the phone talking to clients all day, became intensely tricky; I could not remember who I'd spoken to, nor what I'd said.

I had tinnitus, which is that ringing sound you hear constantly from nowhere. I could not use any headphones to listen to any music. If I did, the ringing got 50 times worse and was actually quite painful. No idea why but my ears would tingle and hurt like crazy after even five minutes of headphone music, no matter how low the volume.

I was pretty gutted about this as I was a bedroom DJ and that was another nail in the coffin of my ex-life. Music is a large part of my life and one of my favourite ways to chill out is to listen to music. I have a huge diverse collection, but now I was into the weirdest ambient music possible, (which is a kind of ultra-horizontal-chillout style). Laying on the floor was the most pain free position for me to be in, so I lay down after work and listened to strange clangs, bongs and pops-in-the-night music and thought this was the coolest music in town. I think there must be a lot of mercury-toxic ambient musicians out there!

I had a chronic sinus infection and a perpetually blocked nose. I always had a cold and I regularly got flu and had time off work.

I felt cold all the time, summer, winter, whatever, I always felt freezing cold. Strangely this constant coldness was a long-term thing that I remember going way back since I was a kid at school. I was at boarding school and during the winters I could be found sitting on 'my' radiator. Now I was beyond cold, now it felt like I was sitting in a freezer all the time.

I had major Repetitive Strain Injuries (RSI) and was unable to do repetitive things with my hands. Writing with a pen was painful as I gripped the pen so hard it hurt. I tried, but I could not grip the pen softly. No computer games for me anymore and typing on keyboards was only in short, controlled, limited periods of time with lots of rest. I had to use a special program on my PC which slowed down my mouse and would force me to break after lots of typing. I had it set at three minutes typing, one minute rest.

It was a standing joke with my mates that I could not sent text messages from my mobile phone other than simple yesses and nos. My fingers could not press the correct buttons and it was too fiddly for my hands to perform. They would send me long complicated requests and would laugh when I replied with a simple 'ok'.

The repetitive strain injury was so bad I could not brush my teeth. The arm and hand holding the toothbrush would seize up, my neck would freeze up. What a sorry state I was in. In the end I had to buy an electric toothbrush. Life was truly difficult in a million little ways.

• • •

So to recap:

My digestion was completely screwed; anything but raw salad made me ultra-sick.

My liver and gallbladder were completely clogged with big and small gallstones.

My kidneys were congested with crystals.

My mind was brain-fogged and swimming with the fairies.

The muscles in my body forgot how to work. They were hard when they should be soft. They were soft when they should be hard. The rigid tension in my muscles had frozen them tight shut. I could not loosen up.

The kink in my spine never unkinked. The pain in my back and neck never unwound. I hurt standing up. I hurt sitting down. I could do no exercise, nor carry anything heavy.

My skin was dry, itchy and flaky; it had that paper texture of old folks, translucent.

Every night I went to sleep and woke up in the morning feeling worse.

I was perpetually weak, tired and drained of energy. I got out of breath walking up stairs.

I had almost zero body fat and looked like Skeletor. People would look at me and instinctively know something was deeply wrong. I felt and looked like the life had been sucked out of me.

All the books said clean the liver. I did and was still ill.

All the books said clean the kidneys. I did and was still ill.

All the books said have a healthy diet. I did and was still ill. I ate ul-tra-healthy organic food every day for nine months, without exception and no cheats, and I was sick sick sick as a dog and I did not get better.

What the fuck was wrong with me?

This part of my life was an utter nightmare and I thank my lucky stars I got out of that hellhole. All the things I did and tried to get bet-ter that everyone said would work, they didn't work on me. Every hope was dashed. All those diets were oh so bloody difficult and tricky to follow. Why was I so different? Why didn't these things work for me? I had to be missing something! What was going on? Ahhhhhhh!

12. The missing link

Eventually I found the mercury forums: Curezone.com, HerbAllure. com and the Yahoo Frequent Dose Chelation group. This is where the 'mercury toxic' hang out and try to figure out a way back to better health. There are many people doing a variety of different protocols and it's all wildly confusing at first with so many diverse subjects being discussed. Remember I didn't really know anything about mercury at this point, but these people seemed to have a lot wrong with them! Just like me.

I was then recommended a book called *Amalgam Illness* by Andrew Hall Cutler. It was all about mercury poisoning, the symptoms, the problems, and how to clean up the mess. I started reading it on the train on my morning commute into work. I was so engrossed I missed my stop! This was amazing: the symptoms and problems he discussed were a mirror image of mine. I couldn't put the book down and every spare moment was spent devouring the text.

He explained what had happened to me. He explained why I was so dreadfully ill. He explained why I wasn't getting any better. His book hit the nail bang on the head for me. I was a perfect match. He has a self-diagnosis checklist and I came in at 99 percent definite for a mercury problem. Even without the checklist, it was blindingly obvious mercury was my thing because everything, every symptom, every problem, fit like a glove.

I was startled too. Reading a book written by someone you have never met or talked to, who lived on the other side of the world, to have effectively predicted the problems throughout my life, was frankly stunning. It was truly amazing to read all my hassles mapped out in black and white like that, and inspiring to see he had plenty of potential solutions to try out.

Through the book I discovered I was poisoned, heavy metal poisoned: mercury poisoned. And this mercury poisoning was my root cause, the source and origin of all my woes. It was the missing link, the most important part of the jigsaw puzzle that was my life and my health: Mercury Poisoning. I also discovered my amalgam removal with no protection had hurt me real bad.

It was pretty scary finding out I was mercury toxic; it's like something out of a spy novel or film. It is a very serious nightmare-like thing to happen to anyone and far far from a minor matter to be so poisoned. But however shocked and worried I was at discovering I was poisoned, I was also gloriously happy. Happy because now I understood, and now I had a chance. To understand was like sun bursting through clouds on a cold winter's day, fingers of gold shining on my face and warming me to the core. I had a goal now, something to get my teeth into.

I devoured *Amalgam Illness* three times back-to-back. I couldn't put it down. After that reading marathon I finally understood what had happened to me, and more importantly a route to recovery. Thank you, Mr. Cutler, I will be forever in your debt. It was such a relief to understand the why of it all. All those years of failing health, all explained, thank you, thank you. You are The Man!

I must say it's not the easiest book to get to grips with; it can at best be described as haphazard. Undoubtedly it makes perfect sense to the author, but the author is a chemist by trade and he also happened to be mercury poisoned when he wrote it! You do get the feeling of mad scientist, but only mad in the sense that writing books for sick people was not his forte.

Figuring out how to safely recover from mercury poisoning was definitely his forte! Genius.

But I understood the book, it changed my life, it saved my life. So it's not that bad; just, he could have used a co-author, or an editor, or something to make it a little more user-friendly, but as I said, I understood it after three reads and it saved my sorry soul.

• • •

Turns out my eight silver fillings, called amalgam fillings, were made of 50 percent mercury. Someone, somewhere deep in the past had managed to persuade some idiots that one of the most deadly elements known to man was somehow safe in my mouth.

Mercury is mixed with other metals so that it can be easily manhandled and put into the holes in teeth and then it sets hard. Amalgam actually means a mixture, or combination. Amalgam fillings are made of silver, tin, copper and sadly, mercury.

As everyone knows, mercury is a liquid at room temperature, but what someone had failed to mention was that mercury gives off mercury vapour too. Just because it was in my mouth did not stop the mercury vapour from being released. This mercury vapour had been leaking out, 24 hours a day, since they been in my mouth, minimum 20 years. All amalgam fillings leak in this way. It's not a question of being placed incorrectly, or corroding, or rotting, or infesting. All amalgam fillings leak mercury vapour, full stop.

Turns out my body didn't like this.

Turns out that when you remove amalgam fillings, when the dentist drills them out, this drilling of amalgams releases a gigantic amount of mercury vapour which gave me a fresh and full load of mercury, kinda like a mobile phone top-up option, except with mercury jacked directly into my brain. Drilling creates heat, heated mercury turns into mercury vapour, and mercury vapour creates mercury poisoning.

Turns out that the unprotected amalgam removal was really, totally, completely and utterly the last thing on earth my poor battered and shrivelled body needed, wanted or could handle. That was why I kept getting worse, and that was why I didn't get any better even after all the attempts I was making.

Turns out I could not get better yet because my body was a toxic dumping ground for the mercury vapour that the dentist had released by drilling me.

Turns out amalgam removal needs to be done in a way that minimises any toxic exposure from the drilling process.

Turns out I bypassed any safety measures in amalgam removal by trusting my regular dentist because my regular dentist didn't use any preventative measures to protect me. He just drilled the fuck out of my face and left me to rot.

Bastard.

Cost me two years of my life that did, minimum. And I was lucky! Lucky I had the drive to keep trying. The bloody dentist even told me he did seven years at university to qualify and he assured me mercury was not a problem. Well, I found out the hard way, found out that what his teachers had taught him was total and utter bull$hit.

I know I made the appointment, I know I made the decision to have one amalgam removed, but I trusted the dentist not to hurt me. If I knew, I would not have done it. If the dentist had known, I guess he would not have done it. But it's the dentist's job to know what he's doing; it's the dentist's job to protect me. He failed miserably.

Oh and apologies for the swearing, both here and elsewhere. I try hard to minimise the bad language, but it's difficult in these emotional parts that caused me so much grief. I am a city boy at heart and swearing is a way of life for my kind. As I said, I will keep the profanity to my absolute minimum.

Further reading: *Amalgam Illness* by Andrew Hall Cutler

13. "Insane in the membrane"
Cypress Hill (1993)

Mercury has always been in our environment, long time, since we been swinging from the trees time, like forever. It's part of our world and the body can cope with mercury in the small doses that occur in nature, but our bodies are not designed to have such large quantities and with such regularity as 24 hours a day leaking directly from my mouth, which unfortunately happens to be pretty close to my brain.

You will not be surprised to learn that the parts of my brain closest to my mouth are the parts that got poisoned by the mercury leaking from the amalgams, makes sense really, although that's not the only reason the brain gets hit hard.

The damaged parts in the brain are the Hypothalamus and the Pituitary and they control the hormones. These glands are hidden between the top of the spine and the lowest part of the brain. Picture that, right in the middle, tucked away so no damage can get them from outside; what God/nature thought was the safest place for these vital glands.

Blood circulates around the body, the hypothalamus and pituitary release hormones sending messages to the adrenal and thyroid glands telling them what to do. The messages are sent via my blood. This happens perpetually. The blood is poisoned by the perpetually leaking mercury, this contaminates the brain: which is, phew, why I got so damn bloody ill: mercury on the brain.

And yeah, wrecked hormones are wildly common in mercury toxic people, more on this later.

But this leaked mercury poisoned me all over my body, not just my brain. Poisoned it in slow motion, bit like watching a tree grow. In fact more like watching a tree die of old age. Impossible to see from day to day, because the quantities are so small on a daily basis, but over the years my body became loaded with mercury.

One of the many different things that can happen to some people, it did with me, was I started clenching, chewing and grinding my teeth together. This released even more mercury from the amalgams. The friction and heat from the tooth grinding was melting the amalgams in my mouth, accelerating my poisoning. Oh bugger!

I had a good three years where I was grinding my teeth all night long, hard. I would go through mouth guards every couple of months I was grinding so violently. My dentists would tut and mutter when they saw my flat, ground-down teeth and shiny smooth amalgams. Even now, thinking of all the grinding I did sends a shiver down my spine. It's not a good thing to do with amalgam fillings.

14. Nine months of hell

I still had seven amalgam fillings at this point, so I embarked on complete amalgam removal. This time, using a specialist dentist who would protect me as best as he could: rubber dam, oxygen, super-fast air hose, specially ventilated room, mega-dosing vitamin C, charcoal. All the things I should have had the first time around, if I had known.

If anyone is reading this and is just embarking on trying to get better, under no circumstances should you skimp or save money on amalgam removal. It must be done with maximum protection from a dentist who knows exactly what he's doing. The mercury forums are littered with people like me who screwed up, cut a corner and massively regretted it. As I said, it is the only regret I have in life.

Thank funk I only had one removed incorrectly. I dread to think what would have happened if I'd had all eight out with no protection. I know people who did and they had a wildly difficult time of it, much worse than me.

But even with all the protection, I still got sick. Doesn't matter what you do, when you are having amalgams removed you are always going to get some toxic exposure from the mercury being drilled out. It's inevitable, but using a specialist greatly minimises the damage and danger. Mercury vapour is released by removal and some contamination is inevitable. It is the price you must pay in order to rid your body of toxic waste.

Most people are fine and amalgam removal is a breeze, but I was so ill, my already severely troubled body protested furiously at the insult I was inflicting on it. I never had the brain fog this bad before.

Imagine playing a game of chess, your opponent makes a move, what's your next move? You think about all the multiple possible moves and consequences, you look two, three, four moves ahead and…and… You know when it gets too much, you have been thinking too hard and everything suddenly gets jumbled up and makes no sense at all and for a split second your mind goes blank? Phuff! Gone. You have to physically shake your head to get a clear picture again.

Brain fog is like that moment when you mind goes blank, but nothing comes clear again and shaking your head just makes you feel dizzy. With brain fog you just sit there staring at the wall for hours, mind a blank.

Occasionally a thought will wander by. What was I thinking about again? But you can't grasp it and it just floats off like a cloud. That's brain fog, and when it lasts for days on end, ebbing and flowing like the tide, working in the office gets pretty tough. Keeping home life together suffers on a grand scale too.

I would sit all day at my desk just staring vacantly into my screen. If someone asked me something it might jog me out of my zone, but the thing with brain fog is, you just stumble back into la-la land a few minutes later without even noticing. It's nice in there, nothing to think about, just looking at stuff, nothing going in. The lights are on, but nobody's home.

Coming out of the fog-zone is horrid, that's when you realise what you have missed, or might have missed. It's dreadful, that realisation that you have gone mental. That's what people get locked up for. Staring into space for days on end. Horrific, scary and part of most mercury toxic people's repertoire of problems, and now mine too.

Work was suffering badly. I went from an aggressive, successful broker to a zombie that just stared at the screen and did the minimum. I was obsessing over every health problem I had. All I could think about was the multitude of aches and pains and how I could figure out a path back to normality. Everything else receded into the background. Everything.

My boss tells me he tried to speak with me, but I didn't make any sense, just blabbered on about weird stuff he had never heard about. To this day I have no recollection of any such discussions. I am thankful that I can't remember anything of my time in the twilight zone.

If I'd been seeing doctors I have no doubt they would have diagnosed me as 'Mad as a Hatter' and found me a nice comfortable cell.

I was warned early on that mercury problems are not recognised by doctors and that my medical health insurance would not cover me. That doctors would just pump me full of drugs, take away my choices and options and could easily lock me away. I consider myself very lucky to have known to avoid the doctors. The mercury forums are littered with horror stories. I repeat: I am lucky I had the drive to get better on my own.

I seemed to be a sensitive soul; after each quadrant of amalgams was replaced I would get major brain fog and all my symptoms would ratchet painfully up up up. The symptoms would last a hard four days and then gradually simmer down for three days and then it would restart again on the seven-day anniversary of the amalgam removal, with all the symptoms repeating again for another week. It did this for about one month, gradually simmering down as the month went by.

Hal Huggins talks about this in his book, *It's All in Your Head: The Link Between Mercury Amalgams and Illness*. It's something to do with the way your body handles a toxic exposure, something to do with seven-day cycles repeating the process the body uses to detox.

I have never read about this anywhere but his book, but there must be some truth to it because it happened to me. I guess it's like when you have a cold or the flu and you think it's gone after a week, but it seems to come back and haunt you and drags on for another week. I guess it's something like that.

After about one month I was just about strong enough (ha, hardly!) to get the next quadrant of amalgam removed and the whole wretched saga of symptoms would repeat again and again and again.

In all, it took me nine months to get all my amalgams out. Nine months of hell. God knows how I kept my job. If I look out the corner of my eye and squint I can mildly chuckle at it now I am better, but that was the lowest part of my life to date, utter misery. I was a complete fruit cake, totally obsessed about my failing health.

On the 1ˢᵗ November 2007 all the dental work was completed and I finally went amalgam free.

Further reading: *It's All in Your Head: The Link Between Mercury Amalgams and Illness* by Hal Huggins

15. Chelation starts here

Some people get miraculously better when they become amalgam free. Their symptoms miraculously evaporate and they go back to a happy, normal life. That didn't happen with me. I just got a load of my usual side effects and horrid symptoms and my problems continued unchanged.

Note the word amalgam. I was *amalgam* free, but I was not *mercury* free. My teeth no longer had any amalgam fillings in them, but my body still had the leaked mercury lodged in it. But now that I was amalgam free, I was free to embark on the next leg of my journey: mercury detox. Chelation here we come! Oh yes, baby!

After extensive reading, I decided I would be using the Andy Cutler mercury chelation protocol. Why his? There were many other mercury chelation protocols that I could potentially have used. But I chose his; why?

There are a few reasons:

He cured himself using the protocol. That might seem simplistic, but many of the doctors professing mercury knowledge never had the privilege of curing themselves.

If I used his protocol, hopefully I would avoid some of the errors of previous generations of mercury toxic people. Errors he identified and wrote about in this book and in his numerous posts on internet forums.

Another reason was because of the Yahoo Frequent Dose Chelation forum. This band of people were all mercury toxic and were all chelating under the Cutler protocol. They all had a multitude of problems, all of which needed solving, and all of which were discussed in graphic detail on a daily basis on the forum pages. Hopefully I could learn from their successes and avoid their mistakes. Also being in close contact with people in the same boat was the kind of support that I needed.

But the number one reason I chose this protocol was because Andy Cutler educated me. His book explained why I was so ill. He explained how I could get better. He explained many of the pitfalls of mercury detox and how I could avoid them. I didn't have to rely on anyone else. His words gave me a clear plan of action.

I had had horrid experiences in blindly following orders. Now I needed to understand the things I did. Cutler's protocol made sense. I could understand it. The decision was easy to make once his words had taught me what was wrong, and how to undo that wrong.

His protocol was pretty simple too: it just meant taking small, controlled doses of chelators (drugs to detox mercury) every three to four hours for three days, even waking up at night to take the pills. Then stopping after three days, resting and letting the body recover. Keeping the dose low would minimise any problems.

When you mobilise mercury, the chelator grabs on to a minuscule bit of mercury, picks it up and moves it out of the body. Once it is out, it can no long harm you.

OK, it's not as simple as that. What actually happens is the mercury is picked up, moved into the blood stream, transported a little, then dropped again. Then it is picked up again by another bit of chelator, transported and dropped again. Picked up, dropped. Picked up, dropped.

All the time this picking-up, dropping-off is happening. And that's fine as long as you have the chelation agent in your blood to do the picking up again. The problem (and misunderstood) part is that the chelators only have a half-life of a few hours. When the chelator runs out of juice, any mercury that has been mobilised is dropped and is not picked up again. Once you have free mercury floating about inside you, that's when it begins to hurt, that's when damage is done.

When a chelator enters the body, it lasts for a very specific period of time. If the level of chelator is kept constant you will have a conveyor belt of chelators moving mercury, bit by bit, out of your body. You keep topping up the chelator dose every three to four hours, keeping the level constant, which in turn keeps the mobilised mercury bound to the chelator—where it can do little harm.

I guess it's like juggling: the chelator lifts the mercury and juggles the mercury out of your body. But the moment the chelator runs out, that's the moment there is free mercury wandering around inside you, i.e. the juggler drops the balls. And yes, free, unbound mercury will hurt wherever it settles.

Each person will have a certain tolerance to the level of mercury they can handle. The lower the quantity of mercury dropped, the easier it is for your body to cope with. So the advice is to start with a low dose of chelator.

Unfortunately because mercury is so toxic, it is not possible to chelate all the time. Even when it's bound to chelators, it is still floating around inside you buggering things up, so you must stop chelating and rest. You must give your body time to recover. People do try continuous chelation, but not many succeed. They always have to have some time off to recover. Mobilising mercury is a serious business and not something that should be taken lightly.

When you end the chelation round in order to recover, you hit the snag, you run out of chelating agent, the half-life is finished, some of the mercury is dropped, *and this hurts*. Sometimes not a lot, sometimes more. The trick is to take just enough chelator so that it does not hurt you when the round ends. Keep the dosage low and you will be fine. Each person is different and will have a different safe dose of chelator.

Maybe you will survive chelating on a big dose, but when the round ends, BOOM!

Big chelator dose = big redistribution event at the end of the round.

Keep the dose low = much fewer, smaller problems when the round ends.

And herein lies the problem with other chelation protocols. So many involve taking very high dose chelator levels, combined with infrequent dosing. Super large quantities of mercury are up-lifted, and super large quantities of mercury are free to re-circulate elsewhere when the chelator half-life comes to an end.

The problems really kick off when mercury is re-circulated into the brain. That can happen at any time when you chelate with very large doses. It's like Russian roulette, you will not get hit every time, but eventually you will be unlucky and the mercury will settle on the brain, and then that person will add their chelation horror story to the pile.

I wanted to avoid these horrors. Cutler's protocol instinctively made sense to me: low doses of chelators to minimise problems, taken frequently to maximise mercury removed, dosage tailored to me and my body. I understood it too, which is oh so important to me.

Important note: Do not attempt to chelate using this book only. There is no substitute to reading Andy Cutler's books about chelation. My description is just a brief overview.

• • •

There are three chelators to choose from under the protocol. Each chelator needs to be treated with respect. Respect because each is capable of mobilising one of the most dangerous and harmful substances known to harm humans.

DMSA (Dimercaptosuccinic acid) is available to buy over-the-counter and you don't need a prescription. DMSA chelates your body, but does not chelate the brain. The brain is surrounded by the blood-brain barrier (BBB), which protects it. DMSA cannot pass it, so will not chelate your brain of mercury. This is important to understand. DMSA can only do so much.

ALA (Alpha Lipoic Acid) is the chelator of choice. This is the real deal, numero-uno, kingpin and the mother of all chelators! ALA is what chelates the mercury from your brain. Oh yes, baby! It is able to cross the blood-brain barrier (BBB) and chelate the mercury out of your head. ALA can also cross the cell membranes and will chelate mercury from all other organs in the body too. Slow and steady is the name of the game and you need to tread carefully, but ALA is the stuff that will make you better again. No doctor's prescription is needed, it is available over-the-counter.

DMPS is another chelating agent, but unfortunately for me, it is prescription only. I could not find a source of supply, nor a doctor to help, so it was not on the cards for me. It is reportedly a good chelator that greatly minimises side effects, better than DMSA. It does not cross into the brain, so does not chelate mercury from your head.

Everyone is different and everyone can handle a different dose. You could start at a high dose and risk blowing your brains to kingdom come. But a much safer method to get better is to start at a low dose and work upwards. I was not willing to chance my luck any more than necessary, so I started low with 12.5mg of DMSA, as per instructions from the Yahoo Frequent Dose Chelation (FDC) group.

Just a quick note to those of you in a rush to get better. Maybe you want to speed your chelation road? Maybe you want to crack on with some nice big chelator doses so you can rush to recovery in double-quick time? Fine, take high doses, but—and this is important—take the high doses later. Take the high doses after you have discovered what your body is capable of handling. Start low and build the dose up. That way you will gently find the level that your body is capable of safely handling. Do not start high and work the dose down. If you do start high, there is a chance your lovely little brain will turn to wibbly-wobbly jelly, and we don't want that, do we! Respect is the name of the game when it comes to chelators.

ALA is not suitable to take until three months after amalgam removal. This is because during amalgam removal, some exposure and contamination from the mercury is inevitable. This free-roaming mercury will be circulating around in the blood.

What ALA does is open the gateway between the brain and the body, allowing mercury to flow between the two. If the concentration of mercury in the bloodstream is higher than that of the brain, then taking ALA will make mercury flow into the brain. What you want is lower equilibrium in the body so that when you take ALA, the mercury flows out of the brain, into the body and then out of the body attached to the ALA. It's an equilibrium thing.

Part of the Cutler protocol is also the recommended supplements. He recommends a bunch: vitamins B, C, E, B12, magnesium, zinc and flax oil. These are the bare minimum and just the start in supporting the body. As I learnt more I added more to suit my needs but I started on these.

I had read up and obsessed about chelation so I knew what to do, but it was still scary as hell. There were so many horror stories about chelation: people going mad, massive side effects, never-the-same-again people, even people keeling over and dying. It's a big deal, chelation. Important to get it right.

But as scared as I was, I was even more excited. Excited to get the show on the road. Excited to get healing. I was sure mercury was my problem, everything pointed to it, but chelation would 100 percent confirm it.

I wondered how long it would take to chelate my mercury out? Two years, or five? I knew I had a lot of chelation to come, at least two years with minimum 50 chelation rounds to do, but yeah, I was excited and looking to the future. Would this get me out of my hole?

Other people had been completely cured using this protocol. Would my healing be fast, or slow, or turbo? I dreamt of telling my recovery story. Telling of how low I fell, and how I climbed up high, high, high again. This was the start, the beginning of my healing!

Or was it?

Time to find out.

On 9th November 2007, ten days after I had my last amalgam removed, I started chelation under the Cutler protocol.

Throughout my detox journey, I kept a detailed diary of everything I tried, every healing action I took, what my reactions were and how I felt along every step of the way. I did this because I am a man of action and I do a lot of different things and not all of them agreed with me. Unfortunately my short-term memory was shot to pieces, so making notes helped me help myself. I needed to remember what caused what. I didn't want to keep repeating the same old mistakes.

And some pretty funky things happened to me along my road too. I found the process of healing fascinating, extraordinary and well worthy of taking notes. I wanted to remember them in the full. They say time heals all wounds, but I wanted to look back and marvel at how sick I'd been and how better I'd made myself, touch wood.

I did a lot of chelation, and there are many more chelation rounds you will read about, but this was the first entry in my mercury diary:

Round 1 – 9th November 2007

Have been amalgam free for just over a week now. I just completed my first round on the Andy Cutler chelation protocol, DMSA 12.5mg every four hours for three days, even waking at night to take the night doses. Waking in the night was no problem, so I did the third night too, to make it three nights.

Had some very good spells, particularly on the second day. I felt like a million bucks for four or five hours, right back to my good old self. But it didn't last and that evening the dreaded brain fog set in with a vengeance and I stared at the wall for four hours like a zombie. The best and the worst of it and all in the same day.

My heart was a bit racy at times and I had some strange sensations and movements in my chest area. These are new to me so they felt odd, but no pain.

I did remember a dream. I don't remember having a dream for years and years.

I smell nasty.

My dumps smell worse.

I have a strong metal taste in my mouth.

I awoke at normal time on Monday morning, after the last dose at 2am, to a massively tingly and itchy right arm. I have a tattoo on my right arm, red and black ink, and it made me think that mercury was in the ink. Not a pleasant thought! But nothing more than itchy, no scabs or anything, just a tad itchy.

Probably had an equal amount of time feeling OK as feeling like $hite.

Today is the first day after I finished and it's basically the same: a nice gentle rollercoaster ride, not too fast, the brain fog comes and goes, but no feeling like a million bucks, nor looking at walls for too long.

All my previous amalgam removals have hurt like hell and have taken three or four weeks for me to get back to normal(-ish). The last was no exception; I would say this first DMSA round really helped. Previous removals have left me unable to function for three or four days in a row, repeating 7/14/21 days later, so what I described above is pretty mild compared to that, so it must have helped calm things down.

I'm real happy I followed advice and started on a low dose of 12.5 mg (the Cutler book recommends 50mgs). That was easily strong enough. No desire to have it any stronger than that.

All in all, a good success. It was very nice to feel so fine, even if it was short lived.

Turns out that the red dye used in tattoos has mercury in it. So there was yet another exposure for me. What a joy! Other colours have other metals, cadmium rings a bell, but you will have to Google it if you want to find out more.

11th November 2007 – Colours!

Two days after completion of my first round of DMSA.

I have had an amazing and wonderful morning. I am less colour blind than I was!

This is totally and utterly and wildly astonishing. I can hardly believe my eyes. Walking to work, I kept noticing how bright everything seemed to be, yet it was a cloudy London morning. I noticed how vivid and clear the street signs were, specifically the blues. Blues have been sparkling at me all day long. Reds and greens are more distinct too. Reading my book on the train was impossible because I just kept gawping out the window at all those new colours. Some pictures seem to have more depth to them, pictures have been leaping out at me all morning, and I kept noticing bright colours across the room, twinkling at me.

Cutler does talk about this. He makes a passing reference to colours being brighter and better depth perception. I always wondered if this could happen to me. Makes me think my mercury issue goes way back, way, way back.

I am very colour blind and always have been. There are three types of colour-blindness you can get: red/green, green/brown and blue/yellow. I have them all and I have been like that my whole life. When I see a rainbow I see the colours blue and yellow and that's it.

The change that has just occurred after this first round of DMSA is not that much, but enough for me to notice immediately. As a wild guess, I'd say my colours are approx five percent better, and some depth perception is back, but it is difficult to gauge.

I always thought that my colour-blindness was a genetic thing, passed down from my grandfather Forsyth. He was also extremely colour blind too. Guess what he did for a living. Yup, he was a dentist. LOL, what a crazy world we live in!

And that's what has come back this morning, colours: most astonishing indeed. Made my day and that's for sure.

Colour blindness and mercury go hand in hand. Back in the good old days people who worked in light bulb factories often used to get mercury poisoned because there is mercury in florescent light bulbs. There are old research papers saying that plenty of mercury poisoned people from light bulb factories lost their colour vision. (See the reference at the end of the chapter for more information.)

Did you know: All florescent light bulbs and all energy-saving light bulbs have mercury in them. All of them! Mercury is required for the chemical reaction that makes the florescent light bulb light up.

Is that so 'green'? To have mercury in our houses? In our immediate and close environment? Did those supermarkets tell you that when they flogged you those expensive energy-saving light bulbs? (LED and halogen are fine, it's just the florescent ones.)

In fact, I just saw on the news some unlucky Chinese workers who have very recently been finding out just how dangerous working in light bulb factories is. Google it. It's happening today in China as I type this. I have none of that toxic crap in my house. I choose not to live with mercury in my home.

Further reading: Google "Colour vision and contrast sensitivity losses of mercury intoxicated industry workers in Brazil".

Round 2 – 16th November 2007
12.5mg DMSA every four hours, three days on.

Two and a half weeks since I had all my amalgams removed. I am still suffering the after-effects of this removal. Specifically the brain fog I currently have comes from amalgam removal, because I've never had it this bad before.

I had another four or five hour period where I felt like a million bucks, really fantastic, followed again by major brain fog although not as bad as round one. I did get a bad headache, my big toe throbbed like crazy for no apparent reason. My tattoo was very itchy again. Sometimes I felt fine, sometimes rough. Each of these symptoms hit me one at a time, each lasting three to five hours before moving on to the next.

I did remember a dream again, as I did on round one.

Now I know what Andy Cutler means when he talks of 'manageable symptoms' – all of my symptoms are 'manageable'. Round two was smoother than round one and I had much less redistribution hassles at the end.

Two days after the end of the round, yellow came blazing back to me ☺

Round 3 – 23rd November 2007
12.5mg DMSA every four hours, three days on.

I love my new colour vision. Round three I have the colour red coming back. I continue to be amazed at this remarkable added bonus. Round one was blue, round two was yellow, now I've got red back too. Happy happy dayz!

The rounds are worth doing for this colour vision alone. Funny how each round gives me different specific colours back. I wonder if this has ever happened to anyone else before?

I want to tell everyone, I want to talk to all my mates and all my work colleagues, tell them how amazing this is, how wonderful I feel at having recovered something that was so utterly, untouchably lost. But no. This is too wild. They already think I'm crazy and this will just make matters uncomfortable. So, no, I will keep this close to home, just my wife and my online mercury toxic mates. That's enough anyway, this kind of news needs sharing.

On the second day of the round in the morning I felt like a million bucks again, just like previous rounds. Then in the afternoon

I felt terrible again, just like previous rounds. Day one and three, I felt OK. Overall it was pretty good, but it is very much like riding a rollercoaster, very up and down!

Although amalgam removal after-effects are still hitting me, the second-day sensations have been basically the same on each round. I asked the Yahoo Frequent Dose Chelation (Yahoo FDC) group and they said I should try to dose more frequently than every four hours. Sometimes people's bodies use up the chelator quicker than normal and they must dose more frequently. Next round I will go to three or three and a half hour dosing.

I also had a heavy-duty redistribution experience 15 hours after the last dose. Ouch! Two hours of mega brain fog. Made me feel like a jittery freak: Cha-cha-cha, cha-cha-cha.

Time to hunker down, close the curtains, shut everything down and everyone out. Just be on my own; interacting with people is impossible when I get like this. Unpleasant really, but it passed like it usually does.

I don't think chelation should be this tough.

Round 4 – 30th November 2007
12mg DMSA, every three hours in the day, four hours at night.
Three days on, four days off.

It is one month since I have been amalgam free and any after-effects from removal should now have subsided. Anything that happens on rounds is now due to the DMSA actions only.

Due to gentle rollercoaster of manageable symptoms, I changed length of cycles from every four hours down to every three hours in the day, but remained at four hours evening/night.

This is acceptable and within the Cutler protocol rules; at night the body closes down somewhat and less chelator is required. Everyone is different and each must find what suits them. This timing does not quite fit evenly into 24 hours, but I want to keep the waking at night to a minimum, so my dose times are now as follows:

6pm, 10pm, 2am, 6am, 9am, 12noon, 3pm.

I started the round at 6pm and at 9:20pm, three hours and twenty minutes after the first dose, I started feeling a bit strange with a little bit of brain fog coming in, but decided to carry on as planned. Unfortunately the round got progressively worse until all hell broke loose two doses before the end of day three.

Oh $hit, oh no, here we go: I had a major mercury attack. Massive muscle weakness hit in my lower back. I felt as floppy as a rag doll, every movement was agony. Energy disappeared, I was tired and weak. I was wildly angry and irritated all weekend, biting back the frustration most of the time, but shouting whenever I lost control.

My shoulders were hurting like hell. My bowel movements changed colour to light tan, I had sickening heartburn and a racing heartbeat. Moderate brain fog set in with the jittery cha-cha-chas returning to complete the madness.

Big time OUCH!

This was my first really unpleasant round, previous rounds were pretty good compared to this nightmare of reactions. Obviously I need to dose every three hours all the time. Think I will change the start and end time of rounds too. I will aim to finish in the evening so that any redistribution events hopefully happen when I am asleep.

So, I need to dose every three hours, even at night. I was hoping not to have to get up twice at night. Oh well...worth a try!

And, I guess I need to reduce the dosage too: 8.3mg or 6.25mg (splitting 25mg capsules). Better safe than sorry.

Today is the second day after the round ended and I have mostly returned to normal now, but that was a horrific couple of days. Muscle weakness has calmed right down, thankfully. This had been one of my biggest problems, and it had been significantly better since I'd been amalgam free.

Round 5 – 7th December 2007
6mg DMSA every three hours, three days on.

I have halved the dose to 6mg DMSA, dosing every three hours around the clock, even waking at night to take the dose, three days on, four days off. I have been amalgam free almost six weeks.

I learned a lot from the previous round, and the result was this round five was pretty smooth, any symptoms were very mild. I could go about my life in a normal manner.

Phew! I have finally found the dose and timings that suit me. Hooray!

This means I am a fast metaboliser. Which means my body burns and uses things up quickly and I have to dose more frequently than every four hours.

I did have a little redistribution event afterwards, but again it was much less than all four previous rounds, just a little itching, heartburn and metal mouth.

Happy.

16. Star Wars Episode IV: A New Hope

Backtrack six months to early 2007, two months into amalgam removal. I went on holiday to France and I started to feel semi-normal towards the end of the week. Within hours of getting home again, my symptoms came raging back. The contrast was obvious, but very puzzling. Something must have been causing me to be sick at home, but what?

I researched toxins in the home. I found a cool little book called *The Chemical Maze Shopping Companion* by Bill Statham. I checked the ingredients on various household products and discovered there are harmful chemicals everywhere: cleaning products, plastics, shampoos, soaps, toothpaste, shaving foam, aerosols. When I realised I was surrounded with chemical and toxic gloop, I took all my toiletries to the muscle tester dude.

He tested me and I came up weak to everything. I was surprised but not shocked, just happy to have discovered another thing that was harming me. Now I could avoid them.

I was intrigued by all this muscle testing. It would be much more convenient if I could do it myself. So I decided to try and teach myself. The muscle tester dude had already explained it to me. I had already seen and witnessed it in action countless times. I knew what was supposed to happen, but could I do it on my own without the muscle tester dude?

I needed a heavy-ish weight, something I could just about lift. Ah perfect! I found my metal briefcase filled with poker chips. It was pretty heavy. I took out a third of the chips et voila. Just my kinda muscle testing device: poker chips.

I took all the household products the muscle tester dude had just tested and proceeded to test everything again, this time on my own. What was supposed to happen was, if something was bad for me, my body would become weak and I would be unable to lift the case of poker chips. The very same poker chips that two seconds earlier I was able to lift.

And wow! I did it straight up, first time, no questions asked: perfect. Whenever I tested something that disagreed with me, I was incapable of lifting the weight. Freak-y!

Muscle testing is not cast-iron and infallible, and certainly for an amateur like me it's prone to misinterpretations, but it's a good guide as long as it is only used as a guide. I take the view that a guide is better than no guide. The most important things are framing the questions correctly, tasting or smelling it, and being aware it applies to the right here and right now.

I consider muscle testing correct about 80 percent of the time, but I never use it for mercury specific issues. It's been wrong with mercury a few times and I don't like messing with the mercury. I don't think my body knows in advance what the mercury will do to me once it's been mobilised. I never muscle test chelator doses for that reason.

It's a cool skill and one well worth learning, one I used repeatedly over the next few years, testing my supplements, the food in my diet and the many things in my environment.

I am fully aware it is considered extreme, but this is not some murky idea a friend-of-a-friend heard from a mate in the pub. This is what I see and feel first hand. I can demonstrate it to anyone, anytime, anyplace.

So anyway, I replaced the whole lot of household products with eco-friendly, toxin-free stuff. There is a market for everything and you can find non-toxic goods if you look: toxin-free hair gel, fluoride-free toothpaste, organic shampoo, eco aftershave, herbal shaving foam. If you look, you will find. It takes a little time to search out, but it just comes down to choice. I choose not to buy products with harmful toxins in them.

From these investigations, I discovered another interesting fact about myself, another problem to add to my long list of woes. When you react to lots of chemicals in your environment it's called 'multiple chemical sensitivities', and I had it in spades!

It was also a huge signal that my liver was heavily congested, which I already knew from the liver flushes, but it showed that even after the liver flushes, I was still clogged.

But even reducing my toxic load by cutting out the chemicals in the house didn't make a blind bit of difference. I remained in deep trouble.

Back to now, six months later towards the end of 2007, after I had been detoxing a little and had radically cleaned up my diet, I went on holiday again. And again I got better whilst away, but this time the getting better was most marked. In the two weeks I was away, I ate like a horse and put on some much-needed weight, but within 24 hours of arriving home, I got sick again. What was going on?

This needed more investigation. I needed to figure out what this meant. Something was holding me back at home? But what?

Further reading: *The Chemical Maze Shopping Companion* by Bill Statham

17. The Great Raw Cat Food Experiment and Me

The muscle tester dude told me something really strange about cats once. He told me that some of his stubborn patients got better when they fed their pet cats raw meat. Weird, eh!

He told me that cats are carnivores. In the wild, in their natural habitat, cats eat birds and mice and that's really all they eat. Cats are carnivores, simple really. Cats did not evolve to eat cooked food. They did not evolve to eat grains, nor rice, nor soya, nor the floor sweepings from the factory floor that is called 'cat food'.

Not sure totally how it worked, I did search the internet plenty and found nothing, not a bean. Sure I found plenty about raw diets for cats, but nothing about its effect on humans. It's something to do with healthy cats being healthy, by eating what cats are supposed to eat, i.e. raw meat, and healthy cats do not excrete some flaky stuff. It's the flaky stuff that we humans are allergic too. Wild, eh!

Now, I have had cats since I was a kid in shorts, must be every day for those years, (except a couple of years at boarding school). And never once in that 35 or 36 years did I ever, ever get sick, or get anything even remotely like a cat allergy. People with cat allergies swell up, sneeze, itch, and all that. Within minutes, this happens to people with cat allergies, and in 35 or 36 years this had never happened to me, not once, not ever. But I was horribly sick in many other ways.

The worst that could happen was the cats refused the raw meat. If they did eat it, maybe the cats would get a little healthier. I assumed the chances of this affecting me and my health to be astronomically low, but I was out of other ideas. I was desperate, frantic, nothing was working and I kept getting worse and worse. I needed to try everything to see if something, anything worked. I could not sit around doing nothing. No stone was going to be left unturned in my hunt to get better.

18. Power Rangers

Unless I wanted a divorce, getting rid of the cats was out of the question, so I started the now infamous experiment: The Great Raw Cat Food Experiment and Me. I fired up a blog on a mercury forum Herballure.com and commenced the mother of all long shots.

I did discuss this beforehand, but the wife was singularly unimpressed.

"Are you mad? Raw meat for the cats? They will get salmonella poisoning. No! Over my dead body!"

So I decided to wait until she was away for a week on holiday before secretly starting the experiment. Yes, I was dicing with death, but I was at my wits' end.

The cats got fed only raw meat and nothing else. It was immediately obvious they preferred bird meat, which I guess is right because cats will never catch and kill a cow or a sheep. Chicken and turkey was good, rabbit was OK in small doses. They lapped up the raw liver.

The cats were young and immediately took to the new food, wolfing it down in the mornings and evenings after I got home from work. Nothing happened the first week, but the second week was more eventful.

It started when my wife got home to discover I'd changed the cats' diet without her prior knowledge or consent. My wife and I argue very infrequently, a couple of times a year, tops, but this was one of those times where I'd overstepped the mark.

"How could you? Experiment! With my cats!"

"Yeah, but, come on, I'm sick, this might help…"

"How could you!"

"But…this….I'm….look…they're fine…seriously…fine…"

"What is this? Why? Tell me again why you started this stupid experiment! This is totally unacceptable! Are you trying to kill the cats? What were you thinking?"

"But…I explained…this is what wild cats would eat…"

"We do not have wild cats! We have pedigree cats!"

"Yeah, but…"

"I can't believe you put the cats at risk with this insane nonsense!"

Yeah, not one of our finest marital moments, but I was frantic to get better. It was a long shot. A wild long shot. I was in try-everything mode.

Three incredible things happened:

Firstly the cats became like Power Ranger Cats. Their fur became ultra-sleek and soft, they became even more relaxed around the house and it was obvious these two cats were ultra-happy and uber-healthy. They started bringing in lots more kills from the garden. Every day these super cats brought in fresh game: birds, mice, rats and even the odd squirrel. Not road kill squirrel, but big Daddy squirrels.

Very impressive that. It was plainly obvious that the cats loved the raw meat diet. But what about me?

19. That feeling of healing

During the second week of the experiment, I experienced a new sensation: that feeling of healing arrived. I'd never felt it before, but there is a 'feeling of healing'. It's a hot, powerful, joyful, energising sensation. If you've never felt it before, I promise you it's a marvellous feeling, one to strive after.

Suddenly it was like I'd felt on holiday, but fifty times stronger. Suddenly I started getting better. It was slow at first, but I was so deathly ill, even small steps upwards were blindingly obvious.

Two weeks into the cat experiment, the feeling of healing was huge. This was a major breakthrough. I had had declining health for ten years, I was utterly miserable in chronic pain every day. Suddenly I was hungry like a horse. Suddenly I was happy again. Suddenly I was in less pain. Suddenly my back did not hurt quite so much and my heartburn relaxed. It was like the sun coming out from behind the clouds right after a huge storm.

Eating took one hour at each meal as I munched through salad after salad. My appetite was huge. I soon realised I could eat a little meat and a small helping of brown rice again. I started bulking up within days of adding these foods back into my diet. The sensation of healing was immense and I basked in its glory as my body kicked into life. A religious person would have said they'd been touched by God. I felt marvellous.

Over the next two months, my body roared into life and I put on 22 pounds (10kg) in weight. Weight that I desperately needed because I was so skeletal.

Obviously my body was making up for lost time after being malnourished for so long. It felt as if a large weight had been physically lifted off my shoulders and I was finally free to start healing at long last.

But make no mistake, this was just the start. I was very ill and it takes a long time to get better after falling to such depths of despair. There was to be no miracle-overnight cure for me, but this was the starting point. All kicked off by the mother of all long shots! A weird diet change for my pet cats!

What an odd world we live in, eh! I wish I could make this more believable for you, some magic bullet that did the trick instead of this weirdness. But all I have is my strange tale. I could not have made this up if I'd tried.

It was a very happy moment in my life, to finally get the breakthrough that I had worked so hard for. I remember sitting at home and just smiling, just sitting around happy, overjoyed and grinning at the wonderful success I'd somehow engineered. The last eight months I'd spent learning and trying many alternative health options, eight months of constant misery, and this was the result, finally, a glorious feeling of healing.

The Pottenger Cat experiments are famous and you may well have heard of them. My cat experiment is the same as the Pottenger experiments, but he didn't figure the human cat allergy connection. I have friends who have cat allergy issues, but they have no allergy symptoms when they come in contact with my uber-healthy cats. A good read that Pottenger book.

After much reading, researching, thinking and pondering, I realised my healing reaction was an indication that I had adrenal fatigue, that my body was unable to tolerate any stressors. The unhealthy cats were a toxin to me and once that long-term toxin was removed and replaced by healthy non-toxic cats, my body was at last able to start healing. It fitted in with my feeling better when I was away on holiday. My body was so weak, even this strange toxin had been holding me back.

I had already greatly reduced my toxic load by cleaning up my diet, by cleaning my liver and kidneys, by clearing my house of toxic chemicals and of course amalgam removal. Seems this cat toxin was the final straw needed for me to start healing. Once removed, a tipping point was reached and I tipped from declining health to regaining health.

I am certain that the many methods I used to reduce my toxic load were collectively the reason for this happening. It is important to understand that this was the result of the accumulation of all the health regaining actions I'd taken in the previous eight months. The removal of the newly-discovered cat toxin was just the trigger that started the healing.

Further reading: *Pottenger's Cats: A Study in Nutrition* by Francis Pottenger
Natural Nutrition for Cats by Kymythy R. Schultze

20. A New Life

A third amazing thing happened during the cat experiment. There is no way of knowing for sure. You will not be able to decide if it was luck, or chance, or fate, or destiny, or coincidence, or BS, or what, but on the third week of the cat experiment, after four years of trying, my wife and I conceived our second child. Nine months later we had a baby son.

Why this happened three weeks into the cat experiment, when I had only just started getting better is astonishing and frankly fantas-

tically unbelievable. But it happened; I have a handsome son who is asleep upstairs right now as I type this. The dates all match up. I was flabbergasted when I figured it out.

Now, I don't believe in God and I don't believe in wishing, nor do I believe in waiting for things to magically happen. I believe if you want something you gotta go out there and get it for yourself. I believe we make our own luck and I believe that's what happened here. The cats became super healthy, I finally started getting better and we started a new life.

I firmly believe we make our own luck.

21. Wrong?

If I knew for a fact I was mercury toxic, why didn't I just focus on chelation? Why not just sit back and wait for the chelation protocol to work its magic? Why bother with all this weird and wacky alternative health nonsense that I'm about to talk to you about? Surely chelation would solve everything?

There are several answers to that question.

I knew chelation was a long-term project and I wanted to be healthy as soon as possible. I knew and understood that mercury had broken almost everything in my body and that there was a lot of cleaning up to do. I knew that any alternative health action would support my mercury chelation and so speed my healing.

I read a lot. I focused, I obsessed and I learned a lot about alternative health. That knowledge stayed with me and complemented my mercury knowledge. Once I learned of some new health adventure, I wanted to try it myself. I didn't want to just read about it second hand, I wanted to experience the healing others had experienced first-hand. I had discovered that there are many different ways to heal.

The solution to my problems was not one magic, all-powerful bullet. How could it be when I had so many things wrong? Chelation was the ultimate solution but chelation on its own would not be enough. I clearly saw that. I clearly understood Cutler's words. There was a lot of support and healing to be done on top of the chelation work. So my story is not just about chelation, it is about detoxing my body in every single way that I found out about. No stone unturned and all that. I didn't just follow Cutler's protocol, or the muscle tester dude's words. I followed my nose. Once I'd discovered it was actually possible, I educated myself and did everything in my power to try and reverse my ill-health.

I did and experienced a lot of pretty unusual, strange and even extraordinary things in order to heal. At first glance you may disagree, curl up your nose, or just laugh out loud at the craziness of it. So I'd like to say a few words about the general-overall-grand-scheme of things.

There is an opposing view to every single health regaining activity I did. Someone, somewhere will have rubbished something I did, said it does not work, said it's harmful, wrong or a host of derogatory things. The internet is full of opposing views. The world is full of opposing views.

Do you believe in Jesus Christ or Buddha? Diet Pepsi or Diet Coke? Brown bread or white bread? Prozac or St. John's wort? Swimming shorts or speedos? Chemotherapy or holistic health education? Blue socks or white socks? There is an opposing view to everything in life and that includes healing and getting better. Everyone has their own special tricks, views and ideas.

I started from a position of minimal health knowledge. I had to read a lot in order to make up my own mind. So I researched everything in great detail. I didn't blindly do anything. I made educated choices. Some were foolhardy? Maybe, maybe not.

If you read my story and disagree with some of what I say and do, that's cool, that's fine, that's good, that's normal because you should question new ideas. But before you email me to tell me I'm a fool for something I did, I want you to ask yourself why you think I am wrong.

Do you really know why you disagree with me? A lot of the things I did are counter-intuitive. A lot of the things I did are taboo subjects rarely talked about in polite society. A lot of the conventional wisdom about health is wildly inaccurate. But the fact remains I got better and everything I did helped in its own special way. Some things I know are not ideal, like all the supplements I took, but I didn't know any other way to give myself that support.

So if you think something I did was wild, crazy, and/or wrong, then please first check out the quote at the beginning of the book, and then search the internet, or read a book or two. You will discover our world is not quite as straightforward as we all thought.

Or maybe it's right for me, but wrong for you? This is just my journey; this is what I did to get better. Don't be boxed in by what I did. There are many different ways to get better. Don't think you must do things my way. People with the same problem as me, they got better using completely different methods than I. If you are sick, you must do things your way. The way that makes sense to you and your circumstances. As long as the final result is the same, my path is no better than anyone else's path.

22. Aliens

Three weeks after the desperate-long-shot cat experiment started, I tried another left-field manoeuvre, another gamble. I had started getting better, but I still had a long way to go.

In the past, I had been tested for parasites many times: muscle tested, blood tested and stool tested. All those tests came up negative. After so many tests I assumed I had no parasites and didn't have a parasite problem. Not a problem I need investigate any further thanks to my fantastic doctor's excellent help and spiffing advice.

Up until now I had done everything that I *thought* was needed. Everything that I had read about, everything that I thought applied to me, I had now tried. Exercise, diet, liver and kidneys. I thought I'd done it all. I thought I'd turned over every stone.

When you research ideas and ways to get better there is a natural inclination to assume some issues are not your problem, especially when you've had tests done that came up negative.

me to try something that I *thought* I didn't have. And
ried many health-regaining activities and they hadn't
my doctors did helped, so I figured I may as well try
had ruled out.

That probably sounds odd, but I was out of ideas, nothing else
seemed to fit the problems I had. Everything else had failed, except
the odd cat experiment. But I knew sitting around doing nothing was
doomed to failure. I'd spent the past 36 years doing nothing and look
at the state I was in.

Turns out 'parasites' does not just mean creepy crawlies with teeth
and thrashing tails from sci-fi films: aliens! Parasites in our context mean
anything that lives on or inside a person that should not. A wart is a
parasite. Athletes foot is a parasite. Candida is a parasite. Lyme disease
is a parasite. Malaria is a parasite. The bubonic plague was caused by a
single-cell parasite. Roundworms, pinworms, liver flukes to name but a
few of the many thousands out there, and in there; they are all parasites.
Bacteria and fungus living inside you are also technically parasites too.

I had been diagnosed with SIBO (small intestine bacterial overgrowth) to which I was given the super-duper-mega-special-diets to follow. I didn't understand what SIBO was, that it is in fact a parasite, a
bacterial parasite infesting my small intestine. This was all new to me after all. The special diets hadn't worked, so I didn't make the connection.

Anyway, even though I was convinced these parasitic aliens did
not live in me because of all the negative tests I had had, I could not
sit around doing nothing, fading away. I am a man of action, so the
parasite cleanse was researched, purchased and started. I decided on a
freshly-ground, all-herb parasite cleanse from an American company
called Humaworm.

You take two capsules before breakfast, two before dinner and drink
plenty of water throughout the day. I was already drinking two litres of
water a day anyway so that was done. Just taking a few capsules filled
with herbs: easy. Most of the herbs I had heard of anyway, like ginger,
garlic, fennel, cloves. Humaworm contained 24 different herbs in all,
with only a minute quantity of each herb in each dose. Probably would

not work anyway. Probably just pass on through.

And whoa! Something happening here, instant satisfaction!

Within two days, I itched all over. Not a scratch-myself-raw itch, just an annoying constant mad little itch on odd parts of my body. The top of my left foot, my right forearm, my knee, then switching to my neck and then my elbow. Constantly hopping from place to place all over, all day and all night. The kind that makes you laugh and cry at the same time, it's so mental.

Everywhere tingled. Strange rashes surfaced and itched like mad. Odd pimples and spots appeared dotted about my body. A nervous twitch in my eye added to the fun. Some weird, hard pinhead-sized pellets painfully forced their way out through my skin, eeeu yuck!

I had wild stabbing pains all down my back. Proper hard psycho stabbing pains too. Really did feel like someone was viciously attacking me with a knife for days on end. Again, so strange it was comical.

Heartburn was nightmare-like. It did vary in intensity, but it was full-on 24/7 for the whole month. A good nine out of ten on the Richter scale for digestive hassles. I hated it the most when I couldn't sleep; the heartburn was so dreadful I had to try and sleep upright. If I lay down the acid would bubble up my gullet, burning me sleepless.

I was amazed at this flood of side-effects. I *thought* I had no parasites. Somehow I was infested with them! The herbs were killing parasites in the millions, the billions. My body was a war zone.

I understood that these side effects were the result of the death throes of these guys getting whacked. I didn't for a moment consider stopping the herbs, which would then stop all this extra hassle. It was intense, but manageable. I could cope with hassle. I wondered if I'd feel any better after all this mayhem?

23. Juicy

At the same time as I was attacking the parasites I also did a seven-day juice fast. I only drank juiced vegetables for a week. Technically

I should not have fasted because it is never recommended for severely underweight people like me. It was a calculated risk I decide to take. I needed to try anything and everything to get better. Now was a time of action, not sitting around wasting away.

And technically I should not have fasted at the same time as the parasite cleanse either. That was not a calculated risk; I just didn't think I had parasites and didn't think it would matter.

Unlike water fasting, when you juice fast, you can still go about life in a normal manner. The juice provides enough vitamins and minerals so you have your usual strength and stamina. That was important for me because I didn't have much energy to spare and I couldn't afford to lose much more weight. I worked a normal office week when I did all this.

Fasting is one of the oldest methods of healing. To this day, Christians fast during Lent, Jews fast as a means of atonement, Muslims fast for the month of Ramadan and Hindus fast routinely. That's a large swathe of the population of the world, so don't immediately disregard fasting as for freaks. Don't forget Jesus fasted for 40 days and 40 nights and he came out the other side a new man.

He saw the devil.

He saw angels.

Large chunks of the western world worship him. That's freaky! If fasting is good enough for Jesus, then I guess it's good enough for me.

A juice fast is not technically a fast either. A fast is officially when you exclude all food. Juice fasting just excludes the fibre in food. Juice is extracted from raw fresh vegetables. You can use fruit too, but I didn't because I couldn't handle the sugar in the fruit.

It takes a lot of veggies to get a pint of juice, triple at least your usual amount of food, so each juice you drink is in effect mega-dosing with huge quantities of raw vitamins and minerals. Not eating any fibre gives your body a chance to rest from the daily chore of digesting your food. That seems an odd thing to say, no big deal even, but digesting your food takes up a lot of your body's energy. Ever felt tired after a big meal? That's your body powering-down, diverting energy to digest what you just ate.

When we fast, we pause the digestive process, this somehow switches our body to detox and removal mode. Feeling rotten is common. Getting much better afterwards is common too.

Being prepared in advance made juice fasting pretty straightforward for me. Whenever I felt hungry and wanted to eat food, I just drank a juice and Bob's your uncle: I didn't need to eat anymore. Fasting is a lot easier than you would imagine.

24. The lady with the pearl necklace

So here I was innocently juice fasting and parasite cleansing. I didn't really expect much. Yes, I was hoping for much, but I'd been hoping for a long time. These actions didn't seem much different from all the other things I'd tried, although maybe the juicing was a little more hardcore than usual.

I was learning a lot about my body and my situation too. Each action I took confirmed I had more and more problems to sort out. One of the things I learnt here was that sitting on the toilet for 15 minutes straining to have a dump was not normal and meant that I was constipated. That is in fact the definition of constipation!

I'm gonna start using the abbreviation BM, short for Bowel Movement, instead of littering my story with words like dump and crap. Using BM seems cleaner and much more acceptable in today's polite society. Sounds almost like a fast car.

Seven days after starting the parasite killing herbs, my BMs stopped completely. This, to those unaccustomed to parasite cleanses, is a bad sign. Yes, even when you fast, you have BMs. It's the body's waste that comes out, not just the leftovers from your dinner plate. No BMs meant I was blocked up inside. It meant the herbs had cleaned me out and killed so much, that now I had a logjam. A parasite logjam. Lovely!

When this happens, all the toxins that have been killed and dislodged get stuck and gum up the works. Then the toxins start re-circulating around the body. They can't get out, nothing can get out.

Around and around they whirl. Nasty really, definitely not good for you, and not much fun either. Heartburn and the itchies went into overdrive. Sleep was difficult.

For three days and three nights, I drank three litres of water a day and didn't have a BM. Everything I read said this was a bad bad sign. I knew it was a bad thing because I was feeling like I'd been run over by a bus. Time for drastic measures. Time for a colonic.

Oh no, did I really have to do this?

This was at the very bottom of my to-do list, but I thought if ever I needed a real reason to pluck up the courage, now was the time. It was an emergency situation. I had to break the logjam or I'd be in even bigger trouble.

A colonic is kinda like brushing your teeth, just one of those daily household chores that's unavoidable in life. It's annoying, it's a hassle, but you gotta do it otherwise your breath smells. OK?

Ha, if you believe that you'll believe anything. OK, I admit it—it's not like brushing your teeth. It's actually just like having a weirdo stick a tube up your bum and turn on the taps!

Oh man, do I really have to do this?

I took a deep breath, thought of England, and before I could change my mind, picked up the phone and made an appointment to pay for the pleasure to have a weirdo stick tubes up my arse. I guess some people get off on having tubes rammed up their rear, but I assure you, I do not.

Oh no, it doesn't hurt or anything. It's just nasty and unpleasant to think about. It's all in your head! Tube in, water tap turned on, swish about with abdominal massage, then the water and any waste is released. Repeated for about 45 minutes. This washes out any 'compacted waste' and unblocks any 'logjams'. Finish off by sitting on the toilet to...dribble.

Even now, after such cool results, I hate talking about this. I totally want to edit this out of my story. I could easily click delete and save myself the humiliation. But as much as I want to edit it out, to not mention it, to blank it out of my mind and your view, getting better was never fun. All the pain and troubles I went thought were a million times worse than having a tube up me bum. So I'm not going to hide behind the delete button. Colonic hydrotherapy here we come. What a joy!

The build-up to the appointment was fraught with doubt and worry, but mostly huge embarrassment. What if someone I knew saw me? Would people know, just by looking at my guilty face?

I was greeted at the Harley Street clinic by the surreal sight of the person in charge of me. Victoria was a 50-something aristocratic lady with the largest pearl necklace and earrings you have ever seen your life. She was impeccably dressed for a night at the theatre! Her voice was the poshest you ever did hear, sounded like the bloody Queen. And here she was, calmly telling me in her plum English accent, to relax and try not to clench as she shoved her tubes home.

I did ask if she was going to the theatre that evening, but she assured me this was her normal attire.

"Relaxes people, better than a white coat which is far too formal." Not sure it relaxed me, but certainly was a sight to behold.

Anyway, tally-ho, off we go, bomb-doors open and torpedoes away.

"Golly gosh! Would you believe it! Ha, in all my years. Look here, can you see that?"

"Errrr, do I have to look?"

"That's compacted waste and toxins coming out. I have never seen so much come out of one person. And especially not someone as slight as yourself. Look, long black ropey lengths of it."

"Is that a good thing?"

"Oh yes, better out than in. Look, it's still coming out. Amazing, must be 15 to 20 foot long!"

Oh boy! Why me? This was her job and she had never seen so much gunk come out! Took me a long time to figure out what that black gunk was. It's pretty important too, but more of that later.

"You may find yourself a tad tired this evening, Sunshine. Your body has rid itself of many toxins, so just relax and take it easy tonight. Make sure you drink plenty of water."

"OK. Err, how long will I be walking like a cowboy?"

"Oh not long, not long at all. You'll be right as rain in the morning. Just take care. Byee!"

Ha, right. I staggered home and for the next three days and three nights, I lay in bed feeling the most drained, shattered, weakened and wrecked I have ever felt in my life. Any gains made by the cat experiment long forgotten as I curled up and went into take-care-of-myself-mode. I can't remember what excuse I gave for not being in the office, but 100 percent for sure it was not the truth.

After the third day, I came to and started feeling a bit better. Not much better, just a little brighter. I was strangely hungry again too, if only the itching and wild stabbing pains would stop!

My BMs became very strange indeed. Easy for a change, but looking decidedly off-world. Either long black gunky rope stuff, or lots of flaky, dark, leafy like stuff, littering the bowl.

Yeah, yeah, I know, it's a technical word that: 'stuff'. Laypeople use it to explain stuff, OK! Just stuff, right! It was weird, murky, earthy, flaky, dark stuff! UFOs. If you really want to know what it looks like, do a parasite cleanse yourself and you try and explain what comes out!

All the time I was bombarded with spots, pimples, rashes and the very odd stabbing pains right between my shoulder blades. Then on the 25th day of the parasite herbs I came down with flu. It was odd because it hit me out of the blue. Usually you get a couple of days build-up of symptoms beforehand. But one moment I was scratching my arse, the next I had full-blown man-flu. For the second time in a month I was bed bound.

Flu lasted a hard three days and then it disappeared completely within two days. It was noticeably short and sweet, but the three days I was down felt overly harsh.

A few days later, the 30-day parasite cleanse finished and BOOM, all the side effects disappeared and I came out the other side a new man. The clouds parted, the sun came out and I felt GREAT! Brighter and livelier, the spring was back in my step.

At first, I stuck diligently to my salad diet, but it soon became clear something was very different; I was craving foods that had been off my menu for a long time. I really fancied a curry, steak and chips, spag bol. I was starving hungry. I rushed back to the muscle tester dude for some more testing.

Ba-Da-Boom! Food intolerances gone! Woo hoo! I was definitely getting better. Awesome! In six weeks, between the cat experiment, juice fast and the parasite cleanse 60 percent of my food intolerances disappeared overnight. BOOM!

I was very careful, but every two days I re-introduced one food into my diet to test my reaction. Suddenly meat was totally OK. Brown rice was fine. No more horrid reactions. Nightshade intolerance disappeared, so I could eat tomatoes and peppers again. Refined food still didn't agree, but basically anything whole and fresh was edible. Holy cow! How cool was this!

This was not like avoiding foods and not getting sick. This was food intolerances gone. Gone and I could eat each of those foods again without reactions. That wasn't avoidance, that wasn't limbo-land, that was cured.

Good news, eh! Happy dayz! At long last, some glorious news. I danced a jig and thanked my lucky stars that I'd kept on battling. Happy I never gave up. Happy I'd ignored my negative test results. Success and from the mother-of-all-long-shots, some juice and a parasite cleanse that I was positive would have no effect. My grimace evaporated and I regained a smile at long last.

I was so excited I rushed to see my doctor. Could he help me better understand my situation? I really needed to fully understand what had happened here. I told him of the amazing results I'd had, how I'd got them and just how much better I now felt.

He laughed in my face.

He didn't believe me, not for a second.

He just laughed a mocking laugh right in my face.

I guess it is pretty funny and having a laugh is important, but still, I wanted to throttle that little twat. I couldn't believe he belittled my success. Success that was so hard-fought. Success that I needed so badly because my world had fallen apart.

I don't seem to have much luck with doctors.

• • •

It's worth thinking about what happened here. Trying to figure out what it all meant. For 30 days I took the herbs and got some pretty wild side effects. During the month I came down with major flu twice. It was short, sharp flu. Lasted three days, disappeared as quickly as it came. By the end of the herbs I had turned a massive corner, I was healing and getting better at long last.

What did this mean?

Why did I get sicker with the side effects?

Why did I get better after the herbs gave me so many hassles?

The flu-like symptoms I experienced twice during the parasite cleanse are what alternative medicine calls a Herxheimer Reaction, also called a Healing Crisis. The first was after the colonic, and I had the second towards the end after 25 days on the herbs. I came out the other side a new man.

A healing crisis is when your body expels bucket-loads of toxins, so many that you feel rough as hell. Toxins that have been locked up inside the body for a long time. More often than not you get a nasty flare-up of your usual symptoms too. When your body has finally got rid of toxins that it was unable to expel on its own, you feel better again.

The colonic was just a quick wash on the inside to unblock a logjam, but the herbs, now those are the boys that enabled me to kill and let go of years of accumulated waste. The juice fast gave my body the added incentive to power out and detoxify. When the toxins were gone, I was free to start getting better.

Many people report significant gains after a healing crisis, just like I did. Plenty strive to have one as it's an important part of the recovery process. It signals the removal of waste is in full force and effect. It hurts for sure, but when the toxins are out they can never hurt again. Short term pain, long term gain. They don't come around too often, so if you get one, just hunker down and slip into take mode and weather the storm.

Doing the juice fast together with the parasite c⌊ turbo charged detox. I only figured that out in hindsight, but it was just my style and just what I needed. I lost a bit of weight, another 3 kgs (6.4 pounds), down to my all-time low of 56kg (123 pounds). But I started getting better, so it was well worth it.

It's difficult to put into words just how good I felt about this success. If you've been long-term sick, if you've had long-term problems that just will not shift, if you've had ten years of troubles; well, close your eyes for second and imagine the joy you'd experience at stopping the rot and turning the corner. Pure joy bubbling up inside.

I was still very ill, but 100 percent for sure I had turned the corner and was at last getting better. The difference was like night and day, one moment I was miserable and had had declining health for ten years, the next I was out the other side, happy, eating again and looking forward to tomorrow.

After searching for so long, the joy of getting some positive results was awesome, it made up for all the hard work in researching so much, for so long. Work and family had taken a major backseat during the time of my ultra-ill health. Maybe I would keep them after all?

Looking back, I can see this breakthrough was just the very first rung on a very tall ladder that was my health. I still had a long climb to the top. I was mightily sick and I knew it would take time to recover. But this was the end of the beginning, hopefully.

Further reading: *Juice Fasting & Detoxification* by Steve Meyerowitz.

If you are going to juice fast, it's well worth getting this little book. Tells you what to expect, how to do it and importantly how to break the fast. If you break the fast eating pizza and chips, you will make yourself sick again! You have been warned!

The Cure For All Diseases by Hulda Clark.

Old skool writing from a little old lady, but she knows her stuff. The queen of parasites!

25. Auto-printout BS

I have done a multitude of lab tests: blood work, urine, stool, saliva, hair and few of them were worth doing. Some have too wide reference ranges, some are too inaccurate and some are just plain wrong. I found it difficult to investigate and impossible to decode many of the results.

The one exception was my hair test. Now this is a splendid investigation and well worth doing. Not a simple test, because the results need close scrutiny in order to figure out what they mean. You can't just look at the hair test and see X, Y and Z are wrong and off you go tra-la-la-la-la. No, I had to read another great big book to figure out what it all meant. But for those who wish to learn, there is an embarrassment of riches to be had. Most people on the Cutler Protocol have done this hair test as it yields so much juicy information.

It must be done by one specific lab. No other lab is any good. All the different companies and different labs use different methods to run their own tests. They use different ranges, different equipment and these differences make it impossible to compare them like-for-like. But if everyone does the same test, from the same lab and it's set out in the same way, then the tests are all comparable. If enough people do it the symptoms are cross reference-able and what means what is decipherable. God knows how they figured it all out!

I snipped some hair off the back of my head and sent it off to the lab. My results did come back with brief notes, but honestly looking at what I discovered from reading that hair test book, and comparing that with the auto-printout-bull$hit notes the test came with, they were not worth the paper they were printed on. Seriously, it was so cheap I could not even wipe my arse on it for fear of putting my finger through.

I know people who have done the hair tests, read the auto-printout-BS notes and left it at that. The amount of knowledge on that test is amazing to behold if you put some effort in, if you know to put some effort in.

Some super-brainy dudes must have figured out this stuff. Thanks again Andy Cutler for writing *Hair Test Interpretation*. Cool book and very relevant.

One of the more important things for me was seeing on paper that I was in fact mercury poisoned: paper proof. I didn't really need to see it, because my reactions to amalgam removals were so drastic that mercury was obviously a massive issue for me. But still, good to see something on paper, something to show people if I needed to.

My hair test levels for mercury came back way up high in the red top range for lots of mercury coming out of me. This high mercury reading confirmed I was mercury toxic. Thank you amalgam removal with no protection for that clear signal! You could almost say it was a good thing having high mercury showing on the test, showed my body was capable of excreting mercury. Almost.

Nine out of ten people doing this test are not so lucky (?) and their mercury levels come out normal or zero on the hair test. This leads many to think they do not have a mercury problem. Most times people cannot excrete mercury and none shows up on the hair test. That's because the mercury is stuck inside them buggering things up. That's why they are sick, because it's trapped inside doing its damage.

When the test shows low, or no mercury levels, you must look at other tell-tale signs to conclude if mercury is lurking or not. It's pretty easy, just follow five 'counting rules' and within five minutes you can tell if a mercury problem is likely or not.

If a person meets the counting rules, this means they have 'deranged mineral transport'. That shows that their bodies are not moving the minerals they get from their diet to the correct parts of their body. Means the mercury is stopping the body from working correctly. Having deranged mineral transport confirms mercury toxicity.

When a person has deranged mineral transport, the test results need to be read differently, because not all the bars and ratios are true anymore, because the body is moving things around incorrectly. That's why you need to read the book, to figure which levels are correct and which are not.

The moderators of the group Yahoo Frequent Dose Chelation (Yahoo FDC) can read the main points on your hair test for you. These cool people read these tests weekly and are very good at it. I did gain much more valuable information about my health from reading Andy Cutler's book myself, but it's cool to have a second opinion confirming my discoveries. Their advice is given freely too.

Those moderators of Yahoo FDC are amazing people, dedicating their lives to helping others struggling with so many problems. Hats off to all of you. Respect.

There is only one mercury forum worth following and that's Yahoo FDC. I read every post for two years. That's a lot of people, a lot of problems, a lot of successes, a lot of failures and I learned a huge amount from my time there. What I learned there saved me years of hassles and troubles. Every person who posted discussing their problems enabled me to avoid the many pitfalls of mercury chelation. Thank you all.

But mercury toxicity is not the only thing the hair test can reveal. If you delve deeper by reading Cutler's hair test book, you can discover many new and interesting things about yourself.

• • •

I found out the following from my hair test:

1) I did not meet any counting rules, so I did not have deranged mineral transport, but they were 'suspicious.' My iodine was very close to the low red, which would tip me over into meeting the counting rules. Could my daily salt consumption affect my iodine level? Maybe? Probably?

2) My elevated hair mercury confirmed mercury toxicity without a doubt.

3) I had very low lithium levels (in the red) together with high calcium; this is frequently associated with mercury poisoning.

4) Aluminium and titanium were both very high, particularly mega-high titanium. These were NOT a toxic problem, but they were a sign that I was mercury toxic.

5) High hair aluminium was a sign of a mercury problem.

HAIR ELEMENTS

LAB#:	CLIENT#:
PATIENT:	DOCTOR: Anna Davis, MD
SEX: Male	Direct Laboratory Services
AGE: 38	300 Mariners Plaza #320
	Mandeville , LA 70448

POTENTIALLY TOXIC ELEMENTS

TOXIC ELEMENTS	RESULT µg/g	REFERENCE RANGE	PERCENTILE 68th 95th
Aluminum	14	< 7.0	
Antimony	0.010	< 0.066	
Arsenic	0.046	< 0.080	
Beryllium	< 0.01	< 0.020	
Bismuth	0.032	< 2.0	
Cadmium	0.037	< 0.15	
Lead	0.28	< 2.0	
Mercury	4.1	< 1.1	
Platinum	< 0.003	< 0.005	
Thallium	< 0.001	< 0.010	
Thorium	< 0.001	< 0.005	
Uranium	0.002	< 0.060	
Nickel	0.20	< 0.40	
Silver	0.02	< 0.12	
Tin	0.03	< 0.30	
Titanium	32	< 1.0	
Total Toxic Representation			

ESSENTIAL AND OTHER ELEMENTS

ELEMENTS	RESULT µg/g	REFERENCE RANGE	PERCENTILE 2.5th 16th 50th 84th 97.5th
Calcium	1220	200- 750	
Magnesium	40	25- 75	
Sodium	12	12- 90	
Potassium	11	9- 40	
Copper	59	10- 28	
Zinc	180	130- 200	
Manganese	0.13	0.15- 0.65	
Chromium	0.33	0.20- 0.40	
Vanadium	0.041	0.018- 0.065	
Molybdenum	0.10	0.025- 0.064	
Boron	0.45	0.40- 3.0	
Iodine	0.13	0.25- 1.3	
Lithium	< 0.004	0.007- 0.023	
Phosphorus	193	160- 250	
Selenium	0.86	0.95- 1.7	
Strontium	2.0	0.30- 3.5	
Sulfur	48400	44500- 52000	
Barium	0.54	0.16- 1.6	
Cobalt	0.007	0.013- 0.035	
Iron	12	5.4- 13	
Germanium	0.032	0.045- 0.065	
Rubidium	0.008	0.011- 0.12	
Zirconium	0.075	0.020- 0.44	

SPECIMEN DATA

COMMENTS:

Date Collected:	9/5/2007	Sample Size:	0.202 g
Date Received:	9/10/2007	Sample Type:	Head
Date Completed:	9/18/2007	Hair Color:	Brown
		Treatment:	
Methodology:	ICP-MS	Shampoo:	Organic

V06.99

RATIOS

ELEMENTS	RATIOS	EXPECTED RANGE
Ca/Mg	30.5	4- 30
Ca/P	6.32	0.8- 8
Na/K	1.09	0.5- 10
Zn/Cu	3.05	4- 20
Zn/Cd	> 999	> 800

©DOCTOR'S DATA, INC. • ADDRESS: 3755 Illinois Avenue, St. Charles, IL 60174-2420 • CLIA ID NO: 14D0646470 • MEDICARE PROVIDER NO: 148453

6) My calcium/magnesium ratios were out of sync. This meant I had blood sugar regulation problems.

7) My potassium/calcium levels were out of sync. This suggested thyroid problems.

8) Abnormal ratio calcium/phosphorous suggested I should have a high fat diet.

9) Potassium and sodium down, with calcium and magnesium up meant my adrenals were not making enough cortisol or adrenaline and the thyroid was somewhat low.

10) Copper was a problem for me. I had very high copper into the red. I needed to NOT supplement copper. I needed to investigate copper and be aware copper was a serious problem that could cause the same problems as mercury. (Oh balls!)

11) High hair calcium levels indicated that I need to supplement calcium.

12) Low potassium meant I have low thyroid function.

13) My cobalt was very low, in the red. This *might* mean I needed to supplement vitamin B12 because I was B12 deficient.

14) Potassium to calcium ratio looked bad, which suggested a thyroid problem.

15) Iron. I should stop iron supplementation. My iron level was a little high.

16) Iodine was very low. Needed investigating. Supplement kelp?

17) Lithium was very low, in the red so maybe supplement lithium? (I didn't in the end because my symptoms did not match those that lithium are supplemented for: mood problems, depression or mania.)

18) Due to the copper problem I should supplement molybdenum.

19) Selenium was low in the yellow, so I should supplement with selenium and vitamin E.

• • •

Now that's what I call a test! Oh yeah baby, pretty cool, eh! Well, not cool to find so many things wrong, but cool to have starting points. Cool to know what needed attention. Adrenals, thyroid, blood sugar problems, liver troubles, copper toxic and the lovely confirmation of mercury toxic. Of course this test just told me what was wrong, now I had to do something about it all, which was not so easy.

The hair test cost about $90, Cutler's hair test book cost $35 and in my opinion there is no finer, wide-spectrum, easy and cheap test than this.

It was also totally empowering. Reading the book, discovering all these things for myself gave me some control over the pain and troubles I was experiencing. Just having starting points for further investigation was more than most people will ever have. Most people just struggle through their pain in ignorance.

The first thing I tackled was copper. The symptoms of copper poisoning are very similar to mercury, so it's a pretty big deal. I had symptoms on top of symptoms and I needed to figure out this newfound copper problem double-quick.

Cutler recommended zinc and molybdenum in high dosages to help remove excess copper. Copper is excreted via the liver and a congested liver will struggle, so liver supports would also help. For this I took taurine and milk thistle.

I also avoided all foods high in copper: nuts, organ meats and lentils were off the menu for three months. There were other foods to avoid but my diet was pretty limited anyway. Avoiding the nuts was tricky because I was so skinny. I was using nuts as a way to try and bulk up, but copper was a serious issue and nuts would have to wait.

I re-did another hair test three months later and was relieved to see much reduced copper levels. If only everything was as easy to solve as that!

Further reading: *Hair Test Interpretation: Finding Hidden Toxicities* by Andrew Cutler

Loads of hair test details, info and instructions here: http://home.earthlink.net/~moriam/HOW_TO_hair_test.html

Lab for hair test: www.directlabs.com and the correct hair test is 'Hair Elements'

Round 6 – 1st February 2008

6mg DMSA every three hours, three days on.

This round was after a six-week break after some mega detoxing, doing some herbal cleanses.

The round started up with a nasty bout of depression. I don't usually get that, so was a bit difficult coping with it, but I battled on and within five hours it was thankfully gone. At the time I wanted to quit my job, leave everything behind and just go somewhere quiet, hide away where no one would find me. Ho hum. But it passed, so all is well.

Rest of the round was the smoothest yet. Did have some heartburn, which was real strange. I was doing a three-day juice fast, as you do, and heartburn suddenly arrived out of the blue. Heartburn should not be able to happen when the only thing I'm drinking is vegetable juice. But again it was short-lived and it passed quickly enough. Did get heart palpitations too, but again they passed after a day.

All in all, the smoothest round to date. The colour yellow was brighter for me on Tuesday. Rock 'n' roll!

I am now officially three months post amalgam replacement, so I can theoretically introduce ALA now, which is the real deal! This is the stuff that can pass the blood-brain barrier (BBB) and get the mercury off me brain. Basically ALA is what will get me better, long-term better. But before I do that, I will see if I can extend the round length. Do more than three days on with the DMSA.

Round 7 – 8th February 2008
6mg DMSA every three hours, four days on.

Managed four days on. Very minor, limited symptoms and zero symptoms after the round. Happy dayz!

26. Steak and kidney pie

Now that I had cleaned the digestive tract and got rid of some of the parasites that had been driving me mad, now that my detox pathways had been freed up a little, I was ready to try another kidney cleanse. I used the Andreas Moritz kidney cleanse formula again, from Presentmoment.com.

This was a collection of herbs that you made into a tea and drank over the course of the day, every day for 30 days. Tasted very bitter to some people. Not to me though, tasted nice, which was an example of my taste buds telling me what I should and should not be eating and drinking. It is important to listen to your body.

My mum did the same kidney cleanse and complained bitterly (ha!) that the taste was super nasty, very bitter indeed. Tasted fine to me! If I crave something, I have it. I use my newfound knowledge to satisfy the craving with the right quality of food or drink. I use my head and don't eat junk; only whole foods and organic foods every time.

I was getting up in the night two or three times for a pee, so this was good reason to do a kidney cleanse. Apparently lower back problems can be caused by kidney troubles, or so I read anyway. I had the mother of all back problems, so worth trying this again. Tiny crystals accumulate inside the kidneys and the tubes that go to the bladder. When fluid goes through the tubes this causes lower back pain, apparently.

It's all weird stuff this, eh! Kidneys and lower back problems, never in a million years would I think that might be a cause of my back pain.

If the liver is congested, which I knew mine was, this leads to sand, grease and stones accumulating in the kidney and/or urinary bladder. The kidneys are delicate, blood-filtering organs that congest easily due to dehydration, poor diet, weak digestion, stress and wild crazy partying late into the night! Most of the kidney stones are too small to be detected using modern x-rays and whatnot. These herbs dissolve any accumulated gunk.

Ingredients: Marjoram, Cat's Claw, Comfrey root, Fennel seeds, Chicory herb, Uva Ursi, Hydrangea root, Gravel root, Marshmallow root, golden herb.

As a general rule, if you have a reaction to a herb, that means it's working. That means there are toxins in there somewhere and that herb/formula got a bit out. Toxins always hurt coming out, which is why it's important to control the flow of toxins removed, too many and life gets difficult again.

Lots of herbs = lots of toxins mobilised = lots of side effects.

A few herbs = less toxins removed = fewer side effects = good life.

Does that sound familiar? Does that sound like chelation? Yes sir. Reactions to mercury chelators = mercury toxic. The Cutler protocol takes mercury out in nice small controlled doses to minimise your hassle. If there is a problem, the problems are small and short lived.

Large chelator dose = large problems.

Small chelator dose = small problems = good life.

The first day I started the kidney cleanse I got a blinding headache, ditto day two. As a rule I only got headaches when I detoxed, so I knew when I cleansed and I got a headache that toxins were coming out big-time-Charlie, it was a sign the herbs were working. There are many different reasons for headaches, but I only got them when I was cleansing or I was stressed out of my tiny mind. And I could tell the difference between those two easy.

There is a simple solution to too many side effects. In this case as it's a herbal tea, I just reduced the amount of tea I drank each day until I had no headache, then gradually increased the dose over the 30 days. This is important. You must live life as best you can and you need to be sensible with the dose. There is no point ramping up the dose to mega-high levels in the rush to get better. You will get better sooner or later if you keep working on it.

After a couple more days, my ankles suddenly inflated like I was wearing six pairs of socks. They were stiff, swollen, hurt and I walked like a penguin. What the funk was going on here? Well, it turned out that the kidneys controlled the fluid in the body, regulated blood pressure, produced urine, and regulated lots of bits and bobs in there in relation to fluids. This swelling of the ankles was called Oedema and old ladies got it because their kidneys were full of crystals and didn't work very well anymore.

It was most startling to have this happen and I did think hard about stopping the herbs, because it was fairly unpleasant. But, this was yet another signal that I was right to try a kidney cleanse in the first place, and that the herbs were working, and that there were toxins in there that needed dissolving. So I reduced the dose and stuck it out. Oedema lasted about ten days.

Had I NOT known what was going on, I would have 100 percent stopped the cleanse and discarded it as 'does not suit me'. Had a doctor given me these herbs and had I blindly taken them and had these strange side-effects, I would have complained bitterly (ha!) to the doctor, and told him he was a fool for giving me stuff that introduced new nasty symptoms. Probably would have reported him or something. Funny old world, eh!

But no doctor gave them to me. I was responsible for my health now. There was no one to blame but myself. Which was why I read and researched so much, so I could make educated choices about my health.

Now that I did understand, I embraced the hassles as proof that I was on the right track and hoped that by coping with the side effects, in the end, I would be better off than when I started; fingers crossed.

Over the 30 days on the cleanse, I had a multitude of spots and pimples, some heartburn, strange rashes on my ankles, arms, torso, very smelly urine and again pretty off-world BMs. Again all these were signals of detox happening, especially the dark smelly urine. Life was tricky and unpleasant, but my life was already tricky and unpleasant, so it was no change from normal. But I had the knowledge, or hope, that by the end I would be better.

The main reason for doing this kidney cleanse was because of my major long-term lower-back problems, and for the duration of the 30 days my lower back hurt like hell. Some days worse than others, but every day was full of back pain. Punch in the kidneys dull throb pain, right inside un-itchable kinda pain. Which again was no real change from normal, but it was definitely worse.

Maybe I'm over-blowing the hassles to you. It was manageable OK. Tricky, painful, annoying, but manageable. For the last five years, every day I had been managing things, I was a pro at managing pain, so this was yet more pain to manage.

So, all in all, another pretty eventful cleanse. Obviously my kidneys were congested with something and I probably needed to do more, because the hassles continued for the full duration of 30 days.

After the cleanse had finished the extra symptoms disappeared and fantastically my lower back was better. Hooray!!! Not cured. Not great. But better, quite a lot better too. Maybe 30 percent better than it was before. Pretty cool, eh!

And when you have been told, 'tough luck', 'it's the dust mites' and 'learn to live with the pain for the rest of your life'. That 30 percent betterness, that 30 days of unpleasantness, all that hassle was massively worth it. I was overjoyed-happy. Jumping around the room happy. Shouting from the top of the roof happy.

Stupid doctors, telling me rubbish that I would never get better again, never be able to pick up and lift up me own kids again. Yeah yeah yeah, I know I have an 'issue' with doctors, but fuck 'em! If this was a court of law and the doctor told me I would never get better, and I did get better, they would be wrong in the eyes of the law. They got it wrong. I was getting better.

27. No sex please, we're British

My libido was shot to pieces after amalgam removals. Really didn't give a toss, not in the slightest bit interested in any bedroom gymnastics. I knew that was not normal because, well anyway, never been a problem before!

This is apparently all something to do with hormones. (I thought hormones was all women's troubles?!) Anyway, I found some stuff called maca powder. I quote:

"It is a cruciferous vegetable from the carrot, radish and parsnip family native to Peru. It has been cultivated and used by the Peruvians for several thousand years, both as a foodstuff and also for its medicinal properties. Maca contains high amounts of vitamins, minerals, enzymes and all the essential amino acids. Maca is an adaptogen so it 'adapts' to your body's metabolism and can help you achieve your optimal level of health and energy."

If you Google it, you will see lots of amazingly healthy things it does for your body, but it is also a firm favourite at swinging parties because it is a natural aphrodisiac and gives you a huge hard-on. Really puts the lead back in your pencil! Oh yes, baby!

OK, it's a bit more subtle than that. More like a jump-start and then gentle encouragement. It's not like Viagra which is a one-evening wonder, this stuff sorts you out a treat, long term.

Talking of treats, when my diet came back on-line and I could eat a whole load of different healthy foods again. I needed to treat myself with something healthy. I was reinventing my cooking at the time and found an amazing recipe for raw chocolate. This stuff is the biz and all I did was add plenty of Maca powder to the raw chocolate and Bob's your uncle: rock hard action all over again.

Didn't take that long really, a couple of weeks of eating raw chocolate, which was hardly a hardship. I had had zero diet treats for five years and this stuff tasted like the food of the Gods. That kinda got me off rock bottom in the bedroom department, then after the next six months of regaining health and chocolate-eating, everything went back to normal and libido was, as ever, ready for action. Since I was using raw chocolate for 'medicinal' reasons I did use a lot of maca powder, lashings of it. Nice.

• • •

OK, minor interlude to give you the raw chocolate ingredients. Seriously, it's piss-easy to make and tastes glorious: raw cacao beans, cashew nuts, carob powder, maca powder, coconut oil and honey. You can add cacao butter, lucuma powder, vanilla pods if you want, but best keep it simple at first. Orange peel is awesome. Cashew nuts are the bulk ingredient. Only thing that takes time is ordering the ingredients. They need to be bought online as they are not that common. All ingredients are organic, no heating is required and you have one very good treat in more ways than one.

Add ingredients in quantities you think best, grind it up a blender, mix it all up and store in the freezer. Takes ten minutes to make enough raw chocolate to make yours the best swinging party in town!

Next batch I think I will use dates or apricots instead of the honey —lovely.

28. Muggles & I wish I had cancer

When that black gunk came out of me during the first parasite cleanse, I asked around on the health forums if anyone knew what it was. Someone told me it was 'probably blood' and that 'I should go to the emergency hospital immediately' because 'I was bleeding internally and I probably had cancer'.

Scary, eh! It's a jungle out there and that's for sure!

I didn't think that was the case, because otherwise why did I get so much better? It was unlikely that if I had cancer, and if I was bleeding so much, that I would get better, but you never know. That gunk was not very much like blood, it was very rubbery stuff.

I found a set of herbs called Essiac Tea, which is an old-skool cancer cure. I seemed to have everything wrong with me. Things that I didn't think would work had been working magnificently, so I thought this worth investigating. I read the amazing story of how the tea came about with Rene Caisse back in 1930s and decided to do those herbs too. It covered the cancer-base, just in case.

It is a big-time detox and pulls a huge amount of toxins out. I did them on the assumption that if it can cure cancer, I'm sure it can cure lots of other things too. I did two months of those herbs over Christmas 2007, drinking the specially prepared tea every day. A good detox and a fine thing to do. I did that at the same time as other cleanses, so no idea specifically what it did, but I am here to tell the tale of my glorious recovery and for sure it helped.

This was a period of major detoxing for me, I was doing the Essiac Tea, the parasite cleanse and the bowel cleanse too, all at the same time. That was a lot of toxins coming out out out. Better out than in! I stopped all chelation at this time.

They were all Humaworm herbs and according to them it's fine to do these specific cleanses at the same time, so I did them all. (For the record: Humaworm, Humacleanse and Hu-mana-tea)

Talking of cancer: if I had cancer, the very, very last thing I would do is chemotherapy. This is not the time or the place to discuss it and I don't have cancer but there are many many things to do to get rid of the cancer before resorting to poisoning yourself on a gigantic scale with chemo. There are many books about cancer for those who wish to take responsibility for their health and chemo would be bottom of my list.

In fact, I wished I had cancer instead of mercury poisoning. Really, I wished that every day for months on end.

Cancer is so much more acceptable in our world. People who have cancer get loads of lovely sympathy and everyone is so understanding, helpful, supportive and caring. You have lots of different options and different protocols to consider.

Poisoned by your fillings and you get zero sympathy, zero support, zero help and zero understanding. Thrown to the dogs springs to mind when looking for help.

I'm not saying cancer is any better or worse than what I had, just that cancer is acceptable and mercury poisoning is not. Not even vaguely acceptable. Which is hard because the problems I had were nightmare-like and to have no-nothing was tough.

An accident would have been OK too. Nice little car crash would have been fine. Three months off to recover from a car crash is morally acceptable.

I quickly learnt never to speak to Muggles about my mercury problems. There is no point. No one understands. No one is capable of understanding and people just think you're a freak and I had a million better things to do than let people think I was a freak. They couldn't help, so best not talk about it.

For those who don't know Harry Potter, Muggles are non-mercury educated people.

29. Village idiot

Mercury is attracted to sulphury foods like onions, garlic and eggs. The molecules get attracted to each other and the food molecules pick up bits of mercury inside the body and move it around inside you.

In some people the body reacts to mercury poisoning by making a lot of sulphury things and any extra sulphur taken in the diet mobilises too much mercury and you get nasty symptoms. Those people need to avoid eating sulphur foods.

In other people the opposite is the case. Not enough sulphur is produced by the body and they get nasty symptoms from that. Sulphur foods makes that person feel great and they need to eat more of them.

The way you figure out how your body feels about sulphur foods is to give up eating sulphur foods for a week. You monitor your symptoms during the week and see if you feel better, worse or the same. At the end of the week you eat a little sulphur food and see what reaction you get. If you feel bad, sulphur foods need avoiding, and vice versa, you get the picture. It's an easy, simple and effective test.

In the past I had maybe had funny reactions to some foods: garlic, onions, spinach, eggs, but it's difficult to know what was doing what. Cysteine (NAC) was a sulphur supplement too and I had a major problem with that, so this was worth doing to figure out if this affected me.

So I found the long list of sulphur foods to avoid and gave them all up for a week. I had done months and months of special diets and so one week was easy to avoid those foods. I did a vegetable juice fast at the end of that week, as you do, three days veg juice only. I tried an egg at the end of the seven days and felt nothing so assumed I had no sulphur problem and went back to the juice fast.

I had been looking at the avoidance list all week but somehow managed to forget I should maybe take it easy on reintroduction. At breakfast on Saturday morning I juiced about seven leeks and a few carrots, but it was mostly leeks. I hadn't had any leeks in the week because they are a sulphur food and on the list. I had a large stockpile that needed juicing. I'd tried the egg the night before and I did not have sulphur problem, or so I thought!

I took a huge gulp of the leek juice, really glugged it down…and oh boy! What a mistake to make! What a village idiot! The reaction was instant, obvious and immense. My body went into spasms as I fell to the floor gagging, flailing around clutching my throat trying to sick up the pure sulphury nightmare I just poured down my gullet. My whole body, every sinew, strained to get this poison out out out.

It wasn't just my throat and digestive tract that retched and gagged, it was everywhere, everything seemed to pulsate, throb, shake and pound trying to get this stuff away away away.

For two full days all my symptoms flared up like crazy and I felt like a sack o' cacko. I seemed to sweat leek juice. I could not shake the stench nor the taste of it for a week. Even now the smell of raw leeks makes me gag.

Today I laugh out loud at that memory, I have a large smile now typing this up, but boy oh boy, that really hurt like hell and never again will leek juice enter my body, my temple.

And that's a top tip: when you do the sulphur exclusion test, take it easy on reintroduction and don't drink juiced leeks! What a Village!

So, yeah, I found out the hard way that I had a sulphur problem. I avoided all sulphur foods after that little episode and took a few more steps up my ladder towards good health. It's an easy test and an important one to do if you are mercury toxic. Avoidance made my life easier.

Further reading: Google 'Sulphur exclusion test Cutler'—that should get you to the right place.

30. Oil

I was having a rough patch here. I felt tired and strangely nauseous each day. The queasy feeling was new too. Something, somewhere was disagreeing. Thinking about it, I had been heading downhill for a few weeks. It seemed to be coming to a head because I felt awful. Wonder what it was? I needed to get my thinking-cap on.

Was the mercury dumping? Was my liver failing? Kidneys closing down? Maybe cancer? Or a tumour? Maybe spiders had laid their eggs in my intestines and were about to burst out? I needed to dedicate some time and energy to figuring this problem out.

24 hours later...

Ah ha! Got it! Muscle testing, I love you! I tested everything I could think of asking specifically about nausea. The food in my diet: nothing. All around the house, carpets and rugs, the walls, the cats, the kids, anything: nothing. Next up supplements: all tested fine. Coconut oil: fine. Ah what was this? Fish oil?

My body gave a strong and firm negative/weak signal to my supplementary fish oil. I gave it a good sniffffffffffffffffffffffff. Ummm, smelled a bit odd I suppose, but I wasn't totally sure. I took a little sip. Yuck! Tasted pretty nasty, but fish oil tasted nasty anyway.

"Wife!"

"Yes, m'lord?"

"Does this smell odd to you? I think it might be causing me a spot of bother."

"It stinks!"

"Really? How can you tell? The bottle is two foot away from you. Is it that strong?"

"It's disgusting! It's rancid!"

"Really? And you can tell from that far away?"

"I don't need to get any closer. I can smell it from here and it's foul. You haven't been drinking it have you?"

"Errr, yeah. Every day."

"What's wrong with you? Can't you smell it? Can't you taste it?"

"Oh, I don't know! Oh boy, I hate this. I guess my sense of smell 'n' taste are busted too. Balls! No wonder I feel like $hit."

"Language!"

So yeah, I learnt the hard way about consuming rancid fish oil. It's not a good idea, and it really does make you feel like death. I also learnt that my sense of smell and taste were severely compromised too. Nothing like a first-hand experience to show me just how comprehensive my mercury poisoning was. Was nothing left untouched?

I chucked that toxic waste away and got better within a couple of days, happy I'd figured out another mystery.

As per instructions, the fish oil had been kept in the fridge and was well within its sell-by date, but why was it rancid?

Maybe my bottle of fish oil sat in an un-air-conditioned depot waiting to be shipped. Or maybe a lorry broke down en route and my bottle was on the top and it roasted in the sun for a while? Or maybe the shop left that carton outside in the back yard in summer for a month while the stock cleared? Maybe some bacteria got in during the manufacturing process? I will never know why that oil was rancid, but it was, and now I always sniff my oils when I take them. Always! And if I detect anything untoward, m'lady checks it for me.

Round 8 – 15th February 2008

6mg DMSA every three hours, three days on.

I am feeling better and better as the weeks go by. Last week I
had two days on the trot where I felt like a normal person. It's
been a long time since I could say that. But saying that, I still
have a ways to go, I still get plenty of bad days along with the
few good.

Now that I am three months post amalgam removal I am free
to change chelation agents. I was using DMSA but now I could
change to ALA, which is the chelator of choice because that gets
mercury off me brain. So, my options:

1) Add ALA? If so what dose? 3mg? 6mg?

2) Increase the DMSA dose to 8mg?

3) Do nothing and stay where I am at 6mg DMSA?

Usually I instinctively know what I should do next, but now I'm
not really sure:

I want to just stay at 6mg DMSA because it's easy and I'm in
the groove.

I want to add ALA because I know I will have to sooner or
later, but the thought of more pain and hassle figuring out the
right dose—I don't need!

I want to increase the DMSA dose to increase the amount of
mercury excreted, but again, potential pain.

It's a scary business this. I never want to go back to the bad
old days ever again. I'm scared, so I will keep things unchanged
for now. I will stick to the 6mg DMSA.

Ahhhhhhhhh! I funked up this round.

Ahhhhhhhhh! I missed my second dose.

Oh balls!

First dose was at 9pm, second dose at midnight was missed
because the alarm didn't go off. Oh no! The 3am alarm woke me
and I thought (in my sleepy head) it would be OK because I'd only

been on round for three hours. I only missed three hours, so I thought it would be OK to just continue the round.

Also I'd been feeling pretty good recently, so I got a bit cocky and just took the next caps. According to the Cutler protocol you are supposed to stop the round if you miss a dose because unpleasant things can happen.

I thought I'd got away with it too, because initially nothing bad happened. I even somehow forgot all about missing that first dose. My memory plays strange tricks with me these days, nothing big, just tricks. I forgot my PIN number yesterday to my cash card. Was a most strange feeling not remembering my PIN... "eh?" I had that same PIN my whole life.

I completed the full three days on round with similar manageable symptoms to previous rounds, but at the end, when the round finished, all hell broke loose with a full blown mercury attack:

Lower back pain is back in full force: total 'mare

Feeling super tired and drained of energy and a bit spacey, tingly, vision is slightly blurred: total 'mare.

I was wildly angry again, completely lost my temper shouting my head off and had a huge row in the office over something minuscule. I freely admit I totally lost the plot.

That was this morning, the anger has calmed now, although I feel it bubbling away quietly in the background. The anger is not new, but usually I hide it away and keep it in check. Pain and anger go hand in hand.

I increased my vitamin C intake to up my maximum, to my bowel tolerance of 15 grams in divided doses 4 times a day. That is not a typo, 15.0 grams. That helped greatly.

It's another painful mercury lesson for me. Two days of hell and a further three days to recover after that. Cutler's words yet again are absolutely spot on. Don't deviate from the protocol!

That hurt, that hurt a lot. I don't want to go back to the bad old days, never, never, ever again. Scary stuff this chelation business. I will stay on DMSA for now.

Round 9 – 22nd February 2008
6mg DMSA every three hours, two days on, then round stopped.

Funked up my round again! Ahhhhhhhh! Missed a dose! Ahhhhh-hh! For some reason I did not take the midnight dose! Ahhhhhhh! But I took the 3am dose! Ahhhhhhhhh! Village!

After last week's adventures I got up and stuck my fingers down my throat! I got the cap out eventually, but that was unpleasant.

I'd rather have five minutes' unpleasantness, than one week's hell. I will not mess with the protocol again. Last week's lesson has been learnt.

After that I stopped the round. Was on-round for two days, and nothing bad happened, the round just finished one day early.

Still at 6mg DMSA only, gonna stay there for now.

All this hassle reminds me how unpleasant this is, so no more rocking the boat, I will stay at DMSA 6mg every three hours for the time being. Not gonna try ALA yet, I'm too chicken.

Round 10 – 28th February 2008
6mg DMSA every three hours, three days on.

In Cutler's book, he recommends to start at 50-200mg DMSA and see how it goes. It's since been updated and the dosages reduced, but still my dose of 6mg DMSA is considered pretty low. But, I'm happy here, mistakes hurt like hell and I will not, cannot rush. The inclination is to rush, push for the high dose, but the pain and misery of a mercury attack screw-up makes me very aware of the downsides. Nope, I will stay at this dose. Need to get a few more rounds under my belt with only minor symptoms.

I definitely feel better on round. Round 10 was very smooth with very few symptoms. I'm in the zone so the waking at night twice to take the capsules is not a problem. It's not great, but I go straight back to sleep with no problem.

Did feel pretty manky on the day after I finished the round, which was obviously a little bit of redistribution action.

I am four months amalgam free and prolly got 24 months chelation every week to go, if I can manage every week. Minimum 70 more rounds to go. Bugger.

31. What the funk is that black gunk?

Back to the herbal cleanses I'd discovered and the parasite cleanse called Humaworm. I had had wonderful results from these herbs and I was very keen to try them again. When attacking parasites it's important to go at them in campaigns. Thirty days attack, followed by ninety days break. This gap stops any super-resistant bugs becoming immune to the herbs.

So, to the day, 90 days after the last parasite cleanse I started another. If you remember I had a whole host of symptoms and crazy side effects the first time round. I wondered what would happen on a second try? Did I get all bugs on the first round?

I started the herbs and immediately the crazy symptoms returned: the itchies, the stabbing pains in my back, headaches, pimples and the rashes. Thankfully not as full-on as before, but still pretty crazy.

Now, remember that black gunk that came out of me? Twenty feet long black gunk? Made me oh so tired for three days long and then I started getting better? That long black ropey stuff started coming out again. What the funk was it?

Thankfully I did not have to see the lady with the pearl necklace again. I took a few pictures this time and asked on the various forums I was frequenting. Did anyone know what this stuff was? And lo and behold someone did. I discovered what it was. It's called Mucoid Plaque.

Now, if you Google this stuff and look it up on Wikipedia, you will discover it is all a load of old cobblers, made up by some weird bloke called Rich Anderson.

According to Wikipedia and the western medical world, that mucoid plaque is an urban legend. One hundred percent it does not exist!
No way, baby! Made up by this Andersen bloke to sell something. Well,
this non-existent stuff was flowing out of my arse, long lengths of the
gunk! That had to make me an urban legend! Ha!

This needed investigating, because it was coming out a lot. I didn't
think it was blood because when it came out I got much much better,
very very quickly. Definitely jumping up another couple of dozen rungs
on the ladder of my health.

So I read a book written by Rich Anderson. Was all very strange
and new to me, but very interesting nevertheless. Interesting because he
described exactly what happened to me. He explained in graphic detail
how my guts worked. I think, technically, the inside of the digestive
tract is still outside of the body. Only when food is absorbed does it
then become officially inside the body. When you ingest something
that it does not like, for example, you by mistake eat a rotten egg, your
body says:

"Yuck, need to stop that rubbish from getting inside me. What I
will do is produce something to trap that crap, so that it does not harm
my body, and then this trapped toxin can be expelled from the body
with all the other garbage." Good plan, Batman!

The stuff that traps toxins is called mucus. You probably heard of
mucus-producing foods, for example milk. Mucus is sticky stuff that
sticks to stuff your body doesn't like. What happens is, you eat the rotten egg, or milk, or whatever toxin it is, body says 'yuck…', body then
produces mucus, mucus then traps the toxin, and then everything goes
out through the digestive tract, down through the bowels and out with
your BM when you have a dump.

It's a fantastic system and works brilliantly and you don't die from
every toxin that goes in you. Thank you, oh glorious body, for saving
me oh so very often!

However, your body is not designed to do this 24 hours a day. A poor
diet will have the body produce lots of mucus at each meal to trap and
expel all this poor food that the body doesn't like. Eventually this sticky

mucus stuff gets a bit clogged up inside, it's like glue, and rather than flushing out the bowels, a little bit of mucus—and whatever toxin it's holding onto—gets stuck or sticks to the side somewhere in the digestive tract. Eventually a layer of rubbery mucus builds up inside. Over the years of your life, it gets as thick as the inner tube of a bicycle tire. Yikes!

32. The Holy Grail

A poor diet in itself is bad enough, but when you add mercury on top of the other household and day-to-day toxins, things get very bad, or they did for me anyway.

Mercury leaked out 24 hours a day from my amalgam fillings for 20 years. It was only small quantities, but it was deadly poisonous, this stuff. Some of the mercury excreted by the body was done so via the bowels. So for 24 hours a day, every day, my body produced mucus to trap the mercury. That's a lot of mucus and this built up into a thick coating, the entire length of my digestive tract.

This mucus stopped bad things, like rotten eggs and mercury, from going inside my body and harming me, which was really cool and saved me from death. But this cool method of protecting me was not designed to be working all the time, because as well as saving me from death by toxins, this mucus built up to such levels that the food I ate could not get through the thick layer of old mucus.

This was why I was so skinny. I had a huge appetite, but was skinny as a rake. I could not digest the healthy food I ate and most of it was wasted because I could not assimilate anything. Things got stuck in the mucus too, festering; it became very dirty inside there. In between the gunk and the stomach lining, strange things started growing, bacteria, fungus, parasites. Yuck!

Just like a blocked drain will stink and smell and strange growths will sprout if left too long. Until you clean out the drain, it will always stink, always harbour germs and disease no matter what you do. And that's what happened to me. The Humaworm herbs, the juice fast, the

cleaned me out. That's what that black gunk was. It was this
ck mucus that coated my entire digestive tract and when it was
ed out of my body, I no longer had that festering gunk inside me
and my body was free to digest the healthy food I ate.

That's why 60 percent of my food intolerances disappeared overnight after the first parasite cleanse.

That's why I became super hungry and put on 10 kg (22 pounds) in
two months after the first parasite cleanse.

Finally after years of being unable to digest and absorb the food I ate,
finally I could up-take my food and my body roared into life. It demanded
more and more food, it was rebuilding itself and making up for lost time.

These are the kinds of things that you must see to believe. I know
it sounds odd, I can scarcely believe it myself even now. But the black
gunk came out of me and I got better, leaps and bounds better.

That's how I understand it. I did not make that up either. Some
people much more intelligent than me figured it out and wrote it all
down. I then read about it, understood it eventually, and realised that is
what happened to me. I am a broker in the city, I dedicated a couple of
years of my life to getting better, but I'm not a scientist, I didn't make
detailed notes, I can't give detailed reference to the pages it's on, but
if you read books by Rich Anderson and Dr. Jensen you can learn all
about bowels all by yourself. Education is key!

If you read these books, the understanding you gain will enable you
to make informed choices about your health. You will not be scared.
You will not be freaked out. You will understand what's happened to
your body and you will understand what is required of you to return it
to good health. If you read the books you will just be curious, just like
I was, curious to know if they are correct and curious to see if you can
get better like they did, like I did.

Mucoid plaque is kinda like the Holy Grail of cleansing. You hear
of the odd story of people getting this gunk out and suddenly getting
rapidly better, just like I did. It is however pretty tricky to get out and
needs some dedication. Fasting is pretty good, Master Cleansers and
water-only fasting report it fairly often, so I guess my juice fast and

parasite cleanse helped me get mine out. People try for months with no success, but those that tough it out and keep making efforts, usually succeed and they add their success stories to the pile.

Funny how I got loads out and didn't even know what it was. If you ever get any of this gunk out, you had better prepare yourself for a leap up your ladder to better health.

Further reading:
Dr. Jensen's Guide to Better Bowel Care by Dr. Bernard Jensen
Cleanse & Purify Thyself, Book One by Rich Andersen

Round 11 – 7th March 2008
6mg DMSA every three hours, three days on.

I'm in the groove now, chelating every weekend. I can only handle three to four days on round then I start feeling it. So three days on, four days off suits me fine. Each round is different, causing different symptoms and reactions.

This round was a little bit like being on speed (amphetamines). Very racy, jittery and speeded up for the first 24 hours. Also had metal taste in my mouth, but the reward was excellent! Got more colours coming back! Happy dayz!

I kind of plateaued out there and had no change for the last four or five rounds on the colours, but blue and yellow coming in bright and clear yesterday. Makes me sure chelation is the right thing for me to do.

Also, I'm doing a one-month bowel cleanse with psyllium. I'm about 7-10 days in now and I have more mucoid plaque coming out. Lots of little black bits and some long rubbery strands too. Green this time, not black. How much of this gunk have I got in me? Whatever, I always feel better when this stuff comes out of me.

Farmer Giles is also paying me a visit which is always a pain in the butt.

Round 12 – 14th March 2008
6mg DMSA every three hours, three days on.

Good round, although have a mild sore throat and feel tired. Got colours coming back, but maybe I should just say everything looks sharper, more in focus. I'm totally in the groove doing rounds every weekend. Still doing the bowel cleanse and feeling pretty good overall. I am a happier person now. Gone are the grumps and I'm looking to the future now.

For the first time, I had real loud ringing and whooshing sound in my ears. Tinnitus. And strange bells ringing, jingling and jangling too. I kept looking up, expecting to see Father Christmas. All rather strange really, I always had the whooshing sound but it went into overdrive on this round.

I have always wanted to try some of those ear-spliffs and here was the perfect opportunity. I set up a mirror, so I could see what I was doing, gently lay my head down to one side, plugged a spliff into my lughole and sparked that little beauty up. Ahhhhh! Lovely!

The burning cone creates a vacuum and sucks up any gunk from your ears. Simple, cheap, easy and works a treat, but best to do it in the privacy and comfort of your own home. It is wildly funny looking at yourself with a huge spliff billowing smoke out of your ear. And don't forget the bolder-burn protector! It's there for a reason!

My ears were a lot cleaner and I could hear clearer, but the tinnitus remained unchecked. Ear-spliffs are good for cleaning the ears, does nothing for tinnitus, but you do feel strangely relaxed and calm after the laughing has subsided. They are officially called Ear Candles, or Otosans. There is no mistaking what they look like.

Round 13 – 28th March 2008
6mg DMSA every three hours, two days on.

I skipped a weekend's chelation because I had a cold. Was minor, but was the first cold I had had for eight or nine months.

Day one felt completely normal.

Day two I was short tempered, irritable, and tingly all over, especially my face and hands. It was most noticeable when using the computer but also watching TV. Mobile phone ran out of batteries in the night, so missed a dose and stopped the round after two days on round. Bugger!

Nothing bad happened after round, everything was normal, except the tingling continues.

Round 14 – 2nd April 2008
6mg DMSA every three hours, four days on.

Going to see if I can extend the round. Four days is cool, five days would be perfect.

Feel I need a longer time to recover in-between rounds, one week recovery would be good.

First day was very tingly. Started to feel it after two and a half hours. Made me think of decreasing the dose timing. Too early for that though, prolly just usual chelation rollercoaster symptoms.

Fourth day I found out the consequences of extending the length of the round by just one measly day. Mercury attack hit me big-time-Charlie: brain fog, muscle weakness, the works came crashing down on my head.

Total and absolute nightmare! Something somewhere did not like that.

was a complete zombie for 36 hours, needed a couple of ys off work, sitting at home looking at the walls and gibbering cha-cha-cha. My face felt like that comedian Jim Carrey: all twisted, contorted and stretched as he makes his silly faces. I was back to normal five days later, but extreme caution will be used next time.

Not sure if this is the six-month dump starting? In hindsight I think it was just too long on round. Three days on is what suits me.

Ouch! That's another painful mercury lesson: I am not ready for longer rounds. Going to stay on DMSA. Too scared what the ALA will do to me.

The tingling continues.

Mercury Attack

After that I developed my Mercury Attack Check-List. When the going gets rough there is a tendency to just sit staring at walls for hours on end in a zombie state, doing nothing to help. So now, when I have a mercury attack, just like on the last round, I go to my check-list and it tells me what I should do.

Mercury Attack Check-List

1. Chill out and remain calm. Relax.
2. Be on my own. Avoid everyone.
3. Be ready for two days of troubles.
4. Digestive problems always happen. Drink plenty of apple cider vinegar even before the heartburn comes, because you know it will come!
5. Detox bath —any type but make it hot hot hot and follow with a one-minute freezing cold shower. Should clear a lot of hanging around mercury.
6. Bowel cleanse of some type—mercury dumps into the

bowels and having a clearout is a great idea. Psyllium or P&B shakes, anything easy and simple.

7. Make sure all supplements are taken.

8. Increase dose of vitamin C to bowel tolerance. Divided doses, four times a day at mealtimes and before bed. *This is very important and will help big-time-Charlie, so do it ASAP.

9. Dry skin brushing. It will tell your body you love it and you will help get that mercury out as quickly as possible. Before a detox bath is great too: wakes up the skin. Help your body help itself.

10. Oil massage after the dry skin brushing.

11. Oil pulling. Lots of it. I did 3 x 20 minutes back-to-back once and it helped a lot.

12. Meridian Massage. Always seems to make me feel better and only takes seven minutes.

13. Self Reiki. Set aside an hour or two, and make 100 percent sure of no interruptions.

14. Don't Worry. This is only short-term hassle. It will pass. It always passes. In a couple of days you will feel good again and you will have learnt a bit more about yourself from whatever experiment just backfired.

Round 15 – 19th April 2008
6mg DMSA every three hours, three days on.

Skipped a couple of weeks, firstly to recover from the last difficult round and the mild cold I had. Second weekend was skipped because I wanted to test out going no supplement. A herbalist convinced me my diet was good enough so I stopped all my supplements to see what would happen. Ouch! That didn't work! I quickly reintroduced them again.

Was mostly OK this round. Mornings I awoke feeling great, but as the day wore on, felt like I should dose more frequently, like every two and a half hours. I felt a little jittery coming up to the three-hour mark. Night time dose of three hours seem good as I usually wake up feeling fine.

Time flies when you're having fun. I am five and a half months amalgam free. I'm happy with the Cutler Protocol, suits me just fine, feeling oh so much better. Every week now I have days where I feel pretty normal again.

33. Understanding

Now that I'd figured out what the black gunk was, realisation dawned on me. Things started to make sense now. The reason why some things worked at getting me better, and why some things didn't work became obvious the more I understood, the more I learned. Why had the parasite cleanse worked and the liver and kidney cleanse not worked? Everything seemed to be equally screwed up and congested, so why did I remain sick when I first did the liver flushes and first did the kidney herbs?

Well, there is an order to cleansing/healing that is required. An order to the parts of the body that need attention first, some things are required before others. It is recommended by all well-educated holistic practitioners, but is poorly understood by the vast majority.

In order for toxins to be expelled from the body, the exit routes have to be open. The excretion routes have to be free of blockages so that toxins could get out.

So, what are the main excretion routes of the body? The main routes are urine, faeces, exhaled air and sweat.

Piss: Urine comes though the kidneys, (kidneys control the fluids in the body).

$hit: If you have less than three BMs a day, it means you are constipated and your digestive tract and bowels are blocked up to some degree. The less BMs, the more blocked. Please note having a dump should be as easy as having a pee, I mean no straining.

Breath: If you smoked cigarettes in your life you will have clogged up your lungs. Ditto been in a smoky pub, ditto lived in a large city, ditto worked around any chemicals. Your lungs are important; they supply oxygen to your brain.

Sweat: The skin is the largest part of the body and you continually excrete toxins through the tiny pores in the skin when you sweat.

If one, or some, or all of those exit routes are blocked up, then some toxins become trapped inside and have to try and find other routes to get out. If toxins can't get out the normal routes, then often it comes out through the skin and you get spots, pimples, rashes, eczema. If toxins cannot get out at all, they get stuck and make you sick in ways that are very difficult to comprehend.

If your digestive tract is blocked up, like mine was with that black gunk, and you then detox the liver or kidneys or whatever, the toxins expelled by the cleanse you have done, those toxins hurt you because they cannot get out. And/or they cannot get out quick enough and they get re-circulated and relocated somewhere else. Having clean bowels is the foundation of good health because they are the major exit route for the majority of your waste. If toxins can't get out, you are in deep deep trouble.

Also your body seems to kinda know that it shouldn't really be doing things just yet, seems to know it's not really ready. Or maybe think about this the other way round: when the exit routes are open, detoxing parts of the body can happen quickly and efficiently without too much hassle. Once the nasty stuff is out of you, it can never hurt you again.

Obviously the largest volume of waste comes out via the bowels, so this is the first, foremost and most important place to start cleaning.

34. First things first
& A drop in the ocean

I discovered I needed to treat my body holistically, which just meant I had to treat each and every part of it. But I needed to start somewhere.

The first job to tackle was the digestive tract. It needed cleaning top to bottom, mouth to arse, to make sure it was clean so that any toxins I dislodged could actually get out, and stay out.

I discovered that three BMs per day was optimal. If you don't have three per day, it means you are constipated. When you eat food, you fill up the top part of the digestive tract. You need to make space for the new food that just entered you. You should have a BM after each meal because this frees up space in the bottom part of the digestive tract for the new food to fill. This is how our bodies are designed to work, when they work correctly. Fresh food in, waste out. If you only have one BM per day it means you need to clean out the pipes to become more frequent. How do you do that?

There are many different ways to do it; it's called bowel cleansing, or colon cleansing. Tubes up the bum is one way. I must say it's not really my cuppa-tea, although it is very fast and very effective. There is a time and place for it, but it only cleans out the lower part of the digestive tract anyway, the bowels. Hey, maybe you will be one of those lucky people that loves it? You never know!

Another method is using a plant called psyllium, pronounced "silly-um". The plant is dried and ground up into a powder. It's a simple scheme: you take some capsules of psyllium and you drink lots of water; two litres throughout the day. The water makes the psyllium swell up to 50 times its original size when it's inside the digestive tract and then sweeps out any congested gunk, top to bottom, as it passes through. It's small stuff and takes time, but it's easy, cheap as chips and very effective over the long term.

It was the psyllium herbs in the parasite cleanse that helped me get all that black gunk out. Some of the other herbs in the formula helped to stimulate the lining of my stomach to dislodge and expel the toxins: (senna and cascara sagrada).

At first, you may have amazing success like I had and get a big load out, but most people don't have fast results. It does take time. One or two days is a drop in the ocean compared to how long that gunk has been building up inside, layer by layer. I believe the reason I had the success when I did was because of the accumulation of all the things I tried up to that point, not least the ultra-strict diet regime I was doing. The juice fast was important too.

It takes a long time to completely cleanse the whole digestive tract too. To date I have done over 300 days when I took psyllium and I still get strange black bits out even now, although no more ropey black gunk.

I understand it takes about one year to completely clean everything out. But it's easy and wonderfully rewarding as your health returns. One or two months of daily use should get results.

Many people take psyllium and initially get congested and clogged up; they then assume that 'this does not agree with me' and that they should avoid it forever more.

Well, the very act of getting clogged up and congested is confirmation that there is stuff that needs cleaning out. If the digestive tract was free of obstacles the psyllium would just pass on through. It is just a fibre and cannot be digested. The only sensible explanation for getting clogged up on psyllium is congestion already inside. Those that do get congested need to drink more water to flush the system and start on a lower dosage.

I know people just pop these caps and assume instant health will be coming their way. Pity the boxes don't come with proper instructions, eh! Do you know why they don't? Ever thought about that?

Most complicated products come with detailed instructions, otherwise how could a company have a great product and sell loads of its goods? Well, in the health business, companies are not allowed to. They are not allowed to educate you. It's against the rules/law. People are supposed to blindly take stuff and just blindly get better. Pity life is not as simple as that.

Once the body can expel toxins, good health returns. It is the foundation of all healing. If toxins can't get out, you can't get better: simple. If toxins can't get out, the body doesn't bother trying things it knows it can't do, so you accumulate toxins. Toxins in this sense means anything and everything bad, including mercury.

My experience is that mercury dumps into the bowels. When you have a mercury attack, large amounts of mercury go into the bowels and gum up the works big time.

With this understanding I did straight bowel cleansing with psyllium, taking it three times a day for a month. Again I used the herbs from Humaworm called Humacleanse. It is the easiest, simplest, least problematic cleanse you can do, it cleans the entire digestive tract top to bottom, not just the bowels. It is vital to do first in any healing quest and as a bonus you don't have to stick any tubes up your arse!

Further reading:
Dr. Jensen's Guide to Better Bowel Care by Dr. Bernard Jensen
Cleanse and Purify Thyself, Book One by Rich Andersen

35. Aliens II

So, the gunk is removed by a bowel cleanse; all those creepy crawlies that grew in the dark 'n' dirty places are feeling a little exposed now! Ha! Their house, their home, i.e. the gunk, has been removed. So now we are in a position to kill the bastards that've been giving us hell. Once the mucoid plaque has been dislodged you can kill the bacteria, fungus and parasites that have been living in that space with special herbs: garlic, wormwood and black walnut to name but a few.

For the annihilation, I used a parasite cleanse from an American company called Humaworm. Theirs is a collection of parasite killers, blood purifiers and waste disposal units, all together in one capsule, called 'Humaworm'. It's just a herbal formula, the quantities of each herb are remarkably small, but it is the combination of herbs working together that somehow works gloriously. I believe the reason people have such great success with these herbs is because each formula is freshly made to order and it's not just a parasite killer,

Ohhh, stop! I can tell some are thinking this gunk is BS. If you don't believe me, I can send you pictures! I daren't print a picture here because it wouldn't be fair; they are pretty disgusting you gag. But if you Google 'mucoid plaque' and click in. see the evidence for yourself. You will see thousands of pi thousands of people that got their own gunk out. If you d see, you will truly understand, and truly believe just how h⟨ ⟩ my body was to get that toxic nightmare out.

Anyway, not just a parasite killer. There are three categories of herbs in Humaworm. The first are the herbs that have the ability to kill parasites, their larvae and their eggs. Different herbs have the capacity of killing different parasite species—some kill the bigger worms, while others will destroy the microscopic ones: these herbs are the Destroyers.

The second category of herbs are the cleansers. They have the ability to sweep through the body and remove all toxins left over from the parasites. Some clean the blood, while other clean specific organs like the liver and kidneys: these herbs are the Purifiers.

The last group of herbs are the digestion and colon helpers. Parasites, larvae and eggs are removed from the body through the colon. During parasite attack-and-destroy missions the digestive system is working extra hard to expel dead parasites and dislodged toxins—this group helps to keep the digestive system running smoothly: these herbs are the Undertakers.

There are no fillers, no dyes, no sweeteners and no man-made chemicals included. This is in sharp contrast to all over-the-counter and prescription drugs. You should recognise half the ingredients too:

Parasite Destroyers: Black Walnut, Wormwood, Cloves, Thyme, Garlic, Fennel, Cayenne, Ginger, Gentian, Hyssop.

Purifiers: Milk Thistle, Marshmallow Root, Pau D'Arco, Burdock, Elecampane, Fenugreek, Liquorice.

Undertakers: Barberry, Cascara Sagrada, Senna, Sage, Psyllium, Yellow Dock, Cramp Bark, Peppermint.

You can look up each ingredient and see what they do, but remember there is only a teeny tiny bit of each herb in each cap; 24 herbs in one little capsule. It is pretty amazing such small quantities of herbs work so well.

And no, I don't work for Humaworm, nor am I sponsored by them. Never been there and only ever talked to the now-retired boss RG on email. Other companies sell similar good herbal cleanses, Dr. Schulze springs to mind, but I never used his herbs because Humaworm worked so gloriously for me.

I know there is a lot of dross out there too, so if you decide to try some herbal formulas, just make sure they are all-herb. You want as many different herbs in there as possible. The more herbs, the more wide-spectrum, the more different species of parasites they can kill. If you can find one like Humaworm that speeds removal of waste too, that will make your life considerably easier.

You don't want any man-made rubbish in there. Patented crud is totally pointless and those are the products you should avoid. As a general rule of thumb, patented things are almost always man-made synthetic products. I always need to see the ingredients in a product and if I can't, if they are hidden, then that product is not for me. I look up everything I take.

• • •

I realised that certain symptoms were due to parasites because when taking the herbs, those problems went crazy and flared right up. Those same symptoms then disappeared for good afterwards.

I had chronic pain in my shoulders and upper back. When I took the herbs, that pain went haywire—remember the wild stabbing pains? When the herbs were finished, the pain then faded away and I no longer had such chronic shoulder pains. The herbs had killed and removed the parasites that caused that pain. Thank you parasite cleanse: job done.

According to Hulda Clark, shoulder pain almost always indicates congestion of the liver and gallstones. I obviously had parasites living in amongst the gunk.

OK, so I was ultra-ill and I didn't get all the gunk out in one go, nor manage to kill all my bugs in one go. But the difference was like night and day. After the parasite cleanse and the bowel cleanse, I was happy, healing and looking forward to the future.

So, gunk gone, bugs gone, what else do I need to do?

36. "Life in all its fullness is Mother Nature obeyed." Weston A. Price

The food I ate ruled the quality of my life so I have read extensively about diet. Tricky subject too. Should we eat meat, or not? Dairy? Wheat? Fat? Eggs? Sugar? Chemicals? Organic? Which oils? Refined foods? What is actually refined and what is not? It may sound dumb, but pasta is a refined food. I was not really aware of this at first. Pasta was just pasta, and everyone eats pasta. Does it grow on trees? Or in fields?

There is a vast array of dietary information to sift through and opinions to consider: who to believe? Conventional wisdom from Tom, Dick and Harry? Mum and Dad? Commercials? Diet gurus? Or random famous people making a quick buck?

I had the short end of the stick too; any false move hurt me. And I was not trying to lose weight like most people, I was trying to gain it. I had to find nutrient-dense food in order to bulk up and rebuild, but any junk was out of the question as that just made me worse.

As is my way, and because I was so damn sick, in the end I tried just about everything. What other choice did I have? Each book, style and method sounded equally persuasive. I just moved through each assessing how I felt. It was not easy as I had so many food intolerances.

After a while all the different diets I looked into blurred into one incomprehensible mess: information overload. There is so much conflicting advice. I need to understand why something is good or bad. If I understand, I can do whatever is necessary. Blindly following orders usually leads me to do the exact opposite!

Why is wheat bad? Why is milk bad? Why is cheese bad? Why should I not eat fruit for breakfast? What's all this food combining rubbish? What's wrong with meat? Should I eat sausages? How can tuna be good for me if it's contaminated with mercury? How can shrimp be good for me if they are bottom feeders? Why shouldn't I cook my food? The questions are endless and I have to know why in order to do.

I tried many different people's ideas on diets; rotation diets, blood type diets, body type diets, Atkins diets, vegetarian, vegan, when to eat, what to eat, how to cook it, or not cook it, I did totally raw foods for a while too. Eventually I came across the missing link, the philosopher's stone, the real deal, the undisputed King of understanding diets. Funnily enough it was a dentist of all people that enabled me to see the big picture.

In the early 1900s an American dentist called Dr. Weston A. Price was trying to understand why so many people in his dental practice, and around the world, had such rotten and falling-out teeth, as well as such poor health. This was at a time of huge ill-health in the western 'developed' world, tuberculosis was running wild, killing millions.

He'd heard rumours of small pockets of isolated peoples free from diseases, and they supposedly had perfect teeth too. He was a pioneer, so he set out to for himself to try and understand how and why these people were so damn healthy.

He looked at the people that had left these isolated communities, those who had stopped eating their traditional native diets. Those who had started eating the western diet of coffee, sugar, white flour and pasteurised milk. Interestingly this was the same diet that his sick and rotten-toothed patients in America had been eating.

There were still a few super-healthy people living there to see the contrast. These were the people who had stuck to their traditional native diets and shunned cheap western food.

The contrast to their before-and-after health was extreme and shocking. The once-happy-healthy people who moved to a diet of western junk all got extremely sick, their teeth rotted and then fell out. They then died in their thousands of nasty diseases like tuberculosis, polio, and diphtheria.

Some of the people still ate some traditional food, but supplemented it with a little western junk food. They also got sick and also had rotten teeth, but not so badly and didn't die quite so painfully and quite so terribly.

The children of the children that ate the western diet also got sick frequently, their teeth also rotted and fell out, but on top of that, they looked physically different too. Their faces changed shape. Gone were their full beautiful healthy faces. Their jaw bones got smaller and their teeth became crowded and ugly due to lack of space. Their faces looked pinched as various parts didn't grow properly because the junk food was not providing them with enough, or the correct nutrients.

Then he saw what happened to the people who moved back onto the local native unrefined diet: they regained their health again. (Although any structural bone damage from childhood remained.)

Once he saw the tremendous changes these people experienced when they changed their diet to one of cheap refined junk, he started studying the original traditional foods they'd been living on in the first place.

It was these traditional diets that had kept those people healthy, fit and well. When they stopped eating them, their health crumbled along with their teeth. It may seem obvious today, but back then, this was a giant breakthrough.

The work he did then in understanding native diets is the foundation of his diet recommendations today. The basics are: eat whole, natural foods, untainted with poisons, prepared in traditional ways, not in ways convenient to industry. He recommends meats, fats, dairy, grains and all manner of tasty treats; but the emphasis being on quality of ingredients and quality of preparation.

This is now how I prepare and cook my food: with care, preparation and quality.

Dr. Weston A. Price is famous even now for his work, and quite rightly so. The things he witnessed and detailed will never happen again. Our world has moved on. There are no pockets of healthy people anymore. Everyone has been vaccinated with poisons, fed a diet of trash and breathed in the fumes of our industry since the day we were born.

I read summaries of his work many times, so I decided to read his original work, *Nutrition and Physical Degeneration*, first published in 1939. This book is a tombstone of old-school English writing and it is a little daunting at first glance, but seriously, if you want to really understand diet, there is no equal, not by a country mile, to this legendry masterpiece of detective work. This book totally changed the way I look at diet, made everything fit together, everything became clear on reading his work.

His book is full to the brim of amazing before and after pictures of the people, the families, the children he met on his travels. He could have called his book 'A picture paints a thousand words'. Pictures so stunning and revealing; side by side healthy mothers and fathers on traditional diets. Next to them their children on a different diet with mangled toothless faces and bodies.

A powerful, inspiring book.

Plenty of today's dietary books have a passing reference to his work, but looking at the wide variety of differing recommendations, I get the impression people didn't read his original work in the flesh to get the big picture. His pictures tell an undeniable story. His words speak with breath-taking wisdom. He stands the test of time. 'Life in all its fullness is Mother Nature obeyed,' is his most famous quote. Wise words indeed.

I highly recommend his book. I feel honoured to have learnt what he discovered. The book is stuffy, old-fashioned and repetitive in places. Just make sure you don't skip the last three chapters which are the diet recommendations.

Sally Fallon wrote a splendid cook book called *Nourishing Traditions*. His findings are used as the backbone to her cooking style. Not your typical cook book either. She brings his discoveries well and truly into the 21st century. She explains why each dish should be prepared in the way she recommends and why other methods might be harmful. She and her book are quite famous now too. Education through cooking!

After being so inspired by these books I embarked on testing these ideas on myself. Theory is all well and good, but what counts is the practical application. Would the diet agree with me? I am a sensitive soul and I knew anything dodgy would soon show up in some funky adverse reactions.

Raw unpasteurised milk is like gold dust in the UK and it took me a couple of months of searching and asking around, but eventually I found some at a local farmers market. Muscle testing showed no bad reaction, so I gingerly tried some. It tasted awesome and best of all gave me no bad reactions whatsoever. Remember milk was the first thing I had to give up, 19 years previously. It's pretty cool to have this success. Gave me a warm rosy feeling to add things back in to my diet, especially something that had been off my menu for so long.

I switched to brown rice and started soaking it to make it more digestible: tasted better and gave no reactions. I reintroduced meat into my diet, all organic. Tasted great, and as predicted, the fat on the meat tasted even better. Again no reactions.

Then I bought a grain mill and started making my own bread using freshly-milled flour. The bread tasted amazing, gave no reactions but also something else. I felt noticeably better, more solid, less fragile and more robust. It was obvious the fresh wheat was rebuilding me, supplying my body with well-needed nutrients, just as Weston A. Price had predicted.

I tried raw butter. Again tasted wonderful and gave no bad reactions. Ditto soaked oats to make home-made muesli.

Happy dayz! Success at last. I had found the diet that suited me. After all the intolerance food hassles I'd been through, finding a diet that made sense intellectually and that actually worked was wonderful. Thank you Weston A. Price and Sally Fallon for helping me help myself.

That's enough of my diet for now, but I will return to it because a first-class diet is an essential part of good health.

Further reading:
Nutrition and Physical Degeneration by Weston A. Price
Nourishing Traditions by Sally Fallon

37. Sleeping on toxic slag

I was sleeping very badly. I woke up each morning feeling worse than when I went to bed. After much reading about why humans sleep in the first place, to recover and recharge from the day's activities, I figured something was wrong. I should have been waking up rested and relaxed. Instead I awoke daily to major back pain and generally feeling like I had been dragged through a hedge backwards. Once I figured something was wrong with my sleeping style, I started to notice that as the day wore on, I would feel better and better, and by the time I was going to bed, I felt OK-ish in an OK-ish-less-bad-way-than-when-I-awoke way. Ummm? What did this mean?

Maybe EMFs (electromagnetic fields) were stopping me from sleeping well? I discovered that cordless home phones emitted microwave radiation continuously 24 hours a day, pulsing, pulsing, pulsing all day and all night long. It is considered bad for your health to have this radiation hammering you all the time, especially if you sleep near it. I hired a detector unit to figure out what waves were hitting my house. The three different phone base units I found dotted around the house were bombarding me and my family, mostly the kids' room. Nice, eh!

So I bought myself a cordless home phone that did not emit that crap 24/7. The new phone emitted that microwave radiation too, but only when the phone rang and when you were making a call. So, 99 percent of the time it was EMF free. Cost the same as any other 24/7-pulse-your-brains phone.

Nothing changed after I bought the new phones. I continued to sleep just as badly. It was just another little toxin, it was no big deal, most people couldn't tell or feel anything. But no matter how healthy or unhealthy they were, every person's body still battled those little pulses of toxins. Every night. Day in, day out. It was like a little pin sticking in you that you were unaware of. Some people reacted really badly to them, but it seemed this was one problem that did not affect me too much. Or, was not causing the bad sleep anyway. Whatever the result, it was down to choice, and I chose not to have microwave radiation pulsing through my house 24/7.

• • •

One Saturday morning I awoke to the usual very painful back. I crawled out of bed. I got up, brushed my teeth and went in to my six year old's bedroom to read a story in bed. As I lay down I thought, Wow, my back does not hurt. That's strange, I thought, because I just got out of my bed and my back hurt like hell. Very strange indeed!

So I got up and went back to my bed and got in my bed again. The instant I got in my bed, my back started hurting. I got out and the pain stopped. I got in my six year old's bed, it was super comfy and no bad back, or I should say, much less bad, or noticeably less bad…whatever, you get the picture…noticeably less pain.

I did that three times and definitely my bed made my back hurt the instant I got in it, and in the other bed, my back was fine/better/less hurting. Yet another strangeness to try and figure out! What the funk did this mean?

I chanced across a passing reference to something called Brominated Fire Retardants (BFR). It was only a small reference but it started the ball rolling. I Googled BFRs and did some reading.

Turns out that Brominated Fire Retardants are wonderful chemicals that stop furniture and fabrics from burning. These are required by law to be impregnated into flammable stuff in your house, so that if you accidentally set something on fire, it doesn't instantly burn you and your house down. These chemical are wonderful *if* you accidentally set fire to something in your house. However they are unfortunately not very good for human beings.

Just because they do a great job of stopping your house from burning down does not mean that they are harmless. These chemicals are in fact super toxic to humans and in the health freak world where some people know about this toxic slag, well, let's just say those people that know about them, they avoid this $hit like the plague. It's horrid stuff, make no mistake: super toxic.

At first I thought it might be my pillows. I muscle tested them myself, they came up weak, so I took all the pillows in my house to my muscle tester dude for some serious testing. He is the man when it comes to muscle testing!

Three pillows I tested weak to, but six others I tested fine? Umm, so that meant I wasn't allergic to feathers, because all my pillows were feather. So there had to be something in those three pillows that I didn't like. It had to be the fire retardant chemicals, the BFRs.

Then I thought, What about my duvet? That tested weak too. Oh bugger, I just bought a new super-expensive goose-down duvet.

So I researched cleaning them with something chemical free and toxic free. I was recommended some highly weird stuff called 'Miracle Soap II'. Claimed to be very effective at this kinda thing.

One of the ingredients was 'prayer'.

Yes, as I said, weird stuff and I would not have bought it if it wasn't recommended. But it was this stuff or nothing, and it wasn't very expensive.

So, everything was washed in this soap to see if I could wash out any toxic chemicals there might be in there. It seemed to work and everything now muscle tested fine. I slept better, but still not that good. Definitely better, but still worse in the mornings...ummm? What had I missed?

My back had been very bad for at least 10 years and about 18 months previously I thought maybe if I bought a new mattress, that might help my back. So I invested in one of those foam mattresses. Super comfortable. Really very comfy, just sink in and oh so warm and cosy too. Very nice and lovely and all, but I still awoke every morning feeling like $hit, even with this new super-expensive mattress.

With my newfound knowledge of fire retardant chemicals I checked out my mattress. I looked it up on the company website and lo and behold, this company proudly told everyone that their mattresses were smothered in chemicals to stop it burning, brominated fire retardants, BFRs, as required by law, to protect me!

I muscle tested the mattress and I was weak to it, big-time weak too.

It was a bit big and heavy to take to my muscle tester dude, so now I was going on trust. Much to the annoyance of my wife, I could see her holding back the frown, I got rid of my foam mattress and bought myself an organic mattress.

Yes, they do exist, I found a cool little company called Abaca making mattresses with zero chemicals, using organic cotton. Handmade to order. Cost a fair amount, but even so, less than the super-deluxe foam mattress.

So, the moment of truth arrived. My beautiful new, organic, toxin-free, metal-free mattress was delivered. Was my research correct? Was muscle testing a load of bollocks? Had I wasted my time on this little saga? Had I flushed even more money down the pan? Was this just another wild goose chase?

Well, as they say, the proof is in the pudding and only if I woke up in the morning feeling fine would this expensive adventure be worthwhile. At first, lying down it felt super comfy, but so did the foam job when I first bought that.

I went to sleep dreading the morning. I had put in a lot of effort in trying to figure this out, in a most unconventional way, another mother of all long shots, and I would be pretty pissed off if this turned out to be a load of old cobblers.

I awoke the next morning after the best night's sleep I had had for over ten years.

I awoke feeling refreshed.

I awoke with a less painful back.

I awoke with a smile on my face.

Amazing, eh? Who would have thought it? The fire retardant chemicals in my mattress, pillow and duvet caused me years and years of pain and suffering. This also fit in with my getting better whilst away on holiday too. I took a dozen more steps up the ladder to better health as my body was at last able to relax and recover when I went to sleep. Phew! Happy with that.

That little saga in fact took me about one year to piece together from various articles and books. I was pretty slow in figuring it all out. In my defence, it is pretty far-fetched to think companies that sell mattresses and bedding also smother them in toxic chemicals that can hurt people.

I figured the pillows first, the duvet six months later and the mattress some months after that. I did smack my forehead and say Doh!

when I finally figured out the mattress was toxic slag too, but I got there in the end and that's the important thing.

I believe some people are now putting two and two together with regard to babies and cot deaths. Not a pleasant thought, eh! The majority of bedding materials you buy are saturated with toxic chemicals, for adults and kids alike. No, not a pleasant thought for sure.

I did not discover this. I did not make this up. I read about it, I experienced it, it happened to me. Someone, somewhere, who sells these chemicals knows it too, and they still sell them. Bastards.

Although I discovered I reacted to these chemicals, and although I could now avoid them, it is important to ask *why* my body could not handle them. Plenty of people love their BFR mattresses and sleep just fine, my wife being one of them. She sleeps like an angel on any mattress.

My strong reaction to these chemicals was a clear indication that I had 'multiple chemical sensitivities' (MCS). It was also an obvious signal that my liver was congested and needed unblocking and unclogging. It was also a very firm and solid clue that I had adrenal problems. More signs, signals and bits to puzzle over. Every symptom and side effect means something. We should all think long and hard about the problems we have, and what they might mean.

You want an 'Analogue cordless phone'? I got mine from a company called 'Orchid'. This website is helpful too: http://www.emfields.org/index.asp

Further EMF reading: *The Powerwatch Handbook* by Alasdair & Jean Philips

Organic mattress: www.abacaorganic.co.uk

38. Me, myself and my hormones

During my investigations of what was wrong with me I saw repeated mentions of thyroid problems and the importance of getting the thyroid supported correctly. Luckily for me that was 'women's troubles' and didn't effect men. Did men even have thyroids? No idea, probably not... or so I thought.

Turns out that men *do* in fact have thyroids too! Amazing all this learning stuff. I never knew that. And unfortunately men's thyroids get just as messed up as women's thyroids, although maybe the symptoms are mildly different, but I'm a bloke so I don't know about women problems!

So, as is my way, I read a book about thyroids. Didn't understand that whatsoever and went away even more confused, but it mentioned something about adrenal glands, which I had never heard of either, and I can confirm men also have them too: amazing, eh!

So I then read a book about the adrenal glands, didn't understand that book too much either. Nor the next book. Thyroids and adrenals is one tricky bloody subject and that's for sure. Remember I only take actions when I understand what's wrong, what needs doing and why. I just kept reading until I got it.

Many people, including the moderators on Yahoo FDC, told me to treat the adrenals first, before treating the thyroid. If I didn't, the extra hormones that were produced become overwhelming and you 'crashed' to even worse than before. Sounded horrid!

The adrenals and thyroid work in tandem together and adjust in relation to each other. I like the car analogy: Thyroid is the accelerator. Adrenals are the engine. If you push your accelerator to the floor and the engine is not working very well, the engine will overheat and blow up. Same with the adrenals and thyroid, if you gun the accelerator (thyroid) before the engine (adrenals) can handle it, everything comes crashing down and you crash, which is why adrenals must be treated first. Otherwise the extra hormones produced by the thyroid will cause imbalances and you get sicker because your body cannot cope.

So, adrenals was first to be investigated. I discovered I did have them, but did I have adrenal problems?

Turns out there are some very easy ways to figure out if a person has adrenal problems. No idea why regular doctors need to get so many expensive, inaccurate and pointless lab tests for these things, but I guess it's something to do with our money, and their pockets.

All you have to do is take your temperature. There are a couple of ways to do this, but I started off by following the very clear guidance from a website by someone called Dr. Rind: www.drrind.com.

To get an accurate reading of what your temperature is, you take your temps three times a day and average them: 9am, noon and 3pm. This gives you a nice precise measurement of your average daily temperature.

Track these temps over a week. Plot them onto a little graph. It's easy and costs nothing but a few minutes of your time each day. Humans are hot-blooded creatures and our temps should be pretty stable. It does change, as your circumstances change, but the three-per-day average is just what you need to see what yours is doing. Your average temperature should be approximately 98.6 deg F (or 37 deg C).

If the 'daily average temps' vary up and down from day to day, then it means your adrenals are not working correctly.

If the temp is above or below 98.6 it means that your thyroid is not working correctly.

If the temp is not at 98.6 and it varies from day to day that means that adrenals *and* thyroids are not working correctly. But adrenals *always* get treated first.

With the ladies, the temp changes daily over the course of the month in accordance with their ovulation cycle. The temps peaks after ovulation, stays steady for two weeks until it gently drops to its lowest point just before ovulation occurs again.

I guess it's a tad trickier to figure out the ladies graph, but only mildly. If the temp is unstable from day to day, this signals adrenal problems. You can easily Google an ideal temp graph that yours should look like, just compare that to yours and Bob's your uncle, instant metabolic understanding. Considering symptoms and temp chart together should give a pretty good idea of what is wrong. All that information is free to anyone who takes their temperature in this way. We are all made the same way.

I took my temps and discovered that my temps were wildly gyrating up and down, and on top of that they were all low low low, well below the ideal 98.6 deg F. I was down at 95.9 one day and up to 97.4 the next. 95.9 deg F is seriously low and the big daily swings indicated major adrenal fatigue. No wonder I was having rollercoaster days! Obviously my temps were also well below normal. After one week of taking my temps, it became clear I had adrenal and thyroid problems.

So now, on top of everything else, I had to embark on trying to figure out how to handle this. I found it easy to figure out what was wrong using the temp graph as a guide, but figuring out what to do about it was super complicated. The books were not very clear: so many different pills, methods and recommendations. I could not figure out where to start, so I did what any normal person would do. I asked for help.

Further reading: www.drrind.com

39. Doctors for the last and final time

I decided to go back and talk to my regular NHS doctor.

"Hi doc, I need some help here."

"OK Sunshine, fire away."

"I need some help in understanding my adrenals and thyroid glands. I know mine are broken, but I can't figure out how to treat them. I don't even know where to start because there are so many complicated options."

"How do you know yours are broken?"

"Well, because my hair test and my temperatures both indicate something is seriously wrong. Here, I brought the paperwork for you to check out."

"Err, OK."

"You can see my temps are all low, which means thyroid issues. You can see the line is all jumpy too, very up and down. I know that means I have adrenal fatigue. And I have all the symptoms too: fatigue, lack of energy, weight loss, mood swings, memory problems, sensitivity to cold and feeling chilly all the time."

"Umm."

"Yes, so what I really need is to understand where to start. Which products? I know I need to start with the adrenals, but what?"

"OK Sunshine, now hold your horses here. All this stuff..." He ruffled my papers furiously. "All this stuff is inconclusive nonsense. It is extremely unlikely you have adrenal problems because that's ever so rare. And it's even less likely you have thyroid problems."

I looked into his eyes; maybe he didn't think blokes had thyroids either?

He looked disgustedly at my temp graph. "I think what we need here are some real tests. Blood tests that clearly show if you have these so-called problems, which I think are highly unlikely. But we will get the tests done and then we can see for sure what the problem is. Thyroid TSH, Liver, Serum C, Bone profile, Coeliac Disease screen, Urea and Electrolytes, Blood FBC, X, Y, and Z."

• • •

A week later, the doc called on my mobile.

"Sunshine, we have your test results and I just wanted to make sure you are OK."

"Wow! You called me. Impressive. Never had a doc call me before. I'm unchanged sir, but thank you for calling to check. I am exactly the same as before. I still have problems A, B, C...X, Y and Z."

"OK, well the results are in. Why don't you come in so we can review them together."

He called! Maybe this guy wasn't such a twat after all?

I skipped in to see him, eager to learn how to help myself.

"Ah there you are. Take a seat, Sunshine. I have good news."

"So, what do the tests tell me?"

"OK, you can see here, here, and here. These indicate you are all in range. And here. And here."

I sat unblinking.

"You see this? Yes that's in range too. And here, here and here: in range. And here, look, in range too."

I sat unblinking.

"The only problem I can see is a sugar problem, see here, out of range, but there is nothing you can do about that anyway, so best just ignore that."

"..."

"and here, liver function, in range. And here thyroid TSH, in range too."

".."

"So yes. All rather good news really. Congratulations."

"Congratulations?"

"Yes, congratulations on a clean bill of health. All your tests came back in range."

"A clean bill of health? Congratulations?"

"Yes, keep up the good work."

"But, hang on a sec! No, no, no. What about all my bloody problems? I told you about them all. I listed them out. You know I've been having a terrible time. I need help in figuring out what to do next, not congratulations."

"You are fine."

"But I feel like $hit all the time."

"You are fine."

"You can't look at those papers and ignore what I told you. I'm telling you again: I feel like a sack o'$hit all the time. I have no energy, I'm weak, and my digestion is terrible. My spine is crooked. Look at my face. Do I look healthy to you?"

"Look Sunshine, your tests are all in range. Your adrenal and thyroid glands are fine. You are worrying about nothing. Go home and enjoy your good health."

"...but..."

"Go home and enjoy your good health."

I stomped out, enraged and disgusted. How could he totally ignore what I told him? How could he look exclusively at a set of lab results and declare me in good health? Civil words fail me. The Doctor and The System were obviously seriously screwed up to miss my multiple problems. I knew 100 percent I was not making them up!

That's when I gave up on doctors for good. What's the point of seeing people if they can't see what's in front of their eyes? If they can't even listen? Even now, I shake my head in disgust at how I was disregarded and thrown away. The disappointment was gut wrenching: on my own again.

That was the last time a saw a regular doc and I hope it's the last ever. When I have a problem now, I find another way rather than seeing a doctor, there are many ways once you know where to look.

I have since learnt why the lab tests all came out 'in range' even when people are sick. It's all to do with, amongst other things, bell curves, averages and how the insurance company classify a person as sick in order to treat that person, or not treat that person, as the case may be.

As an average, they class only five percent of the people that they test as sick. All 95 percent of the rest of those tested, must be, by their definition, fit and healthy. The top 2.5 percent and the bottom 2.5 percent of the people tested are classified as 'sick' and eligible for some type of treatment. Everyone else is fit and well. There is no grey area, only black and white.

So you gotta be at death's door to be classified as sick and then be treated. From the insurance company's profit point of view that's great news because lots of people will die because treatment's been left too late and they will not have to pay for their expensive treatments. The treatments don't work anyway, and the drugs don't work either, just masking symptoms or cutting the problem away, rather than dealing with a root cause.

Bold statement? Looking-for-trouble statement? From my perspective, all the treatments and drugs I received from western medicine failed because I was so ill and remained ill. All the holistic treatments I did worked because I got better and kept getting better.

I am not alone in this opinion. I didn't make it up. It's written in all of the holistic healthcare books I read. Written by much more intelligent people than me. Every alternative healthcare book, it's in there, whether it says it directly, or indirectly. I kid you not! Took me a lot of reading to figure that out.

I also know my experiences with doctors were not isolated incidents. I know many people with serious health problems have been similarly let down on a grand scale too. Only the brave get out of this hellhole.

40. Incurable, my arse!

Whilst I'm distracted by this discussion, along my journey I cured my mother of an Incurable Disease. She was diagnosed with an Incurable Disease called 'Lichen Planus' and told to live with the pain and just suffer.

It's a skin disease, hard ugly bumps and lots of painful itchies. It's not normally lethal, but it's very painful and if left unchecked can lead to other horrid problems which in turn lead to a miserable death. It's just not fun. Nothing they could do and sorry. My mother came to me and discussed what was wrong and I figured out a way that might help.

We ran through the options of:

1) Doing nothing and suffering as per doctor's orders,

Or

2) Trying something her sick son had said might work.

So she tried some herbs that I recommended and in 30 days her incurable disease disappeared. Cool, eh! One proud son and one happy Mum.

But the point is, my Mum went back to the people that diagnosed her incurable disease and told them of her incredible success and complete curing of this problem, and how happy she was, and wasn't it so exciting!

And you know what? They didn't want to know. Said something like, must have been misdiagnosed in the first place and that they couldn't use those herbs on other people. They completely dismissed her cure.

This was the first time my Mum had experienced this, don't know what to call it, mind-blocking? Brain-washing? No idea what to call it, but the fact remains, these specialists in skin disorders, that saw many people with this problem every day of their working lives, they didn't/couldn't/wouldn't consider anything outside of whatever training they had had, *even* if it cured someone. Don't know what you call that, but I call that funked up!

Funny the way I wrote that, eh? Makes it look like everyone would give some herbs a try if it might reduce the pain, but I have since met people also suffering with Lichen Planus, told them The Story of My Mother's Incredible Cure and they didn't want to try it. They preferred the traditional method of problem-solving which is burning those bumps out with a hot poker. I kid you not! And the hot poker method doesn't even work, they told me it didn't work! It just hurts like hell and the Lichen Planus remains and you have nice big scars too.

For the record: I spent some time carefully researching Lichen Planus. It was a pretty fruitless task because it's an 'incurable disease' and there are no cures for 'incurable diseases!' From the little that is known about it, I discovered that it is some kind of growth on or under the skin. So I concluded that this must be a parasite. That is the definition of a parasite: something that lives on/in you that should not.

These bumps and lumps were growing, so they must be parasites of some type. So I gave me Mum a parasite cleanse, yes, the same one I used, Humaworm. Good stuff those herbs. Pretty amazing company Humaworm is too, selling all those herbs at such cheap prices. They also tell you exactly what's in the formula. Not many companies do that. Very few do, in fact.

Cost to cure an incurable disease $29.95.

Oops...I am going off on a tangent here! Where was I? Back to main event: thyroid and adrenals. What a tricky subject!

41. White Gold

My doctor sent me home to 'enjoy my good health'. He was incapable of helping, so I was on my own again. Just me, myself and my books, oh yeah and all my online toxic mates too. There are some wonderful people out there online. Thanks again, everyone!

I figured a plan of action which was to take all the vitamins and minerals as recommended in the books I'd read. I started with salt.

Not table salt, because that comes out the arse-end of a chemical factory. Industry requires a very pure salt for making its products: soaps, detergents, chemicals, plastics etc. So chemical companies strip out all the trace elements to leave a product called 'Table Salt'. Table salt is made of sodium and chloride and a few extra fun-lovin' chemicals, like anti-caking agents. This turns the salt from white gold into a poison. Table salt does not appear anywhere in nature. It is a manufactured product.

So no, I would not be using table salt. I would be using the crème de la crème of salt: Himalayan rock crystal salt.

This stuff is the business. It was laid down 250 million years ago, when man was not around polluting the oceans. Then the Himalayan Mountains sat on top of it for 250 million years and crushed the salt so much that the salt turned into a crystal. Like carbon turning into a diamond, but with salt instead.

This turning into a crystal is a big deal in the world of minerals and makes it wonderful for your body. Eighty four elements from the periodic table of elements can be found in crystal salt, which is all of them, except the gases. This means Himalayan crystal salt contains all the natural minerals and trace elements that are found in the human body, mostly in minuscule quantities: parts per billion! This is in sharp contrast with table salt that, as already mentioned, comes out of the arse-end of a chemical factory and contains just two elements.

Ever wondered why table salt is so cheap? Because it's little more than a waste product from the chemical industry. Luckily for them they found a huge market to sell their poisonous garbage to.

Anyway, I started taking one teaspoon of Himalayan salt spread throughout each day. If you are shocked by this and worry that I will die from salt poisoning or something, you are thinking of table salt. Table salt and Himalayan salt are completely different things. Ditto sea salt and table salt. Sea salt is perfectly fine to eat, but the Himalayan crystal stuff has the bells and whistles because it's been turned into a crystal by the massive pressure of the mountain sitting on it.

If you take too much sea salt or Himalayan salt you just pee out the extra because it's water soluble, but you do have to drink plenty of water each day. I was drinking two litres a day already.

I was tracking my temps daily and within three days my wildly gyrating temps calmed right down. Not perfect, not by a long way, but instantly obvious that the salt worked doing its thing in helping the adrenals. Pretty cool that and very happy was I too. Over the years I adjusted my salt intake. It does vary over the months, from between a quarter to two teaspoons per day.

Now I salt to taste. Your tongue is there to tell you if something is good for you or not. So now I salt all my water and if it tastes nice then that's the correct amount of salt. Too much salt and it tastes disgusting, too little and can't taste anything and need a bit more. Exactly the same way as you salt the food you eat.

I been on that much salt for three years and I continue to regain my health. I start every day with a half teaspoon of solution of water and Himalayan rock salt, it's called Sole and it's 26 percent salt. It is a fine way to start the day.

I added various vitamins and minerals too, one at a time, tracking my temps and each time I added something, my temps calmed down and life got a bit easier. Vitamin C, B-complex, vitamin E, B6, pantothenic acid, magnesium, molybdenum, ashwagandha, kelp. Kelp was particular good. Liquorice was good too, but only in the mornings, otherwise I could not sleep at night.

They all helped and life got slightly easier, but as was obvious from tracking my temps, and from my continued ill health, I needed something stronger, so now on to the real deal: ACE!

Further reading about salt:
Water & Salt, The Essence of Life by Handel and Ferreira
Timeless Secrets of Health and Rejuvenation by Andreas Moritz

42. Ace, Ace baby!

I started Adrenal Cortex Extract (ACE) to support the adrenals, made from crushed-up adrenal glands from cows. Nice, eh! Yum! But much nicer than any man-made synthetic substitute.

I was pretty well-read by now and was pretty confident on what to do and expect. ACE was awesome stuff. This stuff did not turn anything off, nor did it suppress anything. ACE supplied all the building blocks so that the adrenal glands could work and repair themselves. Oh yeah baby, that sounded a millions times better than any other side-effect-laden-plus-shutdown-options available.

I started at 50mg Adrenal Cortex per day (Thorne Research) and worked my way up to 200mg over the course of the next couple of days. At first I felt mildly better, in patches anyway, but very quickly I got a load more new symptoms and side effects to add to the others I already had. I had to stop the ACE and after a couple of days, the new symptoms disappeared.

A week later, I tried again and got a lot more even worse side effects and symptoms: itchy skin all over my body and weird mental symptoms. Ever seen that film Jacob's Ladder? Just like that, mind-jerking jitteriness.

Ummmm? Everything I read said this stuff was the dog's bollards! What was wrong? I re-read the books to try and figure what was going on, but nowhere did I read of ACE causing problems. My online mates could not help either. Was I allergic to the stuff?

Most people went straight onto the hard stuff, Hydrocortisone (HC), which is synthetic and I would only try that if all the natural stuff failed. I was determined to try and use natural rather than man-made chemicals to get better. All the other man-made drugs I had ever taken had resulted in me remaining sick and ill for the long term.

All man-made drugs cause a wide variety of side effects; headaches, dry skin, fatigue, kidney stones, liver problems, to name but a few. The list is endless and I already had these problems anyway. I didn't need to add to my troubles! HC was bottom of my pile and I would exhaust all other natural ways first.

From what I read, ACE had a proven track record dating back 100 years and should 100 percent work. Why did it make me sicker? Almost seemed like I was intolerant to it? Very peculiar indeed.

My NHS doctor was convinced I wasn't even sick, so no point in seeing him, so I looked for someone else to help me. I asked on the forums and was recommended a Dr. Peatfield.

I was told he believed in treating the patient and not the lab results. He believed in listening to the patients and only using man-made chemicals as a last resort. He had a very loyal following in the UK and many people lived normal healthy lives again because of him.

I read his book *Your Thyroid and How to Keep it Healthy* and his methods totally echoed my understanding and my ideals, so I tracked him down.

"I need some help in understanding how to treat my adrenals. I have been tracking my temps for a couple of months now and they indicate I have adrenal fatigue. I have almost all the symptoms associated with adrenal problems. My thyroid is crushed too. See here, here and here: my temps are all low, but I know I should be treating the adrenals first, otherwise I might overwhelm the thyroid glands. I have mercury poisoning. I just removed my amalgams and I'm currently chelating under the Cutler protocol. Ever heard of him?"

"Yes yes, jolly good protocol too."

"Oh cool, you have heard of him! And I have had some pretty good success with cleaning my damaged body too: bowel cleansing, liver cleansing, kidney cleansing and various other herbs too. That's all helped, but I have hit a stumbling block with the adrenals."

"Go on…"

"Well I started taking all the recommended supplen
mins A, B, C, D, E, calcium, magnesium, zinc, coQ10
and they all helped, but it is obvious I need more support
I'd try the Adrenal Cortex next. But when I tried it, it gav ...ic all these
horrid side-effects. I thought Adrenal Cortex was supposed to be bril-
liant. Why does it disagree with me?"

"What did it do to you?"

"Well, all my symptoms flared up and I had the most awful scratchy
itchy skin thing going on, and my mind was all over the place. At first
it felt OK, but the side effects overwhelmed me after a couple of days."

"OK, so why are you here?"

"What?"

"Why are you here seeing me?"

"Well, so you can help me figure out what to do."

"But you already know everything."

"…"

"Yes. You speak like a college graduate. You know everything already."

"I don't know everything, because…"

"Well, it's a pleasure to meet you young man. You are obviously very
much on top of your situation. Sad to say I don't meet many like you,
Sunshine. I must commend you on everything you've learnt. Very impressive. Very rare too. Yes, very rare to meet someone like you. Done
your homework haven't you."

"Thanks, doc."

"Tell me everything about your Adrenal Cortex experiments."

"Well, I started at 50mg and moved up to 200mg after a couple of
days. The side-effects started almost immediately and went into overdrive on the second and third days and I had to stop taking the supplements."

"A couple of days? You moved to 200mg within two days?"

"Yup."

"Bingo! That's what you are doing wrong. You are increasing the
dose too quickly."

"Why's that important?"

"It's important because your body has been lacking in these hormones for a long time. Your body needs to re-acclimatise itself gently. It takes time, that's all. You are doing all the right things, just too quickly."

"Oh, OK. The books didn't say anything about that."

"When the adrenals are fatigued it takes time for them to re-start and re-build. I suggest you re-start the Adrenal Cortex on a very low dose, say 50mg, but stick on that dose for seven to ten days. After your body has had time to adapt, then raise the dose gradually. That way you don't flood your body with too many hormones. If you do get side effects, just back down again and go even slower."

"OK cool thanks. How high do I go?"

"As high as it takes, just go slow. Adrenal Cortex almost always works; you just have to dose correctly and have some patience. Slow and steady wins the race when rebuilding the adrenal glands. Remember: the Adrenal Cortex is rebuilding and supporting your glands, it is not like flicking a switch."

At last! A decent doctor. Hooray! Someone who listened. Thank you world!

• • •

I started at 25mg ACE and gradually increased the dose, going up to 50mg after a week and then an extra 50mg every week thereafter. I had an initial target dose of 200mg. No nasty side-effects or symptoms harassed me, phew!

I was impatient to get better and every time I rushed it and increased the dose too soon, the weird symptoms returned and I had to reduce the dose again. After six weeks I reached the target dose of 200mg, but had no change to my health. My temperatures were still gyrating wildly which indicated adrenals not working correctly.

Next target was 400mg. 400mg of Adrenal Cortex was an expensive eight capsules per day of the Thorne Research brand. So I switched to the Nutricology brand that sells 250mg in each single cap; much more affordable. I found mixing and matching the different brands totally fine.

A month later I reached the 400mg target, but nothing and no change.

Next target 600mg: nothing.

Next target 800mg: nothing.

For four months, I gradually increased the dose, during that time nothing changed in my health. The temps remained very up and down, which signified adrenal fatigue.

It took a lot of courage to keep on taking the pills for four months with zero feedback and remaining sick. I assume many people would not have the patience and would have given up and tried something else, but I did have the patience. Why did I persevere for four months with nothing to show for it?

Well, because I had educated myself. I wasn't blindly taking instructions from anyone. Adrenal Cortex really does have a long history of working very well indeed. I had educated myself and I *knew* that it would work, eventually.

In the grand scheme of things, the reason I got better was because I educated myself. It took a long time and I spent many many days and hours reading and learning. Health education well and truly took over my life.

Education is key and if anyone reading this wants to get better, they had better continue reading books and learning to the max. Only then will you understand, and only when you understand, will you be able to make the right choices in your quest to get better.

All the answers are out there. Every single problem anyone ever had, has been had a zillion times before, and out of those zillion times before, some of those people got better, and out of those few that got better, some of them wrote it down for you to read and learn. Once you have learnt, you will be in a position to help yourself.

Andy Cutler is one of those people who wrote it all down. Dr. Peatfield is another and there are many many more. Anyone who ever wrote about how they got better is one of them. There are thousands of alternative health books to buy. All the answers are out there, we just gotta keep reading until we find what fits us. I was lucky, I had so many different problems; everything was applicable to me!

Anyway: Adrenals, ACE. After three months I was able to increase the dose much quicker with no nasty side-effects, moving up 100mg each seven to ten days. The last dose increase from 750mg to 1000mg was done a week after the previous dose rise. I could handle the higher level of hormones and when I reached 1000mg ACE: BOOM! My temps levelled out and became almost the same each day, and my symptoms calmed down from a difficult Richter scale eight, down to a nice tranquil level five.

Phew! Success at last! It worked! Hooray! I took a couple of dozen steps up the ladder to better health. Rock 'n' roll cool!

It was very satisfying getting it right. Very satisfying indeed helping myself get better. Made me confident in my ability to help myself.

Once adrenal support was in place and working, as shown by a level and constant temperature I was free to move on to the next level: thyroid support.

43. Crushed up thyroid glands

Next up was the thyroid. My temps were very low—around 36.0 degree C (96.9 deg F) so I knew my thyroid was screwed up too. I started thyroid support with thyroid glandular (Nutri Thyroid), which was crushed up thyroid glands from cows. Nice, eh! Yum! But much nicer than any man-made synthetic substitute!

This was the whole thyroid glandular concentrate, and it was fairly mild stuff. It did the same as the ACE, but for the thyroid gland instead. It provided the raw materials for the thyroid gland to work and to rebuild itself. Again, this was my kind of supplement: natural, strengthening and rebuilding. Lovely.

I knew not to overdose my body too quickly, so I started at 50mg and gradually built the dose upwards. This time I had no trouble with weird sensations or strange symptoms like with the ACE, just nothing immediately changed.

I pushed the dose up to a whopping 780mg of Nutri Thyroid. That was ten pills a day. Woohoo! I kid you not! Pretty sure I was over the recommended dose! But I knew what I was doing, and I'd had the thumbs-up from Dr. Peatfield. He said to keep on gradually raising the dose until it kicked in. Track my temps and monitor my symptoms.

Including the work on the adrenal glands, I had been tracking my temperature daily for 11 months by now. Yes, you read that correctly, daily for almost a year. Patience was needed again, but after three months on the thyroid glandular the temps started to rise and I started feeling much better. My temps were still a little low and a little unstable but, BOOM, for the first time I had average temps that were close to normal at 36.6 deg C (97.9 deg F). Hooray, only a few tenths of a degree off normal!

When the temps came close to normal, virtually all my symptoms and chronic problems with my health receded. All of them! No more chronic muscle pain, back pain gone, much more energy, and my brain seemed to be working pretty well too. I even restarted my daily yoga workouts, which further accelerated my recovery, rebuilding and strengthening me.

I'm gonna say that again because it was a big moment for me: *virtually all my symptoms and problems with my health receded.* Woooohoooo! Happy dayz!

When I first started following the mercury forums, I used to ignore the adrenal and thyroid posts because it was so confusing to start with. There were so many different methods, drugs, styles and problems to figure out. But I always saw people saying how important it was to get to grips with this tricky subject. About how much of a difference it makes when these things were correctly supported. Well, now I knew just how true that advice was, because at last I felt like a normal person again, which was amazing considering how terrible I had felt 12 months previously.

Getting the adrenal and thyroid support supplements in place and at the correct dose for me was one of the most important things I had done on this health quest. In all, it took over one year of gradually increasing the dose of adrenal and then thyroid supplements to get it right. I had plenty of two-steps-forward, one-step-back when I rushed increasing the dose too much. Plenty of frustration, plenty of hassle, but I had learnt what to do, I had a plan, and stuck to the plan. And it worked a bloody treat!

From the many many emails and posts I'd read on the mercury forums from all the mercury toxic people, seems this subject was one of the most important to get your head around. It would make the difference between a good life and a miserable life.

• • •

My rules for anyone investigating this would be:

1) Educate yourself.

2) Natural stuff only, no man-made synthetic chemical substitutes whatsoever.

3) Always treat the adrenals first.

4) Daily temperature chart.

5) Patience.

If you avoid man-made chemicals you will naturally have fewer choices to make. Many drug options will automatically be crossed off your potential to-take list and will make your journey simpler.

Most people attack these problems with synthetic drugs. This is because the drug companies market, promote and sell so much of what is available. They dominate the market in every way, with their education, their doctors and their drugs. Synthetic hormone therapy is for life and these companies make billions and billions. People naturally trust the companies and the doctors, and think nothing of taking man-made drugs.

They ignore, or don't know about, the huge list of side effects the drugs cause. The vast majority don't know what I discovered, that there are non-toxic, natural alternatives with proven, long-term track records, that work just fine. The only problem with the natural stuff is no one can make billions and billions out of selling crushed up and dried thyroid glands. Sad, but true; everything comes back to the money in the end.

Anyway, more of this later. I did in fact have a major step-back when I started chelation with ALA. So I will return to this subject because other funky stuff happened and it got tricky again.

Round 16 – 29th May 2008
5mg DMSA every 2.5 hours in the day, every 3 hours at night, 3 days on.

I just completed my third Humaworm parasite cleanse, extra strength this time. It was another big success. Symptoms and side effects now much reduced and feeling fine afterwards. Time for some more chelation.

After the last jittery round I think I should try dosing more frequently. I feel the need to reduce the interval between doses to 2.5 hours in the day, but will stick at 3 hours at night: 9pm, 12 midnight, 3am, 6am, 8:30am, 11am, 1:30pm, 4pm, 6:30pm. Dosing nine times each day. Let's see if that's any better.

I have also reduced each dose from 6mg to 5mg which is a total of 45mg DMSA per day. This is 3mg per day less than before. Better to reduce the dose than increase the dose, and remember to only change one thing at a time, so I know what does what.

Overall this was a fine and smooth round. I had one three-hour patch where I felt a bit rough, but was only mild. Had some mild redistribution at the end, but this coincided with some bowel cleansing, so could have been that.

All in all, the new timings are OK. Will do one more round like this before raising the dose. Also I will wait longer in-between rounds and not chelate every week.

Round 17 – 13th June 2008
5mg DMSA every 2.5 hours in the day, every 3 hours at night, 3 days on.

That was just about the perfect round. I could just tell something was going on, but was ultra-smooth, no rollercoaster whatsoever with almost zero redistribution at the end. Looks like I have found my optimum dose timings. Hooray!

First day of the round I did have some muscle weakness in lower back but I still managed yoga with no problems. I was feeling pretty tired at the end of the round and almost did not take the final dose. The day after the round ended I'm feeling fine. I am very keen to do more yoga now. All in all: perfect.

I was gonna increase the dose, but maybe I will have a couple more rounds like this. I deserve easy rounds!

Round 18 – 20th June 2008
5mg DMSA every 2.5 hours in the day, every 3 hours at night, 3 days on.

Had some heartburn for the last two weeks (this is written two weeks after this round finished) and I finally found out why: the walnuts I had been eating are rancid. Pretty happy with my detective work in figuring that out. Muscle testing confirmed it. So anyway, round 18 was OK, but had heartburn during and after the round...now I know it was the walnuts.

Yoga's going well too. I'd love to introduce ALA and/or increase the dose, but what I'm doing feels right and I am scared of hurting myself. This is the best I have felt in a LONG time, and the thought of any backwards steps fills me with dread. Work is going well and I am much more focused and 'with it' now.

Round 19 – 3rd July 2008
5mg DMSA every 2.5 hours in the day, every 3 hours at night, 3 days on.

A little bit of heartburn yet again. Seems I am in a heartburn phase at the moment. Chelation certainly brings it on. I have been drinking ACV daily to combat it.

Overall yet again another fine round. Did have a couple of strange moments, a couple of hours where I felt peculiar. But I am still back to being a normal person again and can work fine even in the odd moments. I no longer have to think about my health 24/7. It's nice, I am very focused at work and working is no problem anymore.

I am so proud of myself for sorting out my adrenals and thyroid. The rewards are fantastic, I love having a life again.

I still very much want to increase the dose, but I still feel it on round and have zero wish to hurt myself by going too fast. Yes I am scared, when it goes wrong it really hurts, but low, slow and steady is winning my race. I will leave two weeks in-between rounds to fully recover. I will stick with 3 days on, 11 days off. Round 19 was a fine round, with no trouble.

I am moving away from the all the mercury forums I used to frequent, I am losing patience with stupid people who have all the answers in front of their eyes, yet are incapable of seeing the wood for the trees, who are incapable of doing simple things to help themselves. I am sick of sick people, which is a good sign for me. I am well enough to be leaving that behind me now. Time for me to move on, time to move forwards, time to try and forget the hardship I went through.

Next up: I'm going to take two months' break from chelation to catch up on some herbal cleansing: Two week herbal liver cleanse, then I follow that with a month-long bowel cleanse with psyllium, both Humaworm. After that I did a month-long kidney cleanse with Andreas Moritz's herbs. I definitely need to keep working on the kidneys because last time I had mild lower back pain, shoulder pain, and smelly wee for the whole 30 days. But all in all, no serious trouble and the herbs continue to clean me out nicely. Thank you very much indeed.

Round 20 – 11th September 2008
5mg DMSA every 2.5 hours in the day, every 3 hours at night, 3 days on.

It's been two months since my last round, I've been doing some very worthwhile cleansing.

Overall a good round. Only a few symptoms, all minor. BUT, they are symptoms nevertheless and I am enjoying life without symptoms these days. Hey, I'm just whining. This was a fine round. Fine enough to try increasing the dose next time.

Round 21 – 29th September 2008
6mg DMSA every 2.5 hours in the day, every 3 hours at night, 2 days on.

I'm feeling GREAT all the time now, life is very much back to normal, so time to increase the dose from 5mg DMSA to 6mg DMSA! Oh yes! Exciting! The quicker I get the mercury out, the quicker I can dispense with all this chelation!

Day one felt FANTASTIC in the morning. Really powerfully good, top-of-the-world good. Had a great yoga practice. Felt awesome to be alive 'n' kicking.

At the back on my mind I was thinking:

'Umm, this is not good because when I feel so GREAT, I always feel so BAD pretty soon right after that,' which is exactly how it turned out.

Felt a bit frazzled and foggy later and just wanted to be on my own. I was rollercoaster riding again: not good. I was thinking maybe this round might get a bit rough the longer it progressed because the symptoms usually build as the round goes on, but alarm failed in the night and I missed the 3am dose, so the round ended early. Chelation making me dozy again.

The first day after, I felt rough, a bit foggy and had bad heartburn.

The second day after was much worse as brain fog set in heavy. Not the worst ever by a long way, but enough for me to want to be on my own all day and sit around doing nothing in a zombie state. Also pulled a muscle in my neck doing yoga: balls!

So the result of my increasing the dose was negative: too early to increase the dose.

What I might do is reduce the dose to 4mg and see if I can get away with no symptoms. That would be cool! For 4mg DMSA I must get the capsules made up by a compounding pharmacist, because splitting capsules to that small is tricky and time-consuming.

I was buying 25mg capsules, splitting them open and chopping them up, drug-dealer style with my credit card, into five equal piles, then putting each into its own fresh capsule. It's not difficult, but it is fiddly.

Note to self: I must not forget, whenever I end a round early I always seem to get worse after-effects than a normal three-day round. But, I had rollercoaster symptoms on day one, so dose was too high.

By day three after the round I was 85 percent OK. Had a headache, but lots of water cured it. Something wrong with my digestion because I had 10 BMs today. Lots of parasite gunky stuff coming out. Painful too. I guess an enema or bowel cleansing herbs would be useful next time I have a mercury attack. Ho hum.

Even when I feel great, chelation still hurts when I rush it.

44. "Wax on, wax off. " Mr. Miyagi, 1984

If you look at someone's face you can immediately tell by the quality of their skin if they are healthy or not. Are they radiant and glowing, or do they look like me?

My skin was appalling. Looking in the mirror revealed acne. Acne in my late thirties? I wondered why. My face was oily, waxy with dry flaky patches near the hairline. I had rashes dotted around my body: under my watch strap, between my toes, on both ankles, hips and the side of my torso. They varied in intensity as the months trundled by, but the rash on my chest was permanent. I'm not in the least bit vain, but still, I knew I looked pretty unhealthy and had mangy skin.

On my travels I discovered one of the body's major detoxing routes is through the skin. Your entire body is covered in the stuff, everywhere there are little holes, called pores. I didn't know this, but apparently it's two-way traffic through the pores. You can rub creams on your skin and the cream is absorbed. You excrete waste through them too, and when you sweat, you excrete even more.

If something inside you needs excreting and it can't get out in other ways—for example via the bowels because they are blocked—then it comes out though the skin. Pimples, spots, rashes, eczema are all example of things your body does not like coming out the hard way. The more crud you have in you, the worse the condition of your skin.

If your body can't handle some of the food you eat, this is where it shows itself. Your skin is like a signpost telling you if you are eating food that disagrees.

In order for the skin to work correctly those little holes, the pores, must be free of obstacles; they must not be clogged up. If you look at your skin you will not be able to see if it's blocked or unblocked. These holes are tiddly small. If your diet is poor, or has been poor, if you have less-than-perfect skin and if you are sick, then it probably means your skin could do with a little help. Unclogging the skin will enable your body to dispose of its waste much quicker and easier.

First up is dry skin brushing. You get a special stiff dry-skin brush and brush this all over your skin in round circular wax-on-wax-off motions, from the soles of the feet, working up and working towards the heart. Takes five to ten minutes and is done before the morning shower/bath. This stimulates and helps remove dead skin. It unclogs the pores so they can do their job of excreting.

I have read, although not sure I believe it, that you excrete one pound of waste through your skin each day. That seems high, but even if it's half or quarter true, that's still a lot of exits. Waste leaving the body quickly is just what you need. It is also a very fine way to start the day and I always felt a bit better after brushing.

Dry-skin brushing is a *little* help for your body. Doing it once or twice will not have much effect. That would be just another drop in the ocean because the skin has probably been a bit clogged for a long time and it takes a while to get things moving again. However, daily dry-skin brushing is awesome and you really will feel better in the mornings and over time your body really benefits from the skin working better.

When your body is encouraged to detox via the skin, this kinda gees up other parts of you, body kinda realises it's detox time. Do not underestimate the power of dry-skin brushing; it is especially good during bowel cleansing campaigns.

I dry-skin brushed every day for about 18 months. It is a small part of the reason I got better, but even though it's a small thing, it is nevertheless an important part of my road to recovery. After about two or three months of regular dry skin brushing my skin changed and lost that papery look. It started looking healthier, blemishes disappeared and it became soft and smooth once more. All it cost was five or ten minutes of my time each day.

45. Rub-A-Dub-Dub

Another way to help the skin is to sweat. Sweating removes lots of toxins from the body. A sauna will do the job nicely. As well as being a good overall detox and a fine way to relax, sweating also detoxes mercury and that's top of my to-do list. Unfortunately I didn't have a sauna in my house.

You can buy little portable saunas that fold away. They have a metal frame and are covered in heat-retaining silver material. You sit on a little stool and zip yourself in; just your head sticks out the top. An infra-red heating unit boils you alive.

Ummm, I guess some people like dressing up in space uniforms and whatnot. I'm happy for those people. Good on you! Enjoy yourself while you get better, why don't you? But my wife, my kids... I don't think they'd see the funny side of Dad sitting in a silver tent with his head sticking out the top, sweating his bollocks off.

"Hi kids! I'm a space cadet!"

Somehow I doubted it would help my home life. On top of that, some of the cheaper infrared saunas are not recommended because they heat the body unevenly and give some people problems.

So frequent saunas were out of the question for me. However I did have a bathtub, and with a bath I could have a detox bath any time I liked. No one would think anything odd and it'd be a wonderful way to relax and unwind. Andy Cutler says a sauna is worth one day of mercury chelation, so I guess a detox bath was gonna be similar given how much you sweat in one.

A detox bath is usually when you put Epsom salts in the bath and soak in it for 30 minutes. Epsom salts are magnesium sulphate. Magnesium is the second most abundant element in a human body and is readily absorbed through the skin. It helps regulate over 325 enzymes and plays an important role in organising many bodily functions like muscle control, electrical impulses, energy production and the elimina-

tion of toxins. Many of us are deficient in magnesium, so bathi
the stuff is a fast way to recharge our batteries.

Bathing in Epsom salts induces profuse sweating. The high saline
concentration makes the bath water more dense than the body's fluids.
Consequently, osmotic pressure pulls toxin-laden fluids out the body.
I love a bit of osmosis! It's such a great word that. It means mercury is
pulled out of the body: nice!

It is important to take things slowly at first because these baths
can be strong and overpowering if you sit in them for too long. Sometimes you will feel invigorated and sometimes you will feel drained.
But really, for me it was the thought of detoxing some mercury that
appealed the most. As is my way, I discovered some more powerful
detox baths. You can add other ingredients to enhance and power the
detox!

A deep bath is run and you add a cup or two of Epsom salts, a dash
of 35 percent food-grade hydrogen peroxide and a cup of bicarb of soda.
You run the bath super-duper-double-triple hot, not burn-yourself hot,
just as-hot-as-you-can-handle-it hot. The more Epsom salts you use, the
more you will sweat and the more you will detoxify, just don't overdo it.

You sink in and the heat opens up all those little pores in your skin
and toxins can be expelled and the magnesium from the Epsom salts
is absorbed. Hydrogen peroxide adds extra oxygen which your body
loves. The bicarb of soda helps detoxification too.

At the end of the bath you need to take a 60-second cold shower. It
takes your breath away for sure, but it's an essential part of the process.
The cold shower closes the pores in your skin and stops any further
toxins coming out. If you don't cold shower afterwards, toxins keep on
coming out and you feel like a sack o'crap the next day. And yes I found
that out the hard way!

The cold shower is very important. You warm up within seconds
after anyway as the heat is infused deep inside your body.

As a general rule, detox baths are done just before bedtime, they
are very relaxing and you don't want to be doing anything afterwards
except chillin'.

When I was at my sickest, I stopped sweating altogether. I felt freezing cold all the time and had to wrap up with extra layers of clothes every day. My body did not even sweat in hot weather. This is a grim problem and indicates something is seriously out of kilter. It's something to do with, amongst other things, thyroid function and it's a big thyroid fatigue signal.

The first bath was an experience. I followed the instructions to the letter, but as usual, I overdid it. I added all the ingredients and stayed in there for the allotted 30 minutes. I loved it in there, it was wonderful. I felt myself thawing out, felt the heat going deep inside, defrosting my bones. Really felt some of the tension melt out of my stiff body.

The cold shower was breathtaking, and oh boy did I feel funky great when I got out! Oh yes baby, awesome! Light as a feather. Now I know what Ali meant when he said 'Float like a butterfly, sting like a bee'. I felt like a spaceman. Felt like I was walking on the moon in zero gravity. And ha, I couldn't stop smiling and laughing out loud. This $hit agreed with me big time.

The next day, I did feel a little rough around the edges. I was following advice from a herbalist on Curezone.com. Yes, there is a forum for everything! He reprimanded me furiously:

"Son, I told you to go easy at first. You should not feel like moonwalking afterwards! You should have got out much sooner and used fewer ingredients. You could have hurt yourself."

Hey, you live and you learn. I didn't know that was going to happen. And anyway, I deserve to feel great when I find something that agrees with me so damn well. I knew from that first bath that I was going to do a lot more of these babies. The heat sinking deep inside me just felt so right. Right like the smug satisfaction after a good shag.

Next time I used a third of the normal ingredients and stayed in for only ten minutes; that was enough. I learnt to gauge when to get out by listening to my body. When you get that first fluttery, odd, peculiar feeling of detox; that's the signal to get out. The longer you stay in the bath after feeling that sensation, the more chances of overdoing it. Today I can handle 30 minutes with lots of ingredients and no problems.

I don't keep count of my detox baths, but I have done at leas\
in the last three years. I was using so much Epsom salts I even boug\
25kg sack and used all that, so that's 50 baths minimum. I have almost
finished my second sack.

If Cutler is correct about saunas detoxing mercury, then my 100
plus detox baths mean I have chelated mercury for 100 plus days more
now. As I said, mercury detox is top of my to-do list.

I've got to mention this one. An amazing detox bath is one with
Epsom salts and one pint of apple cider vinegar (ACV). Gotta be unpasteurised ACV too.

Oh yes, it stinks! Sounds like just another crazy idea from the world
of alternative health eh, but wowza! When I first did this bath I could
hardly believe my skin afterwards.

Totally amazing: my skin was as soft as a baby's bum, unbelievably
smooth. I'm a bloke and I don't really give a toss about having skin that
soft. But when it arrives outta the blue like that, it's a fine feeling to get
such silky-smooth skin.

ACV baths are excellent for any skin problems: rashes, pimples or
eczema. Now when I do an ACV bath, my skin no longer feels different than before the bath, and you know why? Because my skin is always
super soft and I can't tell the difference between before and after. Ha!

Full detox bath details can be found from a simple internet search.
Please note the baths do not agree with everyone. Some people have
a problem and struggle with too much heat. Obviously these people
should not sit in a wildly hot bath sweating like a loon! We are all different, after all.

If you just want to keep it simple, just have a bath with one cup of
Epsom salts. If you have the bath so hot you sweat, then make sure you
have the cold shower afterwards. If you miss the cold shower because
you are a pussy, you will feel like you have a hangover the next day. You
have been warned!

Further reading about detox baths: http://www.massagetherapy.com/
articles/index.php/article_id/309/Water-Wealth-

46. Sole bath fantastic

I read a book about what amazing stuff Himalayan rock crystal salt is. It recommended a special detox bath called a Sole bath. It was a bit expensive, but since I seemed to have tried everything, I thought I would try this too. A Sole bath is supposed to have the, and I quote:

"Cleansing effects of a three-day fast. The toxins are released into the bath water through osmosis, while the minerals from the sole are absorbed through the skin. This reduces the acidity in our body and balances the pH factor of our skin. Bioenergetic deficits are rebalanced and weak links become strengthened, reactivating our body's electric current. It's like soaking in a sea of energy as the body's electrical currents are reactivated. The organs' functions start to resonate with the natural frequency patterns of the sole. This activates the natural regulatory mechanism of the body and its self-healing powers…" Funky eh, osmosis! Sounds just like my cuppa tea.

When I first did the Himalayan salt bath I had done dozens of Epsom salt baths and four or five straight sea salt baths. I had just done six Epsom salt detox baths in six days, so I wasn't really expecting anything out if the ordinary when I tried it out.

One kilogram (two pounds) of Himalayan sea salt. In a bath that was as hot as I could handle. For 30 minutes. Mildly expensive at a cost of £10 ($20). (Epsom salt baths cost a tenth of that.)

Phew! How do I describe this experience? Fantastic, exhilarating, glorious, this made me feel absolutely wonderful. That was one of the strongest healing sensations I have ever experienced. Really really strong and I had a great day, I was dancing around the house all evening. I think I overdid the bath really; I should have got out after 15 minutes, or maybe started on less salt. But I do lots of baths. The sea salt baths worked fine and they were 30 minutes long too. But wow and double wow, that Himalayan stuff totally and utterly blew me socks off. That is much much stronger than anything else I've tried. Powerful, now that

is a good descriptive word for them. Yes, powerfu
Blew the cobwebs away, that's for sure.

Whatever that bath did, it was another couple
der.

I don't get that super-powerful healing sensation anymore. I don't
do them very often because it's an expensive habit, but on the odd occasion I do, I just feel good afterwards.

Further reading about salt:
Water & Salt, The Essence of Life by Handel and Ferreira

47. Warm and fuzzy

'Liver flushing' with Epsom salts, olive oil and grapefruit juice took
two weeks to recover from and I decided this was too powerful for me.
I needed to find another way to help my liver. I frequently had light-tan
coloured BMs which is known to mean that not enough bile is being
produced and available for the digestive process. Bile comes from the
liver, via the gallbladder. I had been taking milk thistle and taurine
daily for ten months, but I still felt the need to do more for my liver.

I read about castor oil packs and decided to check them out. As is
my way, I researched them online, and then read a book about them:
The Oil That Heals by William A. McGarey. Was a very weird book
about a chap called Edgar Cayce. A very strange fellow indeed: he was
a psychic. I don't know anything about that kind of thing, but apparently he is quite famous.

Anyway, the book was full of praise about castor oil and all the
many ailments it cured. Oddly enough, the book never actually said
how it did it. It just said, It's wonderful stuff and cures everything but
not sure how it does it, but it *really is amazing stuff.*

Ummm, oh well, I decided to give it a try. All you do is soak some
cloth flannels in castor oil. Apply this to the part of the body that needs
the help. Between the chest and tummy for liver issues, mid to lower

back for kidney troubles. Wrap in plastic (cling film) to stop the oil getting on your clothes and furniture, apply heat in the form of a hot water bottle, sit in front on the TV for an hour and a half wrapped in a towel or two.

Afterwards wash the area with bicarb of soda, as any toxins drawn out can get stuck in the skin. They need removing, otherwise you get a nasty rash, which yes, I learnt the hard way and took months of itching to figure out.

Pretty simple stuff, eh? And pretty unlikely to work, but it works a treat. It's also a very civilised way to detox too. No fasting or anything else is required. You get an all-over-warm-fuzzy-glow too. When you feel a bit fuzzy or woozy, it's time to stop. You are supposed to do three in three days.

When cleaning the liver, after the third pack, it is recommended to drink two or three tablespoons of olive oil. The next day you get a strange BM with a load of bile from the liver. I have even got some gall-stones out once in this way too, which is pretty amazing, satisfying too.

I don't keep count of my castor oil packs, but I suppose I have done at least 50 of them. It is a very nice way to detox, so much more civilised than those nasty liver flushes which are so heavy-duty, but you need to do a lot more of them; collectively, en masse, they work well.

Further reading: *The Oil That Heals* by William A. McGarey

48. Lung Cleanse June 2008: I didn't expect that!

I was doing so well with the Humaworm herbs I decided to try their herbal lung cleanse. I did not have any symptoms that I could associate with my lungs, I was just having such success with the herbs, I wanted to see what this set did for me.

I started smoking at the tender age of 15, smoked 40 a day for three or four years, been in a zillion smoke-filled pubs and clubs, lived in a big polluted city all my adult life and I thought maybe it would be good to do something for my lungs. It's a two-week cleanse, taking two caps in the morning and two in the evening.

Lung cleanse ingredients:
Elecampane is the 'king' for cleaning the lungs. It will remove old phlegm and clean the mucous membranes. Helps with asthma, bronchitis and upper respiratory problems.

Fenugreek softens and removes old hardened phlegm from the lungs. Traditionally used for tuberculosis.

Thyme is a natural expectorant that will help remove phlegm. Used for asthma, bronchitis, croup and whooping cough.

Fennel is a great expectorant. It is used in many modern over-the-counter cough syrups.

Ginger is another expectorant that helps with asthma, bronchitis, and congestion due to colds and flu.

Hyssop helps with congestion due to colds and flu. Good for asthma and will help to remove phlegm.

Marshmallow root soothes irritated mucous membranes.

Barberry helps to reduce bronchial restriction.

Cloves help with asthma and helps to clear mucous.

I must say, it felt like a long two weeks and I was very glad when it was done. I had: mild heartburn, moderate heartburn, medium heartburn, bad heartburn, nasty heartburn and mega-nightmare heartburn, strange BMs, my pee smelt, I smelt, a very mild cough, a very minor sore throat, strange top-of-my-head-lifty-off sensations, and generally feeling mildly under the weather.

Oh yeah, and haemorrhoids (piles). Farmer Giles only comes to town when I have some heavy detoxing going on and that is basically what'd been going on for the past two weeks: loads of toxins coming out.

I had these symptoms one at a time, not all at the same time thankfully, except the heartburn which made life miserable. They say the way to a man's heart is via his stomach: I can confirm that when I had heartburn, when my digestion was screwed, I was one miserable and grumpy sod.

Also did a P&B shake a couple of times and was rewarded with some more mucoid plaque. Happy dayz! I'm sure the herbs loosened things up inside and made releasing this junk easier.

P&B shakes? Psyllium and Bentonite clay drunk a couple of times a day. Just another way to do bowel cleaning. The clay sucks things up, the psyllium moves things on through.

A week after I had finished the herbs, I took a moment to see what was different about me now that all those annoying symptoms had stopped. Physically I felt a little stronger but I was surprised to realise the overriding sensation was that I was mentally sharper. Woah! How cool is that!

My head was clearer and I was thinking straighter. I didn't expect that. I was over-the-moon happy about it too. Not bad for two weeks' worth of herbs that cost $19.95. Personally I would pay thousands and thousands to get mentally sharper. These herbs rock 'n' roll big-time-Charlie.

How could two weeks of lung herbs affect my brain? I believe it's something to do with more oxygen getting through the lungs, and hence more oxygen getting into my brain. Amazing, eh!

Looking back this was when I started feeling mostly normal again. Everything in life became a lot easier as my brain started working again. I was more with-it at work. Ditto at home. It was like waking up after a long Alice-in-Wonderland dream. Oh, I do have a job to do. Oh, these are my colleagues. Oh, this is my family. Hello wife, sorry I was away. I was in la-la land. It's *great* to be back. Goodbye zombie state. Hello world.

It's a very fine set of herbs, fit for a king. The mental sharpness gained was permanent too.

Happy dayz!

49. No Dumping Please

Some people have what is called a Dumping Phase five to twelve months after amalgam removal. The body suddenly realises that there is no more mercury pouring out of the amalgams and that finally, phew, it can get rid of some of its stored mercury. The body then starts dumping its toxic load and symptoms flare up like crazy and life gets painful and complicated all over again.

Some people don't get this dumping phase. I didn't get it. Why? Why didn't I get what so many other people do get? I was just as poisoned as everyone else, maybe not as bad as some, but still my life was in pieces. So why do I think I didn't get the dreaded slump?

Well, I did a lot of detoxing, in every-which-way that I could, so that helped me greatly. But I think the main reason was because I chelated from the start. I educated myself, I believed I was mercury poisoned and in the face of many scare stories I chelated from the beginning. I started chelation ten days after amalgam removal.

I would guess—and I am totally guessing here so don't read anything into the numbers—I would guess that 55 percent was because I chelated, 40 percent was because of all the cleansing and 5 percent luck. But I believe we make our own luck, so I will add that onto my 55 percent chelation score to make 60 percent. Which means, I think, I guess, that the reason I avoided the dreaded dumping phase was because I chelated from the start.

This is a powerful incentive for people to chelate from the beginning. The dumping phasing is a nightmare-like time and I thank my lucky stars I avoided it.

50. Who's the Daddy!

It was just under a year since I had my final amalgams removed and started chelation. My health was now considerably better than it had been. The reactions to the herbs had relaxed right down; gone were the wild rides I endured when I first tried them. Chelation with DMSA was not so bad and I had found a dose that I could safely chelate with. My thyroid and adrenals were working OK. I had energy, life was almost back to normal and I was happy again. So now I felt strong enough to face the next stage in my detoxification. Now it was time to try something that was almost guaranteed to be hard, difficult and tricky. But I was going into this with my eyes wide open because I really needed to get the mercury out of my head.

Alpha Lipoic Acid (ALA) is the chelator of choice. This is the stuff that lifts the mercury off the brain. Chelation with ALA is unavoidable if I want to get long term better and live to be 100 years old. The other chelators cannot reach inside my head, and I can't get better if I have mercury on my brain. So I must use it, must find the right dose, and chelate lots and lots with it.

I have not found a safer way to detox mercury yet. Note the word 'safe'. There are many suggested ways to detox mercury and in my opinion the Cutler protocol is the only safe one. I have had meetings with posh mercury specialist doctors in Harley Street to discuss this. They charged me a small fortune just to talk to them. They specifically chelate mercury using large, infrequent doses of chelators, and they categorically assured me that what they were doing was totally safe.

Luckily for me, I checked things out in advance and didn't just blindly follow orders. I have met loads of people on the mercury forums who found out the hard way just how wrong the doctors are. Loads of people get seriously hurt with this large, infrequent dosing style of chelation. When I say hurt, I'm talking years-to-get-back-to-square-one hurt.

I chose to listen to these people who got hurt. I wasn't willing to trust doctors' promises anymore. The mercury forums were awash with their victims. Every week someone new popped up crying for help after incorrect chelation. Slow and steady would win the race and Cutler's protocol made sense to me. Mercury was much too dangerous to take chances on. I'd taken advice and I'd been burnt too many times to trust anyone now.

Who would you trust? A doctor who said his protocol worked great, or someone who used that doctor's protocol and got hurt so bad that their life was ruined?

Go on, ask yourself: Who would you trust? Ask yourself the question seriously. Would you follow a protocol if someone said they got really hurt by it? Or would you trust the doctor who said it was completely fine?

It's a difficult question. A lot of people will close their ears to the people who got hurt, shut them out, just take the easy option and go with the flow, just go with the doctor because they don't have to think. Trusting doctors is what people instinctively do. It is what I did for most of my life. I guess the vast majority don't even know to question them. That's a sad state of affairs in our world today. Make sure you have a good, long hard think about what your doctors tell you to do. And when you ask for a second opinion, don't ask another doctor!

I must say, Andy Cutler has not let me down yet. He gave me options so I could make choices all by myself. His words educated me, so my choices were educated choices. I didn't have to blindly trust anyone. He enabled me to make up my own mind. That is a very powerful position for me to be in. I am empowered. I am strong. I understand. I have the power to control my own destiny now.

Even though I champion Andy Cutler and his mercury chelation, I did a lot more than just his chelation protocol to get better. But the point is, he enabled me to understand mercury poisoning. He explained what had happened to me. He explained how my whole body, every organ, every corner, was poisoned, poisoned with mercury. And with that understanding, I was able to take multiple actions that got me better.

Andy is a biochemist. I have gone more of a herbal route in my path to recovery. He got better, and so did I. There are many different ways to get better, but they all involve educating oneself to be in a position to make educated choices.

The people who get better are the people who understand, who are able to take many different actions. We have to because we have so many things wrong with us.

Andy's book is a dazzling piece of work. To have figured out mercury poisoning, when he was mercury poisoned himself, is a seriously impressive thing to have done. And to have written a book that a non-medical person like me could understand. Man, only a few people in life have that gift. We are lucky someone figured it all out.

There is only one 100 percent cast-iron solid proof of mercury toxicity, and that's if you react to chelating agents. If you get a reaction from a chelator that 100 percent means you have mercury in you.

I get reactions, side-effects and after-effects when I take chelators and that confirms I have mercury in me. If I wish to remain fit and well for the rest of my life, then I need to get this mercury out. I don't want to go back to the bad old days ever again. So I must get the mercury out of my body and my brain too. For my brain to be chelated, ALA is required. ALA (Alpha Lipoic Acid) is the only chelator that crosses the blood-brain-barrier (BBB). ALA is the Daddy of chelators.

It was proving impossible to increase the dose of DMSA, and/or increase the length of the round. My dosage was so low, I would not combine ALA and DMSA like many people did. I couldn't keep putting it off. It was time for me to try ALA chelation.

Round 22 – 10th October 2008
4mg ALA every 2.5 hours in the day, every 3 hours at night.

First trial of ALA here we come!
Ohhhhh bugger, what an anti-climax! My alarm failed after 24 hours and I missed a dose. Village! No messing with the protocol,

so I stopped the round. I know from bitter experience not to continue the round after missing a dose.

When I was on-round, I felt odd, felt like my body was getting used to a new way of detoxing. I had two wild and nasty nightmares on the two nights I was taking ALA. After the round ended I had a massive headache for a day. I had a detox bath and drank an extra two litres of water and that seemed to do the trick. Yeast flared up a little, no heartburn, but pretty itchy and shoulders hurt a bit. It may have been the garlic I ate? But 50/50 it could have been the garlic or ALA, not sure.

No need for the Mercury Attack checklist, but I was in take-care-of-myself-mode. I always feel worse when a round ends too early. But, all in all, not so bad, I will definitely try that again.

Round 23 – 15th October 2008
4mg ALA every 2.5 hours in the day, every 3 hours at night.

Managed the full three days on ALA only! Hooray!

Did the whole round whilst at work with no trouble whatsoever! Hooray!

The smoothest and easiest of all my 23 chelation rounds so far! Hoo-bloody-ray!

Again, at the beginning, it did feel like my body was getting used to this new way of detoxing, but overall a major success. I did have a super-furry white tongue, so I took extra ACV, in-between-herbs, kefir and garlic and I had no troubles whatsoever. Garlic tasted so sweet!

First day after the round was fine, but the second day I was tired all day, could not do yoga and I was very irritable in the afternoon. Definitely the mercury doing that to me. I did a detox bath in the day, but I think they are best in the evening prior to bed, because I was whacked out afterwards.

Overall this was better than a DMSA round and I will stick with ALA rounds from now on.

Ha, all that worry about ALA and I find the rounds easier than DMSA! I felt like I could have chelated for more than the three days too, but will do another couple of three-day ALA-only rounds first. If I continue to get the end-round irritation, then extended round length will be a priority, especially since I chelated during the week at work with no problem.

I discovered a special vibrating watch for blind people, totally awesome for chelation. Vibralite8. It's big, it's ugly, but so big and so ugly its retro-chic! Oh yes baby! It vibrates on your wrist so no one but me knows it's gone off, which is ideal for work. No snooze on it, so pill must be taken then and there.

Also got a new alarm clock for the night, with multiple alarms, settings, and brightness: very good and will not let me down like the others, touch wood. I now have three alarms on my bedside table. One main alarm with multiple alarms, and two standard backups. Both backups are set ten seconds slower than the main alarm, so they go off just after the main alarm. A tad fiddly, but once set up, just what I need: backup alarms. I also put in the backup batteries in case of a power failure. All the settings are saved if there is a power outage. Should have done this rounds ago.

Clock with multiple alarms: *Neverlate Executive* by American Innovative

Vibrating wrist watch: Vibralite8

Round 24 – 20th October 2008
4mg ALA every 2.5 hours in the day, every 3 hours at night.

Oh man, missed another dose, this time after one and a half days. I'm not used to the new vibrating watch. Village! I was in the office and I forgot a dose because I was talking to the boss when the alarm went off and forgot to take the cap afterwards.

Ummmmm, not impressed with myself.

Had zero problems when on the round, but had a real bad headache the second day after the round ended early. I was alright the third day after. I must admit, I also had a hangover on the second day and this combo of booze and chelation was not ideal. I must be getting better if I chance mixing those two beasts!

I am still well keen to do the next round, just not keen to end early because I messed up. I keep screwing up rounds, ending early. This is not good and I will end up hurting myself. I must be more focused and much more consistent. In the office I must accept that people will occasionally see me talking the odd pill, I must just live with it. If they ask, I will just say I'm doing a detox and need to take pills regularly. It's no big deal and it's massively more important that I do full rounds, rather than being a little embarrassed about taking a pill. Messing up rounds frequently will drive mercury into my brain: STOP FUCKING UP!

Round 25 – 29th October 2008
4mg ALA every 2.5 hours in the day, every 3 hours at night.

Oh man, left the house in the morning and forgot my pills at home. Grrr! I must focus, focus, focus! Chelation is obviously making me dozy. I had to rush back on the train. I ran up the hill to my house and took the dose 55 minutes late.

The protocol rule is you can take a pill late, but no later than one hour late. If over 30 minutes late, then the next dose is to be taken at whatever is your usual interval, in my case, 2.5 hours later, after the last dose.

I did get a super-nasty headache that came on within the 55 minutes. It went away after drinking tons of water. A hearty lunch also helped. Round was slightly more eventful than usual, little bit of heartburn, which again, lots of water cured.

All in all I like the ALA better than DMSA. I know ALA is the chelator of choice, so I will stick with ALA for now. I will stick on this dose 4mg too.

I would have tried to extend the round, but after taking the dose 55 minutes late I decided best not to chance it. Three day round was good, next time I will go for four days!

ALA rounds are harder on my body. I feel my adrenals and thyroid being stressed, I feel a little colder than usual and my yoga workouts are in deep trouble. Yoga has stopped for now, lost the urge, don't seem to have enough energy, nor the will. I need to break for two weeks in-between chelation rounds. If I can get my rounds longer that would be better, I might try longer next time.

That was four rounds in one month. Now I will do some cleanses. Humaworm here we come!

Note: I had a detox bath on the evening of the last dose and had almost no redistribution side effects after the round! Cool! Do the baths minimise redistribution side effects? Make a note on each occasion!

Humaworm #4 – 2nd November 2008

All wild excitement is finished for my parasite cleanses. This fourth was mostly uneventful. Just a little rough around the edges; a cough and a few headaches, but small fry compared to the volcano of reactions in the past.

No need to do these herbs so often anymore. Once every six months for maintenance?

Round 26 – 20th December 2008
4mg ALA every 2.5 hours in the day, every 3 hours at night.
Third day 4mg DSMA only.

I did two days of ALA only at 4mg, followed by one day of DMSA only at 4mg. Day two of ALA had a nasty headache, but once I switched to DMSA the headache disappeared. As at end of day three everything is going fine. All in all, smooth as clockwork apart from the bloody headache. I had zero digestive problems on this round.

On round I had a bit more get up and go. I did more things. I felt like doing stuff. Nothing grand, but I had more life in me. I went to the cinema, spent quality time playing with the kids, had lunch out at the local Italian, and repaired the broken door handle to the playroom.

No colours coming back. Feeling tired all the time when off round. No yoga possible anymore. Not good.

Detox bath at end of round and had limited redistribution symptoms after the round. But but but, no energy and no yoga. I am finding ALA chelation hard work on my hormones. I will have to think about this.

What does it mean and what shall I do about it?

51. Trouble at t'mill after introducing ALA

After introducing ALA I started getting tired again, started losing some of the vitality I'd reclaimed. Even when you take mercury out small bits at a time using the Cutler protocol, it is still seriously poisonous. I could not work out anymore after starting ALA and generally things became hard work again.

I had very strange heart palpitations which were new to me. I'd had them occasionally before, but never like this: all the time, day after day, pounding away. It was quite worrying too, having a racing heart all the time. I could feel my heart thumping big thuds 24/7.

So I got my books out, read up and researched it. Turns out one of the things the kidneys control is the blood pressure. I had a stock of kidney herbs at home, so I decided to see what would happen if I took some. Within five days the racing heart problem was gone. Pretty happy about that. I wish everything was that easy!

But I still had other things to attend to. I was getting jittery again, I felt faint and lightheaded some of the time too. It was getting worse and difficult in the office.

After a while I figured it was more intense before eating, and after eating I was fine. Was definitely something to do with food. Maybe this was what the hair test had hinted at? Maybe this was the blood sugar/glucose problems it said I should investigate? Maybe this is what my dumb doctor had told me about, 'but nothing you can do about it anyway'? Maybe this was the sugar problem?

The only food allergies I had left were sugar in all its forms, refined and un-refined, so this was worth investigating. I was puzzled why all fruit gave me nasty reactions: heartburn and bloating, as well as the tingles. I was pretty confused because I could not eat carrots or beetroot anymore. Odd, eh! Looking back now, I realise it was a sugar issue; carrots and beets are both full of sugar, but was baffling at the time and none of my toxic mates understood why carrots and beets should be so totally off my menu.

Eventually I figured out that eating small frequent meals every three hours sorted out the jittery hassle. I then discovered these were hypoglycaemia symptoms and that yes, I did have hypoglycaemia too. It's common in people with adrenal fatigue.

Once this light bulb had flickered on in my head, I read a few books about hypoglycaemia, and I re-read my adrenal books, and re-read Cutler's book *Amalgam Illness*.

Cutler recommended 1000mg Chromium Picolinate in total each day, in divided doses at meal times. Within a month the jittery symptoms disappeared along with the strange eating requirements. I no longer needed lots of small regular meals either. Not totally sure if the chromium was the reason it went away, because I did a lot of different things and it could have been one of the herbs, but pretty sure it was the chromium. The books are pretty clear: chromium is great for blood sugar problems.

ALA chelation had made my hypoglycaemia much worse and it was important to figure this out and then take actions that helped. Must say it's pretty tricky figuring all this stuff out. I never see doctors anymore and I have to figure it all out myself from my symptoms. It takes time, but I am happier this way. I have lost faith with the medical profession. There is no point seeing people I don't trust. They will be right sometimes, but I have got to the stage of automatically disregarding all their advice simply because it was from them. For me, it is best to just steer clear of all doctors. They seemed to just muddy the waters, sending me off in wrong directions. So, it's just, me, my PC, my books and my online toxic mates.

Anyway, always makes me feel like a champion when I figure something out and I take a few more steps up my ladder to better health. Very satisfying indeed considering my doctor said there was nothing I could do about my little sugar problem.

52. Armour

Heart palpitations sorted. Jittery sorted. But I was still tired and still could not do my beloved yoga anymore. I was finding out ALA chelation was hard on my body.

I was tracking my temps daily still and although my temps were stable, which meant my adrenals were still OK, the temps were now lower than before ALA chelation. So I figured the thyroid support I was taking was not strong enough now that I was hitting the hard stuff, the ALA.

It's fairly common in mercury toxic people to have thyroid problems. I would say that some adrenal and/or thyroid support is essential to almost everyone when chelating. Certainly everyone needs to at least investigate it. Diagnosis is easy with the temp graph. It's a pity it is so difficult to understand and figure out the treatment. It's a pity most doctors don't understand this stuff. It's a pity when they think they know what they are doing, and it's a pity when they prescribe synthetic man-made drugs because that is one sure-fire way to not get better.

I find it strange that I understand my metabolic problems but my doctors do not. Sure I had to study hard, read loads of books and research lots on the internet, but surely that's what doctors did at med school? For all those years? I didn't discover anything new. I read six or seven books about it. All this stuff is known about. I just educated myself from other people's research/findings. Anyway…

I was taking ten pills per day of the thyroid glandular supplements I was on, and decided taking even more was probably pointless. Time to move on and move up to something more powerful. And no, I was not going to do anything synthetic yet, man-made chemicals were at the very bottom of the list.

Now I would try 'Armour' which is crushed up and dried pig thyroid glands. Yummy! It is natural, comes from nature and has history of over 100 years of working perfectly well, thank you very much. The pig thyroid is very close to a human thyroid and has all the hormones in the right balance for us. It is stronger than the other cow thyroid glandular I was taking.

Armour just about passes my non-synthetic rule. The thyroid part is natural, but the company that makes it adds magic bits and bobs to make it 'theirs'. I don't need, nor want the extra bits and bobs; I just want those lovely crushed up piggy thyroid glands.

I have yet to find just the thyroid glands alone in a supplement. I assume someone somewhere sells it? I guess I will come across it eventually? Maybe?

Armour is not prescription so I don't need to see a doctor to get it, I just ordered it direct from the company in America.

So, here we go again; thyroid supplementation. Would it take me months and months again to build up the dose just like with the other stuff? Or would I just be able to ramp up the dose nice 'n' high and get better in double quick time?

HHuummmmmmpppppfffff! Took me bloody ages! It took a year! Man oh man, patience was most certainly required! Well, when you understand what's going on and why, it makes it do-able. My health was climbing on a weekly basis anyway during that year due to the increasing Armour dose. I was not bedridden like many other people are when they finally figure out their thyroid is trashed. So I could handle it, but it would have been much better if I could have taken nice high doses and just got super-better in double-quick time.

I did try to increase the dose quickly, but each time I pushed it I got a load of strange symptoms. Mostly tingly sensations all over my body which was fairly unpleasant, annoying and certainly not much help to me trying to work in a busy office. Pushing it was not an option, so I had to go slow again. Anyway, I was mostly better, like I was in fourth gear and could not get into the top fifth gear.

I started at a quarter of a grain (which is how this stuff is measured: grains) and increased the dose as quickly as I could, which in the early days was a quarter grain every two or three weeks. When I got to two grains per day I had to raise it much slower, a quarter grain every four to six weeks. Yes, that's minimum of four months to increase by one grain.

Oh yes, this is a long-term project.

I had to go slowly because my body could not handle the extra hormones any quicker. Seems I had this problem a long time, seems my body would take a long time to adjust back to normal. Another signal that my health problems go back, way way back.

So that's what I did. As the months trundled by I just gradually increased the dose and I slowly got better. There are no short cuts in this game. If I wanted to get better, this was the way. I did my research. I understood what was wrong. I understood what was required. I had a plan of action. I stuck to that plan of action. Fingers and toes all crossed.

Here's what the year of increasing my Armour dosage looked like.

Round 27 – 30th December 2008
4mg ALA every 2.5 hours in the day, every 3 hours at night.
Fourth day 4mg DSMA only.

It's a new year and I have set myself a target of chelating more than I do the herbal cleanses. I am mostly better now and it's chelation that will cure me long term. Twice a month is the goal to try and chelate. Time to try lengthening the round too. Four day rounds here we come!

A good round, smooth. I did however get a rash all around my middle, waist, lower back, lower stomach and top of legs. Odd, eh! Itchy too! On the morning of the third and fourth day of chelation I had the $hits. Oh the joys of chelation. Lovely!

No colours coming back.

Again, whilst on round I did things that I normally would not have done. I sanded the front door and varnished it! This is unusual in the extreme! I love ALA if it makes me do things and enjoy life more.

I just realised my back does not hurt anymore! Touch wood! Not at all. Not even a little bit. No, totally free and easy! Wow! I have had 11 years of real nightmare-like bad back troubles; really, the mother of all bad backs. But now: no twinges, no aches, no pains, no nothing. This is awesome! I feel loose, supple and ooh so fine! Happy dayz!

Ten days ago I had a week off work and decided to give a Christmas present to my body. I went back to the lady with the pearl necklace and I did three colonics in three days. I wonder if that's part of the reason my back is pain free? I think it was *a* factor, important even, but my pain-free back is the culmination of everything I have done, not just one action. It has been getting gradually better as the months flowed by.

I love it when a plan comes together. It was odd realising I had no back pain. Was like forgetting to put your watch on in the morning and keep looking at your empty wrist throughout the day. It's like, come on, everything's fine now, you don't have to keep checking.

I never ever thought I would have a normal back again. My back hurt so much, for so long. I was almost a cripple at one point, hobbling around like an old man. To have a normal back again was like winning the lottery. Ahhh, all the things I can do now I'm better! Like more cleansing.

On one and three quarter grains of Armour—feels like we are moving in the right direction, temps are rising, but still a way to go yet.

Humaworm kidney cleanse #6 – 7th March 2009

In the past few months, I've done a second lung cleanse. I felt mildly better after that—but don't think I need to do these herbs again. I followed that with a kidney cleanse that was fairly eventful, plenty of symptoms and for sure it will need repeating. Then a bowel cleanse where I got the itchies and lots of black bits and bobs coming out most of the 30 days, so that will need doing again too.

Next up, a repeat of the kidney herbs. This needed doing again because the previous set of kidney herbs gave me hassles. Again I felt under the weather for the whole two weeks and by day 12 had a stinking cold. This could be a healing crisis? Or it could be because I've been drinking booze? Or something else entirely? I had flu-like symptoms that lasted a hard three days and then disappeared very quickly. I'd say a 75 percent chance of being a healing crisis. Anyway, it passed and I felt better than before, so all is well.

My energy levels are still not enough for workouts or yoga yet, but I am gradually growing in strength. The months pass quickly and I do feel as if I am making steady progress up that ladder.

It takes a long time to clean these organs out. This was my sixth kidney cleanse and they still need repeating due to the side-effects. Hummpf!

Round 31 – 23rd April 2009
4mg ALA every 2.5 hours in the day, every 3 hours at night.
Last 4 doses 4mg DSMA only.

Rounds 28, 29 and 30 passed without incident, but in the last seven weeks I have noticed green has come back fairly significantly, which is super cool! It's spring time and I can see all the different types of green in the trees as the new leaves grow. This is a first.

When I say a first, I mean it's the first time in my life that I have been able to appreciate green as a colour. Green was always just a dirty, muddy, cloudy colour mixed in with brown and red; a nothing colour for me. So, to see green for the first time was an amazing sight. Made me feel like a kid again. Wonderful.

Anyway, this round has started with me in a great mood and a taste of metal in my mouth. Spent the weekend in Scotland and I even had a drink or two. I was fine. Nothing serious, just a couple of beers, but it's nice to have a drink now and then.

Let's keep at this dose for now. That means I can chelate regularly with no problems and lead a normal life. As a general note I feel almost completely normal these days. I can't handle yoga yet, but I just skied every day for a week, and if I can ski, I can yoga! Oh yes baby!

Doing the yoga breathing exercises pranayama every morning at the moment instead of yoga. This will make yoga better when I can restart.

Yes, you read that correctly. I did go skiing. If you remember this was where my story all started: at the top of a mountain with my back giving out. I had been on a family ski holiday the previous year in 2008 too, but for me that was a hiking holiday. Everyone else skied except me because my back was so weak and feeble.

But this year, the winter of 2009, I skied. I skied every day for a week. Happy dayz, eh! I didn't plan on skiing, but when I got there, I was feeling oh so fine, I thought I would give it a bash. And all was well. Only a couple of hours a day, but nevertheless I skied every day. I had a fantastic time. It was as if I had never been ill. Happy happy dayz indeed!

I can't say it's like a dream come true, because in all my wildest dreams, I never in a million years thought I would ever ski again. I had the mother of all bad backs. I was told I was unlucky and that I would be in pain for the rest of my life. And yet I skied every day for a week. Ha!

And, I also found a fine way to describe the colours returning to me. Picture ski goggles. They also make sports sunglasses like this, but let's stick with the ski goggles because that's how this came about. Some lenses in expensive ski goggles enhance, or make certain colours brighter, so you can see where you are going more clearly in the snow. If you've never worn any, just forget this description, but if you have, the colours returning to me is exactly like putting on that type of ski goggles: enhanced vision!

I'm up to 3 grains of Armour. It's a slow process increasing the dose, but I know it's worth it because my temps are rising towards normal, and most importantly I am feeling better. I continue to climb up my ladder.

Round 33 – 9th May 2009
4mg ALA every 2.5 hours in the day, every 3 hours at night.
Last 4 doses 4mg DSMA only.

Uh-oh, dodgy round. Day one, had muscle weakness in my back and felt pretty ropey all afternoon. Day two was OK, but day three (at the office) was shoddy; tingly all over and a little obsessive. Totally needed to avoid everyone, hide away and be on my own. After-round redistribution side effects were feeling cold and more muscle weakness in my lower back, worst on the second day after the round.

Overall an unpleasant round, but nowhere near what my bad rounds used to be like at the beginning of chelation. On the plus side, I got more colours coming back; green, blue and yellow look amazing!!

After three swift rounds in quick succession, it's time for some more herbs. Humaworm is next.

Round 35 – 25th July 2009
4mg ALA every 2.5 hours in the day, every 3 hours at night.
Last 5 doses 4mg DSMA only.

This round comes after a Humaworm parasite cleanse followed by another kidney cleanse. I'm still getting reactions, so I will continue interspersing them between the rounds.

Did this round whilst on holiday to France and felt totally normal the whole time. I recently got up to four grains of Armour to support my thyroid and wow, I feel great these days—four grains of that stuff rocks! I feel strong and powerful. I have restarted my workouts too. Nice!

For the first time in 11 rounds I did not have a detox bath at the end of the round. First and second day after round, I felt horrid, really ropey. Heartburn, muscle weakness and my shoulders really ached. BMs went light tan colour too. This confirms my discovery. Now I know those detox baths rock 'n' roll. Now I know they limit my after-round redistribution side effects.

Sweating is known to help excrete mercury and I guess these baths—which I do right after the round ends—help mop up the stray mercury that hangs about after the round ends. My body also loves the large dose of easily absorbed magnesium that they give. The baths are part of my routine now and I need to make sure it happens at the end of every round.

Going to stick at this dose of 4mg ALA only, with the last four, five or six doses DMSA. I have bought a load more compounded ALA 4mg, so that should keep me from trying to rush chelation. Cutler says find a dose, stick at it and chelate lots and lots. I will follow that sound advice. No need to rush because 100 percent life is back to normal. Happy dayz are here again.

Compounded chelators from : www.livingnetwork.co.za/ products/

The guy that runs this show, Dean, he is mercury toxic, chelates using the Cutler protocol, and has an amazing mercury helpful website: http://livingnetwork.co.za

53. Armour II

Seven months after starting Armour, in May 2009, my dose was high enough and BOOM! Glorious good health hit me smack-bam in the face. My remaining symptoms of ill-health fell away and I could call myself back to normal at long last. Happy dayz! Yoga restarted, fatigue disappeared, energy returned and I had a huge smile on my face every single happy day.

My health crashed at the beginning of 2007. In early 2008 Humaworm started off my healing, and now in May 2009, I was mostly better. All major symptoms and problems vanished. I was back in the land of the living and happy. My wife reclaimed her husband. My kids reclaimed their dad. My office reclaimed their broker.

That was a long, hard slog. Not many people recover from the lows I hit. Plenty do, but many more people just stumble through life in pain and misery. Once I was better, I thought hard about jacking in the job and living a bit. Maybe travel the world? But, I liked my job and I was good at it once again. People started depending on me again. The money was good and I figured I owed someone something for not sacking me when I was so sick, so I stayed.

Now I was better, I appreciated life so much more. Normal day-to-day things became fun. My commute to the office, once a painful misery, was now me-time where I could catch up with the world by reading the newspaper. Simple stuff was a joy. Running for the train became an option. Sure, there is much more to life than running for a train, but after almost losing everything, running to catch a train was a pretty cool thing to be able to do, if I chose.

I bought bicycles for the whole family. My youngest in a little seat just behind me. I had lost and reclaimed all these things that people take for granted. Happy all my hard work paid off.

• • •

During the saga of addressing my thyroids and adrenal glands, I declined the use of synthetic man-made hormones that the drug companies have separated, formulated, masticated and marketed. Very often they are individual hormones that you must somehow mix-and-match to levels that change as the body's requirements change. The idea that man-made chemicals are better, or are even the same, as natural in-nature alternatives is wildly deluded. The only reason synthetic is available is because people/companies can make money out of selling them. There is no other reason.

Every time you see me use a $ instead of an S when I write bull$hit, that's to remind me, and now you, that our world revolves around money. It is bull$hit that the pharmaceutical companies make multiple billions every year by selling drugs that don't work and that people must take for life. Bull$hit.

Natural hormones from nature are better every single time, without exception, and without a shadow of doubt. Why would I want to take individual synthetic hormones when I can take whole animal hormones in one pill that directly replace everything that I lack? Replace them all in the right balance for humans. That strengthen and rebuild my body's glands. And, on top of all that, have no nasty side effects.

The animal thyroid glands are the same as ours and importantly they have a 100-year-old history of working perfectly well. You don't need to muck about adjusting the dose to two to five different branded synthetic hormones. You take Armour and adjust that dose to a level that suits you, and it provides all the hormones your body needs at the correct levels.

The downside is it takes time to get right. The upside is you get no side effects, you get better and it's almost guaranteed to work, eventually. Contrary to what your doctors will tell you, contrary to what those companies that sell it will tell you: synthetic hormones don't work. And what gives little-old-me the authority, the power, the balls to say such blasphemy?

Look around you, open your eyes, see all those people on synthetic rubbish that remain ill and continue to struggle and trudge through life. Look at the people dedicated to promoting the natural stuff, read the books, talk to people that are on natural stuff and hear it first-hand just how much better they are now, now they've switched to the natural substances.

The last thing in the world I want is for people to just blindly follow me, or anyone else. If your thyroid is trashed, read a few books, hang out with some people in the same boat. You can rebuild your life if you want, it's just a matter of education. Everything you need is available over-the-counter (OTC). You do not need a doctor's prescription to buy these things.

Understanding adrenals and thyroids is difficult and tricky even when you do it correctly. There are plenty of man traps along the way. Other things happened afterwards that I was not prepared for, but in May 2009, when my Armour dose hit four grains life went completely back to normal, for a month or so anyway, then things started to get funky again…

Further reading:
Your Thyroid and How to Keep it Healthy by Barry Durrant-Peatfield.
Adrenal Fatigue: The 21ˢᵗ Century Stress Syndrome by James Wilson
www.drrind.com

Round 36 – 9th August 2009

4mg ALA every 2.5 hours in the day, every 3 hours at night.
Last 6 doses 4mg DSMA only.

I had very hot feet for most of this round. No idea what that means. Overall a 'tired' round. The tattoo on my arm did form a scab on a small part at the tip of the lower black part, which has never happened before.

In-between rounds I continue to be back to my good ol' self again.

Round 37 – 17th August 2009

4mg ALA every 2.5 hours in the day, every 3 hours at night.
Last 4 doses 4mg DSMA only.

Chelation is suddenly hard on me. I seem to be feeling the side-effects well after the round has finished. I feel a general air of tiredness most of the time now. Yoga has stopped again. I need to have more than six days in-between rounds. If feel the need to break after this round.

Muscle tester dude emigrated to Australia, that's not very helpful! But before he left he said my liver was stressed, so will do Humaworm liver cleanse next to see if that helps.

Taking my temps in the day average 36.7-36.8 C (98.1-98.2 F) which is excellent. I moved up my Armour dose and I'm now on 4 ¼ grains.

HW Liver Herbs – 22nd August 2009

I'm tired and I need a break from chelation, so time for some liver herbs. I know it's not a break from detoxing, but it is not in my nature to sit around twiddling my thumbs. I feel the need to do something for my health all the time. All the light-colour tan BMs when I chelate indicate my liver gets stressed and this needs doing. These sign posts are important to read and together with the muscle tester's advice, I feel the time is right for this two-week cleanse.

First day of the herbs started with a splitting headache, together with a flutter of heartburn. The headache went after a day, but the minor stomach hassle dragged on for ten days before fading away to nothing. ACV and plenty of water control these side effects nicely and the last five days were easy. I assume that the easy last days means the herbs have worked: no side effects = no problems inside. Cool!

Bowel movements have gone nice n' dark too. Not quite dark enough, but darker than before. Dark BMs mean my liver is producing enough bile and that enough is passing though my unclogged gallbladder, into my digestive tract, which in turn enables me to digest and absorb all the lovely grub I eat. Dark BMs is a wonderful signal that these herbs rock 'n' roll big-time-Charlie. Another signal of success is that I have bags of energy and yoga has restarted. Nice! I love these herbs.

I know chelation is hard work on my liver, so I must remember to do these herbs more often.

Round 38 – 10th September 2009
4mg ALA every 2.5 hours in the day, every 3 hours at night.
Last 6 doses 4mg DSMA only.

Second day after the round was a little bumpy. Felt tired and grumpy, neck hurt, leg hurt, foot hurt, sore throat and generally felt like I got out the bed the wrong side. I desperately needed to yell at someone.

On the plus side, I was rewarded with a little colour and things are sharper and more in focus. Makes me grin like a mad man, yellow and blue back this time, but still, this is frustrating, I was enjoying life symptom-free.

Thinking about things overall, I guess I'm in the chelation zone where nothing much good happens. Just plodding along with no real change. As a guess, I will have to chelate 300 rounds before I finish. What a horrid thought. I wish I could rush chelation.

Humaworm Antibiotic – 15th September 2009
"It's good to have fun - but you have to know how!"
The Cat in the Hat

I caught a bad cold and terrible sore throat after the last round. Felt like I swallowed barbed wire. Must be strep throat. This used to be regular for me, and it's not fun getting it back. Chelation is hard bloody work. Cold is not going away quickly either. Two weeks and it's still lingering and dragging. Something's wrong, not sure what.

Strep throat is usually treated with antibiotics. I don't use that stuff anymore, so I did a Humaworm antibiotic herbal version instead. Never done this set of herbs before. Usually the first time I try a new set of herbs I have a bumpy ride! Let's see what these do.

First three days were a nightmare of mega bad headaches, real pounders. Not had headaches like that since I was a kid. Buckets of water and feverfew did little. I just had to chill and stay low. I stuck with the herbs in the knowledge that it would pass, and pass it did, as it always does. Side effects and symptoms reduced to nothing by the end of the 14-day cleanse. That's a good sign, means the herbs cleaned me out of whatever should not be visiting.

Overall this new set of herbs worked OK, something was cleaned out of me. Sore throat eventually calmed down, but it wasn't the solution to whatever the problem was. I didn't feel wonderful afterwards. Something was still wrong.

To make matters worse, I went on a business trip to Geneva and got well and truly smashed out of my tiny mind. A long lunch turned into a long dinner, followed by a club and then a show. The booze didn't stop flowing all day. We were so drunk we all got on stage and danced around with the performers. Ha, crazy night! Not had a hangover like that in years either. Ouch.

Unfortunately the getting smashed seems to have allowed some bugs to take control and I definitely feel worse now and it's not going away. I am even more tired and have less energy. Every morning now my tongue is now coated with thick white gunk. I need a scraper, yuck! Annoying, very annoying indeed. And a good lesson for me! It's good to have fun, but you have to know how! Getting totalled like that does not help in my quest to be healthy.

I also have the racing heartbeat again. Maybe this is a signal that my kidneys are getting stressed by chelation? I need to try a kidney cleanse to solve this, but: colds, sore throats, racing heart, Humaworm antibiotic cleanses and kidney cleanses mean I cannot chelate as much as I wish. I want to chelate all the time. This year the plan was to chelate as much as possible, but chelation is hard and forces me to solve other things that chelation brings on.

Hey, life is still mostly normal and I only have minor hassles when I chelate. I could just chelate and avoid the cleanses, but that seems stupid because I am lucky enough to know how to solve the problems that chelation causes. Seems dumb to avoid them and make myself sicker by just chelating.

I am finding life tough at the moment. Still no yoga. This is not going according to plan. Something is out of kilter.

54. "Well, here's another fine mess you've gotten me into!" Laurel and Hardy

In July of 2009 when I hit four grains of Armour, suddenly I started feeling superfine. Yoga restarted and I practiced five days a week that summer. All my symptoms of ill health disappeared. I started gaining weight. I was totally back in the land of the living. Hooray! Happy dayz were here again…or were they?

The happy dayz lasted about six weeks. Then I noticed my chelation rounds were getting harder and harder. Something was out of whack. I started getting coughs and colds, yoga became impossible, I lacked energy and was tired all over again. I was constantly aware of my heartbeat and the heartbeat thuds seemed way bigger than normal. Something somewhere was wrong. I'd had my two steps forward, now it seemed it was time for one step back.

As you see in my diary entries, I did what I usually do in these circumstances, I hit the herbs: parasite cleanse, kidney cleanse, liver herbs. Doing those cleanses took three months, but this time the herbs did not work. I remained troubled, hassled and tired.

Although the herbs did not work, I now knew that my problems were not due to parasites, nor kidney, nor liver problems. I could cross those ideas off my potential-cause-list, which was important in itself. Must say I was confused because the herbs had served me so well in the past. Why were they failing me now?

Then in September, I got that horrid sore throat, along with a cold that refused to go away. The yeast flared up big time too. All signals that something was now seriously out of line. I tried some new herbs to combat the very bad sore throat: the herbal antibiotic. But after two weeks of herbs, still nothing had changed.

Maybe I was doing something wrong? What had I missed?

Eventually I thought to check my blood pressure. I had taken my blood pressure in the past and it was always fine at around 120/70. I bought a little machine, cost £50, and I discovered it was now 164/94. That would explain the big thumps of heartbeats I was feeling!

I didn't know much about blood pressure, so I Googled it and discovered my levels were considered to be 'in the danger zone for heart attacks'. Oh, what a joy!

The 94 in the 164/94 was high, not wildly high, but 'moderately' high nevertheless. I looked it up: if I had gone to see a regular doctor, they would have put me on beta blockers. People are put on those drugs when blood pressure is above 140/90. I had already made the recommended lifestyle changes in diet and whatnot, so I knew I would be a lovely textbook case, nice and easy for them to 'cure' with their miraculous drugs.

I quote: 'Common adverse drug reactions associated with the use of beta blockers include: nausea, diarrhea, bronchospasm, dyspnoea, cold extremities, exacerbation of Raynaud's syndrome, bradycardia, hypotension, heart failure, heart block, fatigue, dizziness, abnormal vision, decreased concentration, hallucinations, insomnia, nightmares, depression, sexual dysfunction, erectile dysfunction and/or alteration of glucose and lipid metabolism.' (Rossi, 2006)

The start of the previous paragraph even used the word 'common'. No disrespect to the doctors and drug companies, but you can stick your side effects where the sun don't shine. The last thing I need is power side effects!

And whatever was wrong with me, whatever was wrong with my heart, I knew 100 percent it was not for a lack of beta blockers or any of the other synthetic drug options available. These drugs were man-made magic beans designed to mask issues, cause other problems and make shareholders oodles and oodles of cash.

So I didn't even bother going to a doctor. What was the point? I would not trust what they told me, nor take any drugs they pushed at me. I would have to find another way to solve the problem. Anyway, I was happiest figuring it all out myself.

Don't think I was treating this casually. Heart problems are serious issues. My father had heart disease in his 50s and this was not something I took lightly at all.

Time for some deep thinking. The questions kept circling my head: why was this happening? What did it mean? Was this just chelation hiccups? Was this the start of heart disease? Was I going to have a heart attack tomorrow? Or maybe a stroke? What had I missed? Back to the books for more reading. Frustratingly I'd lent out my copy of Dr. Peatfield's book and couldn't review that for ideas.

The muscle tester dude was in town for a quick visit so I went to see him. Maybe he could help me figure this out?

I told him I thought it might be one of the 15 supplements I was taking daily? And recently I had changed the brand of my thyroid support, Armour, maybe it was that? Or maybe it could be chelation being hard work, or maybe kidneys, or liver, or adrenals, or maybe something else? What did he think?

We talked long and hard about what I'd been doing in the past year. All the different herbs I'd tried, the chelation rounds, detox baths, dry-skin brushing.

First up, he discovered I was not handling some of my supplements very well: molybdenum, magnesium, niacinamide, zinc all gave negative reactions. If I was reacting badly, that had to mean I was getting better! Ha, cool! Very encouraging. A year ago I could not do without them.

Then he discovered I was overreacting to the thyroid and the adrenal support. Very odd! This needed thinking about. Why would I be overreacting? Were my doses too high?

I retraced my steps. In order to track, monitor and understand my adrenal and thyroid glands, I was taking my temps. My average daytime temp in the day was steady around 36.8 deg C (98.2 deg F). This was less than the 37.0 deg C (98.6 deg F) that I had set as my target. I was 0.2 deg C below target. I figured I still had a little way to go and still need to keep increasing my Armour dose in order hit the magical 37.0 deg C. I had moved from 4 grains to 5.25 grains in the past few months.

FREEZE!

STOP RIGHT THERE!

STEP AWAY FROM THE ARMOUR!
PUT YOUR HANDS IN THE AIR AND STEP AWAY FROM
THE ARMOUR!

Bingo! I found it. I had made a major mistake here. OK, it was a little mistake, easily done, nowhere near as big as the blunder with amalgam removal with no protection, but still a big-ish cock-up. Did you spot it?

A body temperature of 37.0 deg C is considered a normal body temperature, but 36.8 deg C is also considered normal too! Turns out that the correct body temperature is actually anything in a range between 36.6 to 37.0 degrees C. Supposedly each person will have a different normal for them. In other words the experts disagree on what is exactly normal. Great, eh!

The books each have a slightly differing opinion on what is the "normal" temperature and that's how and why I aimed too high. So people don't aim for exactly a specific temperature, they aim for anything close to 36.8. But most importantly: how you feel around this temperature.

I felt great at 36.8 deg C and that was my gaffe, my screw-up. I should have understood this and then stopped raising the Armour dose. I relied too heavily on my temperature chart and forgot to think of my actual health. I was at the correct Armour dose all along: 4 grains. My temperature was smack-on already. I just assumed 37.0 was correct and aimed at that. I kept increasing my Armour dose higher and higher, trying to get to 37.0 degrees. I moved up from 4 grains to 5.25 grains of Armour, which was not unheard of, but it was fairly high.

Muscle tester dude also noted hyper symptoms of 'pressure on my eyeballs'. Hyperthyroidism causes the eyeballs to stick out more than normal and by feeling my eyes, he could feel they were under pressure: another clue to confirm the theory. How he knew that, I have no idea, but he is very well-read.

Three months prior to all this kafuffle, to make things even trickier, I was forced to switch brands of Armour. In 2008-2009 the company that made it changed the formula in a way that half the people using it got sick. There was also something wrong with the supply of the raw materials used to make it. The American regulators clamped down on the company and the supply dried up. This was fantastic for someone who loved to tick boxes, but less fun for the millions of people who needed the stuff to carry on with their lives!

So I changed to a generic brand from Thailand. This stuff cost a quarter of the price, was delivered within a week and was made using the old Armour formula that everyone had been using for 100 years and caused people—and me—no problems.

Switching Armour brands to one that worked correctly also had a major influence in my symptoms and side-effects. I was on a dose of 5.25 grains of the stuff and this flipped me from hyp*o* to hyp*er*-thyroidism. That meant I went from too few thyroid hormones, to too many. Oops!

I could not do yoga anymore, I felt tired, I got regular coughs and colds and I was aware of my loud thudding heartbeat hammering away all the time. I learnt these symptoms were some of the many problems associated with hyperthyroidism, i.e. of too many hormones in the body.

I knew something was wrong, it just took a while to figure out. The thyroid and its treatment is one tricky bloody subject to get your head around, and this was not the only project I was handling! But I figured it out eventually and that's what counts. Phew!

I made the mistake of not taking my blood pressure to gauge my progress. I did take it in the beginning when I first started, but forgot and ignored this simple test to track my progress over the long months of building my dose. I over-medicated for four or five months. Switching Armour brands was like a jet-rocket boosting me up, up and away.

I should have known a stable body temp of 36.8 deg C (98.2 deg F) was completely normal for a male. I should have seen my blood pressure rise as I raised the Armour dose. I did also feel pretty damn good when my temperature hit 36.8 deg C and I should have known that was my signal to stop raising the thyroid support. I should have used my lack of symptoms as a signal that I'd achieved my goal of supported thyroid glands. I just thought 37.0 deg C (98.6 deg F) was the target, was blind to everything else and went too far.

Anyway, must say, I was gloriously happy at figuring this out, very proud of myself indeed. Muscle tester dude was essential, but I would have got there eventually. If I'd have re-read Dr. Peatfield's book, it says quite clearly on page 21 what all my symptoms meant. I'd bought a second copy and that was next on my pile. The racing heart and raised blood pressure were pretty clear and obvious signposts that I had flipped over to hyperthyroidism.

Knowledge is power.

So, I figured out I was taking too many supplements. I seemed to have flipped over to too many hormones. The next job was reducing the ACE and Armour dosage to a level that suited me. How difficult could that be?

55. Cold Turkey

I guess I should have tapered the Armour and ACE dose down gently. I should have gradually lowered the doses, just as I had done when I gradually increased the dose. But screw that! I knew the Armour and ACE were hurting me and I wanted to stop that hurt right now, not in God knows how many weeks or months. So rather than gradually reducing the dose, oh yeah baby, I went cold turkey!

It was a calculated risk and that's the decision I made given my health and understanding of the situation. Looking back in the cold light of day, I admit this was a bit drastic.

Understanding that I am not infallible is just as important as understanding that I know exactly what I am doing! Although I'd made a cock-up, overall I was pretty good at all this. I decided to take a chelation break too. Adrenals and thyroid were mega-important to get right and I did not want to have chelation rounds muddying the water while I found the correct doses for each. I would need a level playing field to figure this out.

So I went cold turkey with the ACE and the Armour. I went from 5.25 grains of Armour, and 750mg of ACE, to zero all in one day. That was after one year building the Armour dose a quarter grain per month and one and a half years on ACE. All the major supporting supplements for my adrenals and thyroid removed in one fell swoop.

Now, to those accustomed to adrenals and thyroids, you are probably holding your breath, squinting and looking sideways at the words, waiting for the crash and burn. Ouch! This is gonna hurt this reckless city boy. I know some of you are thinking it, but it's OK, you can breathe again and look straight, everything was cool.

As with many of the things that I have done and experienced, it took time, about five months to get it right. What happened was not a miracle because loads of people get better, but what happened is pretty unusual. It's the kind of thing that people on thyroid medications dream about.

The plan was to use all the tools in my belt to track and monitor my situation. I was to take my temperatures three times a day which gave me my average temp. I took my morning basal temperature too, which is my temperature at rest after a night's sleep. I also monitored my blood pressure, my pulse and I made a note of all my symptoms daily. All this would tell me what my adrenals and thyroid were doing.

I was planning to re-introduce the Armour as soon as the temps dropped.

I was planning to re-introduce the ACE as soon as the temps fluctuated.

That was the plan, and I like a good plan, Batman.

• • •

For the first week of cold turkey my temps fluctuated from 36.4 to 36.8 deg C. I did have good days and bad days which coincided with the high and low temps. Because my temps went down and then up again to a normal 36.8 deg C, I concluded that this was an adrenal issue showing itself. Remember large fluctuations in temps between days means adrenal problems.

I was originally on 750mg of ACE, so two weeks after going cold turkey I re-introduced ACE at 500mg to support my adrenals. Within two days I had a raging heartbeat going bananas and my body obviously disapproved furiously of ACE. I stopped the ACE.

Maybe it was a thyroid problem? So next I tried re-introducing Armour. I took 4 grains of Armour, 1.5 grains less than before. Within one day I had a racing heartbeat going bananas and my body obviously disapproved furiously of Armour. So I stopped the Armour.

Back to Cold Turkey for a week. Temps fluctuating again. I re-introduced ACE again at 250mg and again within two days I had a racing heartbeat going bananas and my body obviously disapproved of ACE. I stopped the ACE.

This was odd. I didn't expect this. The reactions to the Armour were worse and I didn't seem to need much/any of that. My temps where still fluctuating so I focused on the ACE and gradually lowered the dose down, down deeper and down.

Each experimental dose took 10 to 14 days to understand. It took a few days for symptoms to arrive and then a few days to go away when I stopped. But with no adrenal supplements my temps fluctuated and I didn't feel right, so I needed something. I just needed the right ACE dose.

The dose got so low I had to change ACE brands to a lower dose capsule because I could not cut the caps any smaller. I moved down to 50mg ACE per day. This was a massive drop from 750mg per day and at 50mg ACE my temps levelled out beautifully. Most significantly my symptoms reduced right down and good health returned to me once again. Workouts restarted too, which is a large indicator of my health. I still had slightly raised blood pressure, but I could not notice it day to day anymore. It was time to re-start the party. This is the healthiest I'd felt to date. No symptoms and restarted yoga. Happy dayz!

But what about the Armour? What about my thyroid glands? Surely they needed help? I was on 5.25 grains of Armour before I went cold turkey. I 100 percent had had thyroid problems, everything pointed to them: my symptoms, my hair test results, my temperatures, my reactions and the good health after supporting them with 4 grains of Armour. What was going on with my thyroid?

As far as traditional western medicine is concerned 'thyroid support is for life'. People never get off thyroid support. Not one of the many books I had read said thyroid fatigue was curable. Thyroid fatigue was only supportable. The books talk at length about the unfortunate people who are taken off thyroid medication by ignorant doctors looking at lab results and those people getting sick again. Not one of the books talks about curing. Not one of those books I read talks about reducing the dose.

Maybe I read the wrong books? I read six or seven of them, surely that was enough? They all talked about thyroid support as 'for life' and getting on the correct dose and staying on the correct dose 'for life.' You find your dosage and stick with it. If a doctor tries to lower or stop the pills, then to ignore the doctor and keep taking them anyway.

Of course there are a few exceptions, a few people say you can heal the thyroid and get off thyroid support, Andy Cutler is one of them. He says mercury toxic people who safely chelate the mercury out of their bodies find that their thyroid glands and adrenals heal up just fine. I have met some of those cured people online and they stopped thyroid medication when they got better after chelation.

But I had only done 38 rounds of chelation to date. Chelation is long-term stuff. People chelate for a hundred rounds to get better. Here I was, after 38 rounds, dosing at a measly 4mg ALA and BOOM, my temps were rock solid 36.8 deg C with the only support being 50mg ACE and zero Armour. Life was totally normal and symptom-free now.

This was not supposed to happen.

I was getting better.

My thyroid had been cured.

My adrenal glands seemed to now only be mildly fatigued now.

That was not supposed to happen.

Oh yeah, the only other people saying you could repair the thyroid without drugs, or even ACE or Armour, were herbalists. Some of them say all supplements are harmful, are completely unnecessary and herbs will work just fine thank you very much. But hardly anyone believes herbalists; they should cut their hair, shave their beards and get a real job!

I believe the herbalists and Cutler are correct.

Cutler said people do get cured from thyroid fatigue with correct chelation: I did.

Herbalist say people do get cured from thyroid fatigue with herbs: I did.

Which herbs did I take? Remember all those parasite, liver, kidney and lung herbal cleanses? Those herbs. Each cleanse had between 10 and 24 different herbs in them. Just because it says liver on the packet does not mean they are only good for the liver.

I am happy to prove you guys right. Well done boys and thanks a mill. You will have to fight amongst yourselves as to who get the credit, but in my eyes, you are both right. My chelation and all the herbs healed me.

I called Dr. Peatfield, the thyroid specialist in the UK. He could hardly believe his ears and was overjoyed to hear my news:

"Congratulations, old chap! What fantastic news! Whatever you are doing, it's worked wonders, keep doing it."

"Does that mean I'm cured?"

"If after three months you don't need any Armour then you can consider your thyroid healed."

It's been over 12 months now. Happy dayz.

"I must say, I am a bit surprised. I was not expecting this. Is it normal?"

"Oh yes, of course some people get better. It's not unheard of, some people get better almost magically and they never even do anything. But is very uncommon and you should be proud. I am amazed. Thanks for calling, that's made my day. "

56. The Curious Incident of the Dog and the Raised Blood Pressure

I have done many more herbs than chelation rounds. I have had wonderful results from the herbs. After each and every herbal cleanse I got better. Sometimes more than others, but herbs I have done the most, because I have felt them working the best. I put the curing of my thyroid and adrenal glands down to: (in this order)

1) The herbs.

2) ACE and Armour providing the raw materials and building blocks to rebuild.

3) My diet.

4) Chelation.

5) Amalgam removal was also essential. I had to turn off the toxic tap.

I firmly believe that it was doing all these things collectively that enabled me to heal. I know attacking the problem from one angle would have not worked, or at the very best, taken a lot longer. And if that hurts your ears to hear me say I needed to do so many different things to get better, sorry, but that's mercury poisoning for you. It's a bitch and make no mistake about it. All parts of your body have been poisoned and all parts need attention. There is no magic bullet and the sooner you get that into your head, the sooner you can take multiple actions to help yourself.

However I had one lingering problem, the high blood pressure. It just wouldn't go away. So, time to embark upon education and figuring out what actions to take. My pulse was normal; down to 70 and sometimes it's in the low 60s. But my blood pressure remained high at around 162/85.

I did notice it too. I felt the big thuds of my heart thumping against my chest. Not all the time, but when I thought about it I could feel it, and it didn't feel right. I knew I should not be so aware of my heartbeat. It was worrisome. It was a bit like un-opened mail. You just knew there were gonna be some bills in there, and someone somewhere was going to have to pay. And that someone was me.

It needed sorting out and this would be my focus in the next few months. This was the start of blood-pressure-lowering tactics.

I hit the books. The first alternative health book said, first stop for blood pressure issues was bowel cleaning. I have already done plenty, but OK, I had a furry tongue in the mornings and got mild bloating in the evenings so let's see if P&B shakes would do anything?

To remind you, the P is psyllium, the herb that sweeps out debris from the digestive tract. The B is bentonite clay that absorbs and sucks up anything it comes in contact with. Don't take it at the same time as food!

I did 13 days' worth of P&B shakes, drinking the murky gunk morning and last thing at night. Always good to do and sorted out the bloating, but it didn't do anything for my blood pressure which remained unchanged.

Much to my joy, one of the side-effects of the P&B shakes was that I had regained the energy to restart yoga. My practice felt good and each stronger and better than the last. This was in stark contrast to previous yoga époques where it always felt tough and a bit of an uphill battle. It was early days but I had worked out three times a week over a period of a couple of weeks. Resuming my yoga felt like the icing on the cake of rebuilding my life.

Further reading about the heart:
Put Your Heart in Your Mouth by Dr Campbell-McBride

November 2009 – Andreas Moritz Liver Herbs

Finding a solution to the high blood pressure continues, this time with liver herbs. Instructions are for ten days. I had eight normal days, but also two harsh days where I was aggressively angry. A real boiling rage. This was during the weekend so the only person to notice anything untoward was my wife, and all she saw was me hiding away. I closed to door and cut myself off from the rest of the world. We never discuss it, she knows when I struggle and need peace, quiet and solitude. If ever social interactions are unavoidable, I hide my eyes, kept my head down and am completely withdrawn. Inside my mind I am holding the fury back, hoping I won't bite someone's head off.

This only lasted two days, so it was manageable. I know why it's happening, because my liver is being detoxed. I know it will pass, because it always passes. I know what to do when it happens: solitude, good food, lots of water and any health-regaining activities I can find the strength for. And I know that after it has passed, I will have removed some old harm, hurt, poison that had been stuck in me for God knows how long. So even when I'm in the midst of a storm, when all hell is breaking loose, deep inside I am happy, happy that I am excreting an old enemy.

What I find amazing is that this anger was caused by me physically removing some crap from my liver. Think about that. The anger came from my liver, not my mind. These herbs specifically detox the liver. I was not angry because I lost money, or had a bad day. There was no reason to be angry, but I was boiling with rage. No, the anger came from cleaning my body. I got mental effects from physically cleaning my liver. That is amazing. That is deep. That is a profound experience of understanding, first hand, how our bodies work.

As ever, it passed, as it always does.

Blood pressure remains unchanged.

What next?

18th December 2009 – Andreas Moritz Kidney Herbs

Next stop in the blood pressure lowering tactics: Kidney herbs. I have done these before and they have helped, so worth doing again. This is just a minor interlude before the yearly whole-family parasite cleanse in January.

I did nine days in total as I need a few clear days between cleanses. By the end I was getting the typical signals: slight lower back pain along with an itchy rash on my arse. I do also feel slightly under the weather, a mild cough and a blocked nose. Nothing serious, just enough for me to know they are working.

By the second day after I stopped taking the herbs I felt noticeably better. Cough, nose, lower back and rash have all gone now. This confirms the herbs were working fine.

Blood pressure remains high.

1st January 2010 – Humaworm #6 + Humacleanse #5

I like to start the year with my yearly maintenance parasite program. As usual I am coercing my wife and daughter to join me on this too. My little girl gets a Playmobil safari park and the wife stays in my good books!

I will be doing the full monty: the 30-day parasite cleanse together with the 30-day bowel cleanse. Being my sixth parasite cleanse, I hoped I would be clear of the buggers by now, and it finally seems that I am. Hooray!

This was by far the easiest, with nothing exciting to report whatsoever. What a difference to three years ago when I first tried these herbs and had all those wild and crazy side-effects.

I had an odd little episode of some colours being sharper and clearer, blue and yellow again. This is the first time I have experienced this outside of chelation. Not sure what it means.

I still have the furry tongue in the mornings. Wonder why that's not shifting?

Yoga has restarted and I am practicing every other day which is super-cool. I love these herbs, every set helps.

Blood pressure remains high.

Round 39 – 12th February 2010 – 4mg ALA

That was a BIG chelation break: five months. I have not had such a long break before. It was necessary in trying to figure out adrenals, thyroids, heart and the pulse problems. So many things to do and get right!

Anyway, today my body temperature is steady at 36.8 degrees C. I am on 50mg ACE and zero thyroid supplements. Yoga has restarted and I'm feelin' pretty damn good. Rock and roll good even! I did 14 days of yoga in January. I'm getting stronger again, more muscle tone, but still a long way to go. Blood pressure is still high.

So, what kind of round did I expect after such a long break? Honestly, I expected a rough round. I have had rough rides after previous mini-breaks of one or two months, so yeah, I anticipated trouble and was a little apprehensive. Heartburn and maybe some anger could rear its ugly head?

I also discovered I am slightly off-protocol when I end my chelation rounds with 3-5 doses of DMSA. Cutler says some people are OK with it, some not. Plenty of people do it and it's up to the individual to decide if they want to or not, but officially it's out of protocol. I get some strong reactions to mercury I like to try and keep things as tight as possible. So from now on I will stick to ALA rounds only. I don't like taking any chances if I can avoid them.

I did a full three-day ALA round with no DMSA at all. First evening I was a tad more tired than normal, but on-round it was velvet smooth.

But the second day after the round ended the hassle started and I did get a little heartburny, tingly and itchy. Even needed a second detox bath but it passed as it always does. On the whole, nothing too bad, certainly nowhere near as bad as I dreaded.

This makes the long-term nature of chelation do-able. God knows what I would have done if I'd had major hassles. Life without symptoms is good and if chelation brings on hassles I may not chelate. I know I need to chelate long-term in order to live long-term.

Round 40 – 23rd February 2010 – 4mg ALA

Felt a little tingly and a bit under-par all round, but I did manage yoga twice and that was fine. Day two and three after the round I was tired and slept a lot. Muscle weakness in lower back was noticeable in the mornings upon waking for about 10 days after the round. Yes, an irritating little round.

Round 41 – 12th March 2010 – 4mg ALA

Blue coming back. Nice!

Third round after the long break and I seem to be back in the groove now. Chelation is easy again. I definitely think chelation hurts more after breaks, takes a couple of rounds to get back into the swing of it.

3rd April 2010 – Liquid Fast

I did a seven-day fast here. Veg and fruit juices, bone broths, raw milk, raw milk kefir and ginger kefir along with plenty of water. All homemade except the lunchtime juices at the office. This fast is not in any books you can find. I made it up, so don't try this at home! I know each ingredient is good for me. Interestingly I felt best when I drank the animal-derived juices, especially the bone broths (which is just stock made by boiling up bones for 12-24 hours).

I had some left-over bowel cleaning herbs too, so did five days of Humacleanse at the same time. I alternated between a mega white coating and thick yellow covered tongue. Yuck!

You wouldn't think it, but it is amazing how easy fasting is. First three days are mildly tricky as you do feel a little empty and hungry, but after that it was plain sailing. Pity I had to stop but I have lots of lunches at work. I could easily have done another week! I was really in the groove.

This was done for the benefits of fasting. I do not want to, or need to lose weight. Within two weeks I regained the weight I lost; 4 kg (8.8 lbs).

My blood pressure remains unchanged and higher than it should be.

14th April 2010 – Andreas Moritz 30 days Kidney Herbs

This is my tenth kidney cleanse. Within three days I have mild toothache and ultra-dry skin on my hands and forearms. The mega white tongue from the juice fast remains.

Eleven days in and I have clusters of itchy spots from the hip upwards on each side of my body. More odd than anything else. The dry skin now extends down my legs and I feel 10 percent under-par, but it's hardly the end of the world. All are signals that I needed to do these herbs: something that does not belong is being removed.

Overall I'm feeling good and these herbs are easy, so easy I decided to chelate as well. Time will tell if that is a wise choice.

Day 24 and everything is cool, chelation round was fine. Still get regular smelly pee, I do feel slightly off-peak but I'm chelating and cleansing so that's expected. Today I have a strange bumpy rash on left foot. Lower back is mildly painful sometimes when I lie down in bed, but it's small-fry and does not affect day-to-day life.

By the end of the cleanse I felt pretty normal. Chelating at the same time was fine and certainly I can kidney cleanse and chelate at the same time now. I can now consider the condition of my kidneys a millions miles better than three years ago. I will concentrate of other cleanses: Liver herbs next.

But blood pressure remains high and tongue remains thickly coated with white gunk. Something is still broken, so I still have some figuring out to do.

Round 42 – 23rd April 2010 – 4mg ALA

I kept staring at the fluffy clouds. I seem to have got some depth-perception back because the sky was looking, like, funky. Check out the colours man! The sunset took my breath away. A real heart-stopper, filled with the most amazing pinks. I never realized what an energetic colour pink was.

Otherwise a normal round.

57. The Big Wake-up Call – 23rd April 2010

The past eight months have been busy, so let's recap what's been going on. The first three or four of those, I finally got to grips with my adrenals and thyroid, but lowering my blood pressure was proving troublesome. High blood pressure is the start of some serious dangers. I needed to nip this in the bud. It was up at 165/85 most of the time, but occasionally hitting a worrisome 160/104. I was aware of the great thuds thumping away. It was not supposed to be doing this.

I had researched blood pressure and did all the things recommended. In terms of holistic medicine I had already done most of the things required for a healthy heart. I was already living a pretty awesome healthy lifestyle, but obviously I needed to be even healthier. As usual I did not bother seeing a doctor.

I chose my usual path, I hit the herbs. I did another full body round, constantly checking my blood pressure and pulse to see if anything made a dent. Thirteen days P&B shakes, 10 days liver herbs, 9 days kidney herbs, 30 days parasite cleanse, 30 days bowel cleanse, 7 days liquid fast, 30 days kidney herbs. All these herbal formulas did me a world of good: cleaning, strengthening and rejuvenating my body, however none of them made a blind bit of difference to my blood pressure.

The most common and widely recommended herbal remedies are garlic and hawthorn berries. So I took garlic capsules daily and ate extra garlic whenever I could. I made a special herbal tea made of hawthorn berries, lime flowers, mistletoe and yarrow. I drank it twice a day for six months. Nothing changed.

Salt is supposed to be a culprit in high blood pressure. Muscle testing said my Himalayan salt was fine, but muscle testing is a guide only. Better to be safe than sorry, so I stopped my half teaspoon a day consumption. Within three days I started to get cramp in my feet and legs daily and got up at night to have a pee. After three weeks of peeing, cramp and no change to my heart, I added salt back into my diet. Table salt was the stuff that gave people high blood pressure. The Himalayan stuff is good for me, not bad.

I tinkered with my diet. I stopped dairy for a while: did nothing. I stopped grains: did nothing. I stopped sulphur foods and that did nothing too.

Perhaps it was my thyroid? I added some mild thyroid supplements, but no change.

Maybe it was just a bump along the chelation road and I just need to chelate more? After the five-month break I did three close chelation rounds, but they made no difference either.

Maybe I needed to physically calm it down? I started mediating daily, but that just worried me more. I was even more aware of my heartbeat when I relaxed and chilled down. Thump, thump, thump reverberated around my whole body when I was under.

All to no avail. It seemed that my heart was stuck in too fast a gear and was unable to shift down. It had one speed: GO!

Nothing I'd done had helped and the longer this went on, the more ideas that failed, the more worried I became. I even thought about going to see a regular doctor. Yes, that's how desperate I was! I did promise my wife that if I did not find the solution soon, I would force myself to go see one. I didn't want to waste my time, but if I was out of ideas, that would be the next step.

In-between I went to see an alternative health care guy who specialized in iridology. I always wanted to see one of these dudes. Fascinating stuff that iridology. These are the people that can read your health by looking at the pupil of your eye. Funky, eh! Old skool healing that is. He recommended supplementary magnesium. Worth a shot, but did nothing.

Next I thought it was time for a hair test. Not done one for a while, so worth seeing if this picked anything up. This would be my fifth. At this point my only symptoms were high blood pressure, blocked sinuses, a furry tongue and not quite as much energy as I would wish. I didn't expect anything electrifying to come out of it. It was an easy option, only cost $90 and I could read the results myself.

The results came in and, oh no! I met Cutler's famous counting rules! That was unexpected. Very unexpected. I'd never met them before. My first hair test showed high mercury being excreted (in the red), but the subsequent three had all reflected exactly what was going on in my life; increasing health with all those bars levelling out and normalizing. This new hair test met two out of three rules and it almost, by a whisker, was meeting all three. That meant I had Deranged Mineral Transport.

I was horrified.

Here I was, 92 percent of my symptoms gone, with only a few issues outstanding and leading a normal life again. What the funk was going on?

And then it hit me.

Boom!

This was The Big Wake-up Call.

Oh $hit!

This was mercury poisoning in all its glory.

How depressing.

Meeting Culter's counting rules on the hair test showed I had De-ranged Mineral Transport. Mercury poisoning is the only thing that can lead to this condition. It means I am incapable of moving minerals around my body correctly.

When I eat my healthy food, my body breaks it down into smaller components that are absorbed and used by all the different parts of my body. 'We are what we eat' and all that. What mercury poisoning does is stop my body from being able to keep the levels of minerals correctly balanced. This is one of the main reasons us mercury toxic have so many problems. And why it is a slow insipid illness, gradually building up a head of steam as the body struggles to function while continuously being starved of the right raw materials.

The hair test results become much more difficult to read because the body is no longer playing by the usual rules. But it's not just about reading test results. It's about my body being so damaged by mercury that it does not, cannot work correctly. Having the wrong bits in the wrong places is bound to lead to trouble. That is mercury poisoning for you. That's why it's such a bitch.

You do hear stories about people recovering for a while, but getting mysteriously sick again. They have amalgam removal. They do plenty to help their health. They get better. They brag about how great they feel. They get on with life for a few years. Then the mercury rears its ugly head again, their health crumbles and they return to the bad old days. These are the people who didn't get all the mercury out of their bodies. These are the people who didn't finish the clean-up job. The mercury always comes back to haunt us if we don't finish the job. I know people like this, some of them quite well too. And it was going to happen to me if I was not careful. That's what these results showed me.

Bloody funking mercury.

When I first fully understood I was mercury toxic I was happy. Happy I'd figured it out. Happy I had a plan of action. Happy I had a goal to aim for. Now I was almost completely better and here I had rock-solid, cast-iron proof that after three years of serious hard-core efforts, I was still wildly and completely mercury toxic.

Fuck.

That sobered me up. It wasn't fun having to face the music, especially after I thought I'd cracked it. Oh man, this is a long road.

I realised that because the mercury was still lurking, I would continue to have to fight and battle until all the mercury was chelated out, even though I was mostly better. The mercury would continue to throw problems at me. Currently it was my blood pressure. Once I solved that I would undoubtedly be faced with some other mystery to crack. Most of the hassles would be solved by the continual herbal barrage my body was under, but mercury is like a stalker, perpetually knocking on my door, sending me obscene messages.

The message was blindingly obvious: chelation is the key to my long-term health. Luckily I was on top of the situation here. I understood what was going on. I was focused and I wanted to live a long and happy healthy life. And if I ever needed something to keep me sharp, to re-focus, to motivate myself to continue chelation; this was a jolly good smack around the chops to wake up and smell the roses.

Not sure why it affected me so much. Most mercury toxic people get deranged mineral transport and it's not like I didn't know. It's just, that, well, I suppose the truth hurts. I wasn't running around hyperventilating, eye bulging, freaking out. No, this was a cold hard, teeth clenched realisation: Chelation was the only thing that would remove the mercury from my body. Chelation was my only hope.

58. "I have one speed: Go." Charlie Sheen Interview, 2011

I needed some fresh ideas about the blood pressure problem so I started asking around on all the forums I frequented to see if anyone had any top-tips. I got the usual scare messages from kind-hearted citizens telling me my arteries were bunged up and I could pop my clogs at any moment. But in amongst the worst case scenarios a lovely lady called Maria sent me a little message saying I should check out something called 'Mukta Vati'. It was getting good reviews and it had worked for her. Generally I have had rotten luck with miracle cures, but I always check out every idea.

Mukta Vati is an Ayurvedic remedy for hypertension. Funny word that 'Ayurvedic'. I can never pronounce it. Ay-ur-vedic. It just refuses to flow off my tongue. It's the Sanskrit name for traditional Indian medicine. Anyway, Mukta Vati is the Indian herbal remedy for high blood pressure, anxiety and insomnia. The first thing I discovered was that it was banned. Intriguing!

I decided to call Big Pharma and have a chat with them about it.

"Why is this stuff Mukta Vati banned?"

"Untested you see."

"But, it seems to have been used successfully and safely for generations in India."

"Oh you don't want to trust dirty people from third-world countries. They live in mud huts and eat with their hands."

"But what about the western people that have used it? They got cured too."

"That's anecdotal evidence and does not count."

"But I found plenty of success stories on the internet."

"That's anecdotal evidence and does not count."

"But if people got better from taking it, why can't I try it?"

"We are protecting you from harm. It's untested you see."

"But it has no side-effects."

"That's anecdotal evidence and does not count."

"But it's really cheap too. I can actually afford it."

"Look son, just shut it, OK. We can't make any money out of that muck because we can't patent it."

"Oh."

"And to make matters worse it reduces our market share."

"Oh."

"Our stock prices might be trampled if word got out there was a cheap cure for hypertension."

"Oh."

"Mukta Vati is a competitor to our products and all competitors must be killed, crushed or banned. Preferably all three."

"But what about all the people that are sick and could get better by taking these herbs."

"Look son, we are running a business here. Not some namby-pamby, beard-supporting, sandal-wearing charity!"

"Oh, so you are just a businessman. You don't actually care about healing or curing anyone?"

"Spot on, son. Now you're getting it. And Humaworm is the next target. Now fuck off and stop annoying us."

"You can't ban Humaworm!"

"Oh yeah, wanna bet! Hahahaha..."

Click.

If they had gone to the trouble of banning Mukta Vati, there must be something to it. The internet was awash with people saying it worked for them, so I decided to give it a bash too.

Just like recreational drugs, you can buy anything if you know where to look. In this case I didn't have to nip down to Camden Town tube station, I just had to order it off Ebay.com. Two days later my little pot arrived. I started straight away with two hits a day.

Nothing drastic happened. I had no side-effects. No weirdness. No rashes. No grumpiness. No blind rages. No nothing, except it worked perfectly. After two days my blood pressure started dropping and within one month it had gone from 160/104 down to 139/65. After three months I stopped taking the pills, but the blood pressure starting rising a little, so I did another two months at half dose. Five months later I stopped taking the pills and my blood pressure remained in the 'perfect' zone.

It was about time one of these miracle cures worked for me!

The way I understood it, my heart was stuck on 'Go'. Mukta Vati worked its herbal magic and reminded my body that it has more than one speed. Calming and normalising my body's functions. This could have just been the tipping point after all the other heart-pressure-reduc-ing-activities I'd tried. Maybe? Maybe not? I didn't really care because it was the end result that mattered.

Yet again another saga. Yet again I had to try lots of different things, but I kept on trying, reading, researching and asking for help. I got there in the end, like I always do. Never give up. Where there is a will, there is a way.

No idea if Mukta Vati will work for other people because I am not a double-blind study, but I'd say it was worth a shot if you have heart troubles.

I must admit to feeling a peculiar unease at the back of my mind about this victory. As a general rule miracle cures don't work for me. It seems odd to find a magic bullet that shoots down a massive problem: this is a first. Don't get me wrong, I am wildly happy about eliminat-ing the high blood pressure, it's just that something doesn't smell right. Really? A miracle cure?

The reason I'm such a Doubting Thomas is because there is a rea-son, a cause for the raised blood pressure and I failed to find it. I found the solution, but not the root cause, which leaves an uneasy feeling, a feeling of unfinished business. Anyway, time will tell. I gave myself a large pat on the back and got on with life.

Round 43 – 30th April 2010 – 4mg ALA

Had a wildly vivid 3D dream the day after the round ended: totally awesome. I love these adventures in the underworld of my mind. This trip was back to the good old days in club-land. Absolutely felt like I was out on the town, living it up large, down all these narrow passageways and on wild dance floors. I awoke hot, sweaty, disorientated and happy. I still don't dream that much, so it felt like a treat.

Round 44 – 14th May 2010 – 4mg ALA

First two days felt no different to normal days. Last seven hours of the third day I was spaced-out and mildly irritable, but I just chilled, kept low and all was fine in the deep dark wood.

I am dreaming a lot now. Sometimes vivid, sometimes just a normal dream, but this is new because I was not dreaming before. Another clear sign I need to keep up the enthusiasm and dedication for chelation. Lots of colours this round, red came back strong and some blue too.

To date I have done 66 days' worth of DMSA chelation rounds, and 66 days of ALA chelation. 44 rounds which is 132 chelation days in total. I wonder how long I will have to chelate to get rid of it all?

Round 45 – 22nd May 2010 4mg ALA – 1 day round

Screwed up this round. Everything was cool as a cucumber on the first day but I somehow turned off both my alarms and missed the midnight dose. I stopped the round when the next dose was due at 3am. A minor blunder and surely a one day round will not hurt that much?

I must have a reshuffle of my clocks so I don't automatically turn them off in my sleep. I have a five-second delay between alarms and I need to make that ten seconds: just enough time to make me pause to turn the second alarm off and take the cap.

And now to the joys of a one-day round: First day after the round I had a nasty four hours where I had Tourette's and a raging fury! I must have looked like death too as my wife could tell I was in trouble the moment she saw me. I had to forcefully bite my mouth shut to stop the swear words from thundering out. I was angry against everyone and everything. It was 98 percent locked up in my mind, but I did slip up once and swore at the kids over absolutely nothing. Not good. I retreated and hid in my room after that.

I don't panic when I get like this because I know it will pass. All I have to do is bide my time, ride the wave, tough it out and it will pass. Hiding away from the world is essential, but it always passes. Why does it always pass? It passes because that's the delight of the Cutler protocol. Because I chelate slowly, I dose only at levels that my body can handle and so the consequences of any mistakes are minor and short-lived. And I promise you this is minor. Nasty, but minor compared to the nightmares I experienced before, and minor compared to the horror stories out there.

This only lasted four hours and I was fine, although weary afterwards.

This round was yet another signal that I need to chelate, yet another signal to show I'm on the right track, and yet another signal to show how important it is not to deviate from the protocol. Come on: FOCUS FOCUS FOCUS. These cock-ups hurt.

24th May 2010 – Andreas Mortiz Liver Herbs

As usual starting out the herbs caused some heartburn, but it's short-lived and by day three everything is cool and I am chelating at the same time with no trouble. Finished on 10 days and it was easy with no bumpy ride. Instructions for the herbs say to do 10 days, but felt like it needed doing for longer.

Yet another cleanse under my belt! Feels good to be strong enough to do the herbs and chelate at the same time.

Edit: 22nd June 2010. Since the liver herbs I have no more digestive troubles during chelation rounds. My BMs have gone very dark which shows my liver is producing enough bile for the digestive process. Perfect! These herbs rock 'n' roll! I am slightly lacking in energy and no workouts possible due to a blocked nose/sinus.

Round 46 – 28th May 2010 – 4mg ALA

This was an ALA round only. First couple of days were fine, but the last six hours of the third day were very spaced out. I zoned out in front of the TV and generally felt fine, but stoned.

First day after the round I was tired and lethargic, so early to bed after my detox bath. Chelating and cleansing is hard work. Maybe I should not push myself too much?

Round 47 – 12th June 2010 – 4mg ALA

Oh man, had a horrid, horrid first day. Total space cadet! Half the time I was in a zombie state staring into space, the other half I was boiling with rage. Snapped at the wife and very much needed to be on my own. Not good.

Day two started out OK, but as the day wore on it became increasingly difficult, spacey and annoying again. I was forgetful and had short-term memory hassles. Not as bad as day one, but a tough day for sure.

Now, when I end rounds early I am almost guaranteed to feel rough as hell, so I will try and tough this out and go for three days. Feels like I am damned if I do, and damned if I don't.

End of day two I did some dry-skin brushing and had a detox bath. More dry-skin brushing in the morning of day three and strangely the whole third day was fine. Just a normal day, as if I was not even chelating. Chelation is odd sometimes.

I love these detox baths, had another at the end of the round too. I know they help big-time-Charlie. Also made sure I drank lots of freshly-squeezed veggie juice; that always helps give me a vitamin boost.

The three nights on-round I was dreaming in HD and 3D: Funky and oh-so vivid! Long, complicated, cool adventure dreams and no nightmares. I love that $hit.

There is a feeling of having broken through, or crossed some barrier in regard to mercury after this round. First two days were bloody hard work, then the third was easy and the end round days were completely hassle free. I didn't even get any heart-burn. I wonder what the next round will be like? More hell? Or easier?

15th June 2010 – Humaworm Lung Cleanse # 3

My nose is blocked, my sinus is clogged and yoga is impossible. I still have the furry white tongue in the mornings, and this seems to be getting worse, not better. This is candida and it's chronic. Humaworm have just started selling a Candida cleanse so I will try those herbs next, but in the meantime, let's see what a lung cleanse will do? No stone unturned, and all that!

This was a two-week cleanse and it was pretty easy. I che-lated at the same time. I did feel a tad knackered by the end, but overall my lungs seem fine. Good to do, but nose, sinus and furry tongue problem remain.

Round 48 – 19th June 2010 – 4mg ALA – 4 days

Something has changed since that last difficult-then easy round. That feeling of crossing a Rubicon persists. I feel different. I feel a little freer, lighter, healthier and stronger. Chelation is easier now, so easy I did a four-day round. Three full ALA days and a full DMSA only day as well. Strong!

After the round I was a little tired for a couple of days. Although it's minor stuff I will stick to three-day rounds in future. They suit me best. Think I will avoid DMSA too. It stirs up yeasts and the candida seems to love it.

Zero heartburn hassles: thank you, Andreas Moritz liver herbs! Seven rounds in two months! Great work, Danny boy!

Round 49 – 2nd July 2010 – 4mg ALA

Grumpy.

Tired.

Fatigue is setting in, and I mean a general weariness is surrounding and swallowing me up. Dark clouds block out the sun. I could not do yoga if I wanted to. Sinuses blocked. Mouth all furry. Energy and will is sapped and gone.

Day two, needed a three-hour morning nap. I am knackered. Something somewhere is wrong. I must think about this.

Am I doing too much chelation? Too many herbs? Should I not chelate and herb at the same time? Do I need a bit more thyroid support? More adrenal support? Do I have tongue cancer? Sinus cancer? Brain cancer?

Time for some muscle testing me thinks. I tested all my food and all my supplements. I discovered the two pills of mild thyroid glandular supplement are making me weak. I had restarted them when looking at solutions for the blood pressure problem. Maybe they have something to do with the fatigue? I stopped the thyroid supplement and went no-thyroid-support. Let's see what happens.

To date I have done 80 days of ALA.

I continue to have funky dreams. Hiiiii-ya!

Round 50 – 9th July 2010 – 4mg ALA

Ba-Da-Boom! I am a Lord! Yet again I crush and banish ill-health from my temple! Glorious success – to me! Oh yes baby!

As you can tell, I figured it out. I always do, eventually. When I'm not screwing up, I am awesome at all this alternative health-care nuttiness. The muscle testing was correct; the thyroid supplement (two caps of NutriThyroid) was draining me of energy and giving me the white tongue. Ha! Take that bitch!

The tiredness is 50 percent reduced and the candida tongue is much less aggressively white in the morning. Nice! The sun has come out and I'm feelin' punchy.

Funny thing supplements. They do so much good when we are sick, but so much harm when we are better. Chuffed I figured this out. Thanks muscle testing, again. It is amazing it gets such a bad press. Is it me? Am I just good at it? No idea. Who cares, works for me and that's all that counts.

You know what this means?

It means my thyroid glands are definitely 100 percent healed. Cool, eh! Not a lot of people can claim that. My scatter-gun approach is working just fine and it's this overall everything-including-the-kitchen-sink method of herbs or chelation all the time that has collectively healed me. I will continue in the same vein, cleaning, strengthening, rebuilding and rejuvenating my amazing body. Who would have thought it was capable of coming back from being so badly screwed-up. We have amazing bodies.

Life is great.

Round 50 was easy with nothing to report out of the normal. Moving up to 5mg ALA should be piss easy.

Breaking from chelation now because of Indian business trip and two-week French holiday.

6th July 2010 Candida Humaworm #1 + Humacleanse #6

OK baby, let's go! New set of herbs, never tried these bad boys before. Candida Humaworm is a 30-day cleanse. This is for the sinus and furry tongue. I expect a hard ride because new sets of herbs always chafe around the edges. I will also do a 30-day bowel cleanse at the same time (Humacleanse). This will speed removal of any waste and hopefully soften the journey. Bowel cleanses have helped with furry tongues in the past. I must remember to drink plenty of water to flush, expel and vamoose the crud from my temple.

After four days I had a BM with major parasite action. A flock of floating dead bodies that I recognised from previous culling campaigns. I love the smell of napalm in the morning!

Twelve days in and I am suffering. A good seven out of ten for hassles. I am drained of energy. I sag in my armchair, deflated like a punctured paddling pool. The typical digestive troubles are bloating me and acid heartburn makes me grumpy. I awake each morning to a carpet of fur on my tongue. Yuck!

It's at times like this that I think dark thoughts. Could this be the dreaded mercury dumping phase? Could my body have decided, enough is enough, let's unload the mercury in a huge dump, crushing me in the process? I don't mind fatigue in small doses, I mean for the duration of the cleanse, but if this is the beginning of something altogether more sinister: man, I don't need that $hit.

Deep down I know it's just the herbs, but these worries do rear their ugly heads in the difficult times. I guess I will find out when the herbs are finished.

I am on a business trip to India in two days' time. I do not need heartburn or fatigue for that tricky trip, so I am pausing on the bowel cleanse and reducing HW candida herbs to half dose.

It's not good having serious discussions with clients when I have hassles from herbs.

Trip was fine and I ramped the dose back up to full power when I got home. I then went on holiday to France and the side-effects were again harassing me. On this occasion I decided that a chilled-out holiday was more important than powering through. So I again reduced the dose to manageable levels and enjoyed France to the max.

Observations at the end:

Every morning I awake gasping and blink away the after-images of yet more super-funky dreams. This is startling, but fun! I love going on adventures. Anyone know anything about lucid dreams?

My weight has gone up, yippee! I have been eating like a horse for the whole cleanse and my weight is up to 71kg (157 lbs), which is the heaviest I have been since I crumpled down to 56kg (123 lbs) when I was uber-sick.

I have successfully reintroduced bread and cheese back into my diet after a two month holiday. I thought they might be affecting my sinus, but excluding them did nothing to help.

Had major white tongue at the start of the cleanse. Much to my joy it is much reduced upon the day I finished: time will tell if it's gone.

The cleanse started with major blocked sinuses and they are much clearer now, but no doubt about it, I still have blocked sinuses.

I have been sneezing hard daily. Real Ka-Pows.

During the cleanse I had heaps of UFOs in my BMs almost daily.

These herbs had a large effect on me and I look forward to the aftermath to see how much better I will feel: will I be able to restart the yoga? I am at least 50 percent closer than at the start of these herbs.

I need to do these herbs again. Second round is always easier so nothing to fear.

Round 51 – 27th August 2010 – 4mg ALA

A straight 3-day ALA round that was a joy. This was one of those rounds where I am full of energy and DO things. I repaired the number plate on the car, made wooden covers for my log stacks in the garden and measured up the veggie patch for the raised beds. I also found some nice cheap wood for them too: scaffolding blanks with slight imperfections. £124 delivered: nice!

Going up to 5mg ALA should be no problem at all. I will wait until this batch of compounded 4mg run out before moving up.

I had a full medical health-check this week for my company health insurance. All my results came up splendid: liver fine, kidneys fine and even had no blood in urine which is a first in 20 years. My heart readings showed I had a good healthy strong heart and my blood pressure was perfect. Blood was fine. They analysed the blood for lots of dietary issues and I came out in the super-healthy league! The top 0.3pct of the people they test for antioxidants. That will be my super-cool diet! Respect!

Not that it means much. When I was sick they couldn't find anything wrong, so what's the hope of them detecting anything untoward now I am actually well again? But still, happy dayz! The doc said "It's nice to meet someone healthy for a change, well done."

My energy has returned after the Candida cleanse cleaned me up. Hooray, the side-effects were worth it! My only current issue is the blocked sinus. Cool, eh! And annoying! The one thing I really miss is my morning yoga and I can't practice because the bloody sinuses stop me being able to breathe through my nose. Ahhhhh!

The health-check doc recommended me a steroid based product to snort up my schnozzle. When she saw me curl my nose in disgust, she said salt water would probably do the trick too, Ha! And indeed it does.

I already have and know about something called a Neti pot.

This a special yoga teapot used to cleanse the nasal passages for easy nose breathing. It is basically a mini teapot. You fill it with lukewarm water and a bit of salt. Mix it all up, stick the nozzle in one nostril, tip your head to the side and let the salted water flow up your nose and out the other nostril. The water sucks out any snot and gunk as it passes through.

Funky and not as difficult or horrid as you might think, although it is a peculiar sensation at first. It is awesome at decongesting noses. Used daily for a month should give good results. I had forgotten about this. Thanks doc. (Google and YouTube "Neti Pot" for more instructions. Oh yeah, you want a Rhino Horn shaped one, or a NoseBuddy: they work best.)

As of 26th August 2010 I am using the neti pot daily. Let's see what happens.

End of round side effects: third day after the round I got a major bad neck, but was a one day wonder and was gone in two days. Odd.

Round 52 – 27th August 2010 – 4mg ALA

Nothing out of the ordinary to report. Did feel mildly tired on first day, but totally easy round. Feeling fine. Feeling normal. Life is great.

9th September 2010 – Humaworm Kidney Herbs

I'm doing this to see if it helps my adrenals. The adrenal glands sit directly on top of the kidneys and I'm working on the assumption that since they are connected to each other, the kidney herbs will help the adrenals. My adrenals are the only thing I take specific supplements for anymore. Everything else is managing fine without support. Cool, eh! And I know this cleanse does not cause me any hassles whatsoever and I can chelate at the same time.

Two weeks later: As hoped for, I had zero side effects from these guys. Kidney must be in good shape. Nice!

So the question is: did they help my adrenals? I really don't know, time will tell. It is autumn now and it's got cold outside, but I still feel warm and strong. I continue to support my adrenals with two caps of ACE (100mg.) My instinct tells me this was a fine thing to do, it also tells me to do it again. If I get no side effects, then I can do this anytime. Herbs only cost $19.95 so it's not expensive.

Oh, and another thing: I am completely symptom free now. My sinuses are clear. My furry tongue is clear. I have no ill-health, no dis-ease. I feel as healthy as can be. I guess you could say I need a bit more energy, yes, definitely, thinking about it, a little more energy would be cool. But yeah, 100 percent symptom free, really, amazing eh, wonderful, wow, damn I'm good!

So, how did I clear the sinus? Clear the furry tongue?

Well, the neti pot was 50 percent responsible. That neti pot is good, real good. Couldn't have done it without it. I highly recommend it, but that's not the whole story. It wasn't the kidney herbs either. No, the other 50 percent was from meditating. Weird, eh!

After all the fun stuff I have shared with you: the cat experiment, the colonic, the parasite cleanses, my colour vision returning, drinking the leek juice, I consider this beyond the thunderdome of weirdness. It is far out of my comfort zone and I have no idea how to explain it. I guess that's why it makes me uncomfortable discussing it.

Energy? Healing energy? Ever heard of that? You might have heard of Reiki? Ok, cool, good: I give up. I'm not gonna try. I will minimise this subject and move on quickly.

I cleared my nose and sinus by meditating. I generated healing energy using a special meditation I discovered along my travels. Something called Hemi-Sync. You listen to this special CD and it, errr, it, errmm, yeah, it vibrates your brain so that you go deep into a medative state. So deep you generate healing energy and can heal yourself. Told you. Funky beyond the thunderdome, I know.

I didn't even mean to. I was just exploring. I just stumbled on it. I was recommended it by a cool friend I met along my travels. It was just a bit of fun. I sat down, played the CD and meditated and Ka-Pow! I was overcome with a warm and fuzzy sensation all over, which focused on my sinus. Felt wonderful. Once I'd got a taste for it, I meditated five times a week for an hour each time. After four weeks of Neti pot use and two weeks of funky meditation, on 25th September 2010, I banished my remaining symptoms. Nice! That's how I roll: Winning!

These energy experiences are very personal and I struggle to talk about it here. I love it, but I don't understand it yet, so I'm not going to say any more. I will however say that if you ever get the chance to do any energy work, any mediation, any Hemi-Sync, any Reiki, meet any healers or do anything beyond the thunderdome: Go for it! They are all just other ways of healing, and you should know me by now; I just love trying out new fun things.

Reiki is getting pretty big now. If you look, you will find. If you ever have the chance to do the Reiki One degree, where you are taught to generate energy yourself: jump at the opportunity. That stuff's rock 'n' roll cool. And anyone can do it. Yes, anyone.

And if you do the first degree, I promise you the second degree is mind-blowing fun! If I ever write a second book it will be about my adventures in the wonderland of my mind.

Round 53 – 17th Sept 2010 – 4mg ALA

Easy round and nothing to report. Small amount of heartburn on day two and three after the round, but time to raise the dose. 5mg here we come!!

Round 54 – 8th October 2010 – 5mg ALA – 1 day

OK, time to try 5mg. I have run out of 4mg and now we will see if I can handle a bigger dose. That's 45mg ALA per day, instead of 36mg, spread over nine doses.

I am excited and worried in equal measure.

Day one was super-smooth but on the second day I missed a dose because I was in a meeting with the boss. I hesitated taking the cap, then forgot about it. I ended the round and nothing bad happened afterwards.

Village! I must focus!

13th October 2010 – Andreas Moritz Liver Herbs

After I got back from the biz trip in Singapore at the end of September I have felt a little tingly. I muscle tested myself asking questions about which set of herbs I should try to solve it and the answer was liver herbs.

Within 10 minutes of taking the herbs the tingly jitteriness returned in full force, accompanied by a massive headache. Plenty of water was required.

That was the first day. Everything has been unremarkable

since then. Day by day my BMs have become darker and darker. Tingly/jittery $hit has finished too. Nice! Another success.

Round 55 – 16th October 2010 – 5mg ALA

First full round at the increased dose of 5mg ALA. On the third day I was a little worn-out, but otherwise an easy round. The following after-round days were fine too.

Orange came blazing back, sparkling and attracting my attention wherever I saw it. I never really appreciated what a wonderful colour orange is! This stuff makes chelation worth it. Maybe when I don't get much colour returning during my rounds that should be a signal to try for a higher dose? Maybe. That's something to think about.

Round 56 – 29th October 2010 – 5mg ALA

"Look at those trees? Amazing, eh! So marvellous to see such beautiful colours. Autumn's a wonderful time of year isn't it, Sunshine?"

"Where?"

"There. See the leaves?"

"Where?"

"There, there, all along, right beside the motorway."

"Errrr, oh yeah, right, yeah, beautiful Mum, beautiful."

I remember being perplexed. What was she talking about? I saw trees. I saw leaves. They looked like normal boring old trees to me.

This is an old memory from my youth that has stayed with me over the years. I was twelve at the time. I guess I remember it because I knew I was missing something, I just didn't know what. I had an uncomfortable feeling of being deficient, of lacking what others automatically had.

And today, after all this time, I finally know what my mother was talking about. Today my eyes nearly popped out of my skull. Today a wild and crazy kaleidoscope of colours bombarded me as I drove down the motorway. All along the hard shoulder I saw the most amazing trees. It's autumn now and the leaves are just running riot with colour. Yellows and oranges shine out madly, dazzling. I even saw huge trees completely covered in red: I mean, the whole thing was, just, red man. Wild. I never seen anything so, anything like it at all.

At first I wondered if it was just a trick of the light, or just a patch of trees? But no, there it was, mile after mile. The vastness took my breath away. Everywhere I went the autumn leaves delighted my newfound senses.

This is what my mother was talking about.

This is what I have been missing.

Amazing. Amazing. Amazing.

• • •

OK, that's enough about chelation and herbal cleansing. I think you get the gist that I am symptom-free, happy and life has returned to normal again. My chelation regime continues, along with the herbs. I know there will be hiccups along my way; I will just have to figure them out as I go along. After all the problems I solved I am confident I can crack just about anything now. I know what to do, where to look and the people to ask.

It's almost five years since my health crashed after I had unsafe amalgam removal. It's three years since I went amalgam free. Three whole, long, full, hard, busy years. That's the kind of time line we are talking to rebuild a life, and I'm still not out the woods yet as I still have mercury in me. Some of the people battling mercury poisoning would consider three years swift.

Re-reading my own words reminds me just how difficult it all was. Looking back I can see the massive effort that was required. I had to do so many different things to help myself. I'm just happy I made it back to normality.

In some ways life is pretty similar to before I got sick. I have the same job in the city and now my health is fine I am good at it again. I have the same wife and kids, with the addition of my son. But the reality is I am incredibly different compared to four years ago when I knew nothing about health. Now I am back from death's door, now I have learnt so much, now I know how to look after myself, now life is good again, now I am happy: I am a very different beast. I guess we all have to grow up at some point. Learn to take care of ourselves correctly eventually. Only took me 40 years.

If you passed me in the street this afternoon, you would see just another city bloke, but I am different both inside and out. Gone are the wild nights, gone along with the temper and the shouting, the bad back, the chronic heartburn, the pain, ignorance and the years of suffering. The grimace is gone too.

The new me is a lot calmer, thoughtful and controlled. I am one of the more senior brokers in my firm and I have a team of brokers working under my direction now. Funny to think only four years previously I couldn't even take care of myself, let alone manage other people. No escaping the responsibility now.

That is the end of my story, and a happy ending it is too. However I will only ever write one book about mercury poisoning, so I'm not going to stop there. I want to get into more detail about my diet, the cleanses I did, and all the things I learned whilst I was sick.

I know that some of you just wanted to find out what happened to me—you can rest assured, I'm fine, life is cool. But I know a lot of you are reading this book because you are poisoned too and you want answers. I know, I was there.

Which is why I wrote this next part for you—to give you a bit more insight into what worked for me. Maybe it will work for you too? The main thing I'm going to talk about is my diet, and that's because diet is a huge topic and still remains absolutely key in my continued health today. But I touch on all manner of subjects because recovering from mercury poisoning changed my life and changed the way I see the world. While I was sick, I didn't have a lot of energy to think about it, but now that I'm well, I've had time to sit back, think and write about what all this means…

Part II

Life, The Universe and Everything—What I Learned on My Travels

59. Voodoo People

Every human has a toxic threshold whereby we can cope with a certain toxic load in our body. When that toxic threshold is breached, we can say our bodies cannot cope with any additional toxins, thereafter we will get sick. For healthy people, this threshold is pretty high. Their liver, kidneys, bowels etc. work fine, they can handle plenty of toxins. But for a person whose liver's detoxing capacity has been impaired by mercury, a small load of toxins can send them crashing over their threshold into illness.

This is why seemingly small toxins can suddenly make life a misery for some of us. It's why one small thing tips people over the edge and they are never healthy again. Ever wondered why people suffer from hay fever? Why some people can't handle chorine in swimming pools? Or mould? Or milk? Or wheat? Or peanuts? Or perfume? It's not just an allergic reaction to that one thing, but it's a whole host of other toxins in that person, tipping them over their toxic threshold, and their bodies are unable to cope. It's a tip of the iceberg scenario.

Mercury is one of the biggest toxins our bodies will ever have to handle, but it is by no means the only one. There are copious toxins on all sides, lurking in the most unsuspected places. Some are obvious, some obscure, some totally non-believable. Certainly I didn't believe when I first started this journey. Back then I would have laughed in your face had you told me.

First up, about one million cells die every second in your body. Obviously they are replaced by new cells re-growing, but the dead cells still need removing.

This dying and renewing process is totally normal. It is why we have built-in waste-disposal units all around our body and why we take so many dumps in our lives. This waste is dead, and unless it is removed in a timely fashion, it festers and becomes toxic. You don't want it hanging around attracting vermin.

Obviously toxins come from our environment too: car and lorry fumes, factory fumes, aerosol cans, fumes from paint, mercury from amalgams. Less obvious, but nevertheless still there: from household products, bleach, detergents, makeup, shampoos, toothpastes, soaps, fire retardant chemicals, chlorine in swimming pools, vaccinations, fluorescent light bulbs, plastics and even tap water has toxins in it from the processing plant.

There is a massive list of environmental toxins that hurt humans, I could go on for pages and pages, and most people would disregard most of that list. Why ignore it? Because it is simply inconceivable that so many things could be toxic to humans. Conventional wisdom dictates that this cannot be true.

Diet is a major source of toxins to us too. Our culture is awash with toxic and poor quality food. Foodstuffs so masticated, pasteurised, homogenised, hydrogenised, refined and mashed-up that most nutritional value is lost and the food is turned into a slow poison, invisible only because the vast majority consume it.

You would laugh if you looked at the supermarket shelves through my new-found eyes. Even I find it spooky and surreal: aisle upon aisle of boxed, canned and spammed food that I consider worthless junk unfit for human consumption. Potato chips fried at super-high temperatures in cheap rancid oil. Pre-made meals made with the cheapest ingredients, wrong oils, maximum E numbers and all ready to be nuked in the microwave. Vegetable oils and margarine both have bad names these days, but the shops are still full of it. Fresh milk with a shelf-life of 21 days? Lettuce surviving ten days in a sealed plastic bag? That's not natural, because it's not natural.

If you see anything that looks too good to be true...then it probably is, and supermarkets stuffed to the gunnels with incomprehensibly cheap food fits that bill with five gold stars. Chickens bred in factories 17 to 20 birds per square metre, that never see the light of day, fed on the cheapest feed they can get away with, that cost the same as two cups of coffee also comes under the too-good-to-be-true category. I guess the cheapness blinds most people.

Then we move on to toxins in the form of sugars, synthetic sweeteners, rancid oils, and chemicals like MSG. They are everywhere and almost completely unavoidable for normal people going about normal lives.

Avoiding the thousands of dietary chemicals takes real and serious effort. The food producers have even managed to persuade our wonderful food authorities that some added chemicals don't need to be included on the ingredients list on the packet. The mind boggles, eh!

This is where the bulk of our everyday toxins come from: our diet. I make impressive efforts to avoid chemical, toxic, bad, lifeless food. And I make even greater efforts to make sure the food I do eat is good for me. The quality of the food we eat is vital to making our bodies work correctly. Every single part of the body is made up of the food we eat. I consider the food I eat as medicine and I require the best medicine available. We are what we eat, and now that I have detoxed I am free to digest what I eat too.

Let's not forget mercury is a gigantic toxin to the body. It is the most poisonous, non-radioactive, naturally occurring substance known to man. There is no safe level of mercury because even one atom will harm the body. It does not target one organ, or even one part of your body. The mercury leaks out, circulates around the body, gets transported in the blood, and poisons everywhere. Everywhere, everywhere, everywhere. It is important to understand this: the mercury is everywhere in the body.

The mercury comes to us in small packages. It's not like we swallowed a bar of gold and can just fish it out in one easy swoop. No, most of us got poisoned by a slow gradual process over many years from a variety of different sources and sizes: mercury vapour leaking from amalgam fillings inhaled through our lungs, vaccinations, travel shots, allergy shots, flu jabs, medicines, fish consumption, even broken light bulbs. All these exposures come in small amounts and are distributed all around the body, accumulating little by little, poisoning us in every nook and cranny.

The mercury concentrates in the parts of your body that detox. That's the liver, kidneys and digestive tract. But even though it accumulates, the mercury still goes everywhere: any fatty tissue it will sit on, nothing is immune. But it always accumulates in those organs because that's their job; to detox you. Unfortunately they get damaged, and then they struggle, and then we struggle.

Yes, we are surrounded by a toxic soup that is incredibly hard to avoid. Sure, some toxins are big and some are small, but even if they are small, which healthy people can easily handle, they are still a toxin that our bodies must handle.

Like my mattress impregnated with fire retardant chemicals. I was so toxic that it tipped me over my toxic threshold and it made me sick. But my beautiful wife slept like an angel on the very same toxic mattress. She was not sick, she was not toxic and her strong body could easily handle that toxin no problem. The toxin was there all the same, she could handle it, I could not.

Individually each little toxin is almost insignificant, but collectively all the hundreds of different little hurts build up and cause devastation to those who have crossed their toxic threshold.

When I was at my sickest, even the smallest of the small toxin hurt me. Remember the Great Raw Cat Food Experiment, the passive smoking, one mouthful of tomato soup, one sip of beer?

Add all the different toxins together, mix 'em up, shake 'em around, smear them everywhere and you have your typical mercury toxic person well and truly over their toxic limit asking:

"Why are so many things wrong? Why does nothing seem to help?"

Let's think about the liver for a moment. If you place your hand over the right side of your ribs, just under your nipple, your hand will just about cover the area of your liver. It has a wide range of jobs, about 500 at last count. It handles waste from your body, makes bile for digestion, manufactures and regulates your hormones and has the job of taking care of toxins coming in from the outside world. It is a busy chap and is the largest internal organ you have.

A poor diet will not help for smooth operation. Toxins from our environment will stress it and once the mercury starts coming in, the harm really kicks in. It's a gradual process, slowly getting more clogged up and damaged over the course of your life. As time passes, it cannot do all its jobs. It gets backed-up and you start accumulating toxins. Not just mercury, but all different types of toxic waste build up and are unable to be removed by the malfunctioning liver. This is when life starts getting tough.

As more time passes, toxic levels build up to even greater heights and make the liver function even worse. The longer this goes on, the longer toxins keep coming in that cannot be processed, the worse the liver functions and the worse we feel. It goes into a vicious circle of ever-decreasing function.

It's not just mercury that this misfiring liver can't handle. It still has 500 other jobs it must do all the time. Not a pretty thought, eh! Obviously this has knock-on consequences all over the body.

This unfortunate situation, vicious circle, applied to everything in me. Most of my internal organs were mercury damaged. The ones that were not directly mercury toxic were fatigued, overwhelmed, congested and backed up because everything else was working sub-standard. The result was a downward spiral of health. In my case it took 37 years to come to a head.

How long did it take you?

Avoiding as many toxins as possible obviously goes without saying. You can't swim in a sea of toxins without getting wet. Learn what is toxic and avoid it. In my opinion avoidance is nowhere near enough for people loaded with mercury. We passed the point of no return a long time ago. Avoidance is essential, it gives the body a chance to recover, but it is just another rung on the ladder.

In order to get seriously better, there are two possible solutions:

First up, chelation can remove the mercury. This is done safely using the Cutler protocol, and unsafely and dangerously via other stupid chelation protocols. This takes two to five years. That's a long time and chelation is hard work.

Second, we can speed the process, lighten the load and make our life considerably easier if we can detox any congested gunk out of the malfunctioning organs, the liver in this example. If we find ways to de-gunk the liver, the liver will be free to work much better than before. Sure, it still has mercury buggering it up, but with the congested gunk gone, it functions oh so much better and you don't feel like a sack o' cacko anymore.

This same thing applies to every organ in your body. If you clean out the liver, the digestive tract, the kidneys, the lungs, the blood and everything else you can find out about, they will all function a great deal better, and you will feel a great deal better too. Chelation will be considerable easier as your body will be stronger and more able to cope with the hard labour of removing the mercury.

Imagine all those toxins and mercury inside you are pins sticking in a voodoo doll. Each little toxin, in each little place in your body, represents a little pin stuck into the voodoo doll. If you are very sick, you are a voodoo doll that is covered head to toe in pins. Each pin that you pull out relieves a little of the pain, but until you remove a lot of pins, or a lot of toxins, you are gonna remain in agony. Alternative healthcare, herbal cleansing and chelation are the tools to remove the pins that are in the voodoo doll, that is your body.

And phew! That's what the all these weird and wonderful things do: they clean up the mess caused by the mercury. It is why I got better even though I am still full of mercury. I know I am still full of mercury because when I take chelators I still get reactions.

You will have to decide for yourself who is holding the voodoo doll and sticking the pins in. Apart from yourself of course! (Ouch!)

60. Good plan, Batman

I had such amazing results from the herbs I did not stop taking them. And why stop? During each cleanse I got plenty of signals the herbs were working. After each and every set, without exception, I felt better than before, and sometimes gigantically better. That feeling of healing is a fine feeling too, addictive. So I embarked on body-cleansing rounds, moving around the body cleaning each zone.

There was method to the madness too. I was not just willy-nilly doing herbs. I was following a well-trodden path. I came across numerous healing protocols out there, written in the many health books, websites, forums and blogs that discussed everything in great and graphic detail. Each person, guru and company had their own preferred style and methods, but the fundamentals were all the same: clean out the body and provide it with the raw materials to rebuild.

The protocol I found the simplest to follow and the best explained is the one online at Curezone.com. It's at the very top of the main page, on an insignificant little tab called 'Health':
http://curezone.com/diseases/health.asp

Curezone Healing Protocol
Diet clean up and food education
Bowel cleanse
Parasite cleanse (can be done at the same time as the bowel cleanse)
Dental clean up (amalgams, root canals, nickel crowns, cavitations)
Kidney cleanse
Liver cleanse

This was my base camp in my dark hours. It goes into detail about each topic, giving plenty of differing options to try, together with examples of people's experiences and what happened to them. Having options is important. Not everything agrees. I dislike sticking tubes up my arse, it's just not cricket. I needed other options for cleansing the bowels. Travelling around Curezone, I found more palatable choices that suited me. To my mind, taking capsules for a herbal bowel cleanse is an infinitely more civilised way to clean out the digestive tract.

The list is not complete either. This is just the starting point. I still had to figure out mercury chelation, adrenals, thyroids, and the lung cleanses I did were life changing too.

After five years of use, the cleanses are straightforward now. Gone are the wild and extreme reactions, gone along with all my symptoms of ill-health. My body is cleaner, so I get much fewer side-effects. I still get a few, which is why I do them, but everything is calm and gentle. I am a pro now too. They are so easy; it's a no-brainer.

In the last four years I have done the following:

Bowel cleanse x 7 = 7 months
Parasite cleanse x 7 = 7 months
Kidney cleanse x 8 = 5.5 months
Liver cleanse x 1 = 14 days
Liver flush x 10 = 10 weekends
Lung cleanse x 2 = 30 days
Essiac Tea x 2 = 3 months
Castor oil packs for liver+kidney cleansing about x 50-60
Detox baths x 100+

In amongst all that I have also done:
73 chelation rounds,
Full environment detox,
Worked my full time job,
Reinvented my cooking,
Wrote a book,
And kept my family!

Yes, life is full and yes, time flies even faster when you are well again.

• • •

Once I started doing the right things, in the right order, I reversed my decline, climbed my ladder and was 75 percent better within 18 months. I would do each cleanse one after the other, with a little gap in-between of maybe three to seven days to let any side-effects dissipate. Bowel, parasite, kidney, liver and any other herbal formulas I found, like the lung cleanse.

The only things I did together were the bowel and the parasite cleanse, because they go hand in hand. It is recommended they are done together, but even those I did separately too, just to see what happened.

Each cleanse is 15 or 30 days long, so it's about four months with no breaks for a full body round of herbal cleaning. But I was chelating in-between too, so it was taking me five to six months.

In the beginning, I didn't know that mercury had smashed everything. I didn't know about any protocol, nor the order of cleansing. I was not thinking of my body as a whole, and that it might need treating as a whole. My health care knowledge was patchy and in its infancy. Consequently I did things as I discovered them, and I did everything in the wrong order.

I did the strongest, most powerful and widely recommended things first. I did the liver flushes, then the kidney cleanse, then the parasite cleanse, all in the midst of amalgam removal. So, according to the Curezone protocol, I did things completely arse-about-face.

In that backwards style I experienced and learnt an incredibly important concept: There is an order to healing the body. Some things 100 percent need doing before others. Some organs need cleaning before others can be cleaned.

I only started getting better when I did the bowel and parasite cleanse. I did lots of things beforehand, but I only started healing when I did the first things first. The bowels must be clean and cleared of gunk in order for whole body healing to take place. This is a basic prerequisite when healing the body.

So far, I have done seven full-body rounds, moving around the body using different sets of herbs to cleanse different parts of me. I am always doing some form of cleaning, be it chelation or a set of herbs. Every week I do something to help myself without fail. To date I've been at it five years. That probably sounds like a long time, five years, but I take one day at a time and it's just part of life now. I think of these herbal cleanses exactly the same as I do as brushing my teeth daily; it's just part of life and no big deal. No one sees, no one notices and no one knows I am detoxing and rejuvenating my body all the time. What's to see, except another city chap strolling around the city?

61. If the herbs are so good, why do I have to keep taking them?

For herbal body cleansing the Curezone plan of action is one powerful and super-fine protocol to follow in your quest to get better. Notice first on the list, before you attack anything, is diet education. Education is key!

Anyone sick and in pain will make great gains in their health if they do this protocol. This is not a special protocol solely for mercury toxic people. It's not secret and you don't need to learn any special hand-shakes in order to do it. It's an all-purpose, general healing regime for humans, used since the dawn of time. The knowledge is free and the tools pretty cheap because herbs are never expensive. Sure the dental clean-up can be costly, but the mercury tap must be turned off in order stop the perpetual flow of poison from polluting the body. The most expensive part of the protocol is your time, but if you don't have time for yourself, then you are doomed in any case.

The answer to every single problem we have is out there somewhere. If you take the time to look, you will find. If you did two full body rounds of herbs, that would take you 8 to 12 months. In the context of how long it took to get sick, that's not very long.

Important message to those in a rush: The herbal cleanses and chelation are powerful things. I have seen plenty of people in a rush to get better. They try lots of things simultaneously in a mad rush to heal. Like parasite cleansing and chelating together, or throwing twenty new supplements at themselves overnight, or thyroid and adrenal support chucked around like confetti. Rush, rush, rush.

It's pretty common; health plummets, they discover a host of new methods to try, everything seems to need doing and they do it all. I did the same too in the beginning. Luckily for me, I was so sick I quickly learned to do one thing at a time!

It's great to be keen, essential even, but you need to keep your head screwed on. You need to think. How long have you been sick? Five years? Ten years? Twenty years? Forty years? How long do you seriously think, and I mean look-me-in-the-eyes-serious, how long do you think it will take to clean up the mess after all these years?

Let's take me as an example. I had amalgams for at least 20 years. I had poor health for over 10 years, 5 of which were hellhole-chronic. Do I think one month's worth of herbs will undo all those years of hurt? Do we really think 30 days is going to heal 10 years' worth of ill health for my liver? Thirty years of poor diet? Thirty five years of mercury poisoning?

No, of course not. No way. Our bodies do not work like that. It takes time. It's important to keep this sense of perspective. It takes time to get sick, and it takes time to heal. Luckily it takes not nearly as long to get better! Only one or two years, but nevertheless, time is required. Each organ will need a respectable about of time and effort to clean, unclog, stimulate and rejuvenate. And remember, things need doing in the right order too.

If you rush and try to do different things at the same time, you may get hurt. Not dead-hurt, but painful-hurt nevertheless. And pain is a powerful teacher. This hurt may scare you away from health regaining activities that could really help. Because you combined it with some other powerful detox, you overloaded your system and now you are too scared to retry.

It's like learning to juggle. At first you start with one ball, then two, then after a while three, but if you keep adding balls before you have learned how to juggle correctly, they will all fall to the floor.

Keep things simple and listen to your body.

When we try a method of healing, we need to read the signs our bodies give us. We need to know what it does to us. If we combine different things together, how are we to know what causes what?

We need to adjust the dosage to a level that suits too. We need to know what causes us to itch, bitch, rant, rave, moan, groan, laugh out loud, get horny, sing with joy, or radiate love. If you get no reactions, maybe that action does not need doing again. If you get loads of reactions, maybe you need to try something gentler.

Keep things simple so you can see where you are going.

Just as chelation is slow and steady wins the race, so it is too with herbal cleansing. It's a marathon, not a sprint. It took us many years to get sick. It will not take so long to get better, but you need to have a realistic timeline for your healing. One 15-day cleanse is not going to undo 20 years of neglect. Take your time because your body needs time.

And yes, I know exactly what it's like when nothing's working and the urge is to do anything and everything we discover immediately. But my strong and firm advice is one at a time, in the correct order. If you have never done a cleanse before, then you should use your common sense and start slow and see how it goes.

I guess at some point you wondered why I needed to repeatedly use the different sets of herbs. If they are so good, why must I keep taking them? They must be rubbish if it takes so long!

It's a good question and the answer is easy: I continue to cleanse because I am still mercury toxic. I still have deranged mineral transport. I still chelate. My organs still contain mercury and they still don't work 100 percent. So I allocate a small part of my life to the herbal cleanses. They keep me well.

Chelation is hard work. Every time I chelate, I drag some mercury around my body. That hurts and damages me a little and my body must handle it, kidneys and liver particularly work overtime when chelating. I chelate at low doses so the damage is minimal, but it's still hardcore. The herbal cleanses clean up the damage caused by the mercury, but also any further damage done on the chelation road too.

Further reading: *Timeless Secrets of Health & Rejuvenation* by Andreas Moritz

62. To supplement or not to supplement, that is the question

I had fun with my supplements! On the surface it seems such a simple subject: pop pills, get better. But the deeper you delve, the trickier it gets. Figuring out what I needed, when to take it, in what quantity, what helped, what made me worse, which company to use, and when to stop taking them is almost an art-form in itself. There are thousands of options and it's all a bit daunting at first.

It's important to get it right because correct supplementation makes the difference between a good life and a miserable life. When I was at my worst I was taking 20 different supplements in divided doses each day; morning, lunch, dinner and bedtime. Some just one pill a day, but others I was popping 10 a day.

This lot kept me up and running after the unprotected amalgam removal took me down: calcium, vitamin D, vitamin B12, vitamin C, boron, milk thistle, zinc, molybdenum, magnesium, betaine and pepsin, GTF chromium, multi vitamin B, taurine, probiotics, Himalayan rock salt, COQ10, ACE, Armour, flax oil and fish oil. I was rattling like a coin in a can.

The effort I put into understanding my hair test proved priceless here as it gave me the starting points I needed. I knew which parts of me were screwed and Cutler's *Hair Test Interpretation* book very kindly recommend the pills and potions to support them. I also cross-checked everything I took in *Amalgam Illness* to make sure I got the correct type, dosage and didn't fry my brain.

At first, I went to the supermarket, bought a load of the cheapest multi-vitamins and just chucked them down my neck randomly. Luckily I was so sick I quickly learnt this was wrong and that more care was required! I discovered that not all pills are created equal. I learnt the best supplements are those that come from nature. Supplements made from natural things that once lived. The calcium I take is made from seaweed for example.

Cheap man-made synthetic options just didn't cut the mustard with me and my mangled body. Seventy five percent of the cheap synthetic supplements just caused me more problems and that was the last thing I needed. I learnt to carefully monitor myself when starting new pills. I checked each by muscle testing and I quickly learnt to go with nature. I just read the labels in detail and if there were too many x, y, z's, that supplement was not for me. If you look, you will find. There is a market for everything, including whole food supplements.

Because I knew specifically the quantity and type of supplement my body might need, I mostly used single-ingredient supplements and shied away from multi-vitamins. That way, when I introduced a new supplement, I knew precisely if it was suitable or not. If you take a multi-vitamin with 20 ingredients and it disagrees, there is no way of knowing which ingredient caused the problem and you will have learnt nothing.

I knew from my terrible experience with cysteine (NAC), when I lost a couple of months of my life, that each supplement needed introducing at a low dose and gradually raising to the target level to ensure it didn't mash me. Some only took a few days, but the adrenal and thyroid supplements turned into a bit of a saga with months and months required to find the correct dosage.

Each new supplement also needed introducing individually when nothing else drastic was going on. Chelation or herbs might give me side effects and I would be unable to see if the new supplement was hurting or helping me. Patience was required, but again I was lucky; I was so ill, every time I pushed it I discovered my error pretty damn quick. I like to think I learn from my mistakes too!

Some of the so-called experts say all supplements should be stopped during chelation rounds. They say the chelation agents somehow suck up the supplements and they are wasted. Cutler says that's wrong. He says that it is the body itself using the extra vitamins and minerals in its efforts to cope with and remove the poisonous mercury that has been mobilised on the chelation round.

I tried both styles and I 100 percent felt better on continuous dosing and from that I believe Cutler must be correct. It is our body working over-time, using extra energy whilst it's got the tough job of disposing of the mercury.

There are a huge variety of opinions on the value of supplements, some people think they do more harm than good and should all be completely avoided. I know first-hand that some are harmful; but which and what is individual to each person. A blanket statement that all supplements are harmful seems fanciful.

Well, one day an incredible herbalist on Curezone.com convinced me that I didn't need my huge array of supplements and that my diet was good enough on its own. I had a pretty cool diet and I was curious to know if he was right. You read so many different points of view out there. Everyone seems equally persuasive and sometimes you just have to suck it and see. Must have been feeling particularly punchy that week!

I stopped everything except my adrenal and thyroid support and went cold turkey on 13 supplements. My health rapidly went downhill with all manner of aches and pains and a general lack of energy surrounded me. I stuck it out for ten days to make sure, but it was obvious I was in much poorer health without the supplements. I restarted everything and within a week, I was back to how I was before.

It was an interesting experiment and I don't regret one dodgy week of trying out a new idea. I'd spent a lot of time and energy getting the supplements right, not to mention my hard earned cash, so it was good to know that it was worth it and that they actually worked. After that experiment I took my supplements religiously every day. If I missed a day it was no big deal, but if I missed two or three days, then my health started to stumble.

Knowing if specific supplements are harmful or helpful is pretty tricky, but what I didn't realise was that stopping them was just as challenging. I used some supplements daily for over two years and I knew they were essential when I was sick. What I didn't know was that when I had recovered, those same supplements would make me sick again. Ha! Crazy, eh! It's not like there was a sign post, or a noticeable turning point reached along the road that indicated I didn't need a pill. I got better gradually, not with the flick of a switch.

And I assure you it's difficult stopping something you think is helping and supporting. In the cold light of day it's easy to point the finger and say what a cock I was for over-medicating with Armour. But at the time, I was sure I needed those pills. Figuring out I didn't need them took time, effort and balls.

But it is not just the Armour that turned out to be a problem; it was the same with most of the other supplements too: molybdenum, magnesium, niacinamide, zinc, vitamin B12, multi vitamin B, taurine, COQ10 all gave me trouble once I was better. As I gradually got better, my body no longer needed so many supplements and because I was better, they actually started to make me sick. Once I understood this, I took 10 minutes out every couple of months to muscle test everything to see if any were harming me. The muscle tester dude helped too. Each time I saw him we tested everything I was on.

It's worth having a chat about oils: I learned that once oils are refined, once they come into contact with the air, they start deteriorating: oxidisation. The cold slows down the deterioration, but there is a definite shelf life for refined oils, just like anything else. This applies to all the oils available: sesame, flax seed, cod liver, borage, rapeseed, sunflower, canola, butter, coconut and olive oil.

Remember my dodgy oil experience when my wife could smell the rancid oil from across the room? That was not the only iffy oil experience either: I had similar problems with all the various oils I took as health supplements, so I'm a lot more cautious with them now. I have ditched all the new-fangled oils and my philosophy is to stick with tradition and Mother Nature: olive oil, coconut oil and butter. There is a reason they have been used down through the ages: they are naturally stable, they last the longest, degrade the slowest, and taste the best.

Fish oil seems to be important, everyone recommends it for the Omega 3, EPA, DHA, vitamin A and D. I occasionally get some, and I buy the best quality I know about (Green Pastures). Not sure why, but it only agrees with me in small doses of one or two weeks. After that it starts harming me. As I said, no idea why when everyone categorically assures everyone that it's essential to life.

When consuming oils, you want virgin where possible too. That means no mucking about, just straight from the plant. All this filtering, de-odorising, hydrogenation; all that refining is to delay the oil from going rancid, disguise the smell when it does, and robbing it of any health-giving properties in the process. The heavily refined oils, canola and sunflower for example, have been messed around with by industry and are too volatile to be of any value to human health. There is masses of literature on how poisonous some of them are, or become, when they turn rancid.

The funky-exotic-rancid-oil issue comes down to money. Some clever people can make weird oils that are cheaper than traditional oils. They then sell you the dream: Magic Bean oil.

Supplementation is for sure a tricky bloody subject. Without muscle testing I have no idea how people figure it out. I guess just trial and error. Stopping each supplement and seeing what happens. I know people don't check their supplements too much. They don't introduce them one at a time to see if there is a good or bad reaction. I know few people muscle test them, or have any method of checking to see if their supplements help or hinder. They buy their supplements and automatically assume they are a help. Pity really, I know it's not as simple as that.

I have greatly reduced the number of my supplements now I'm better, but I still chelate and chelation is hard so I continue with a few. The adrenal supplements (ACE) are essential to my well-being and I will be on those until all the mercury is out, or one of the cleanses heals them up. I did try going off them in January 2011, but had to reintroduce them after six weeks of dwindling health. In May 2011, when I have no symptoms of ill health but am still chelating I supplement: vitamin C, calcium, magnesium, chromium and 100mg ACE.

63. Meet the Fockers

The lifestyle changes and looking after myself extends to my family too. My wife and kids are all healthier now because of the much better diet we eat and the toxin-free household we live in. Their diet is no-where near as wild as mine, but it is a million miles better than many others. At least the choice of healthy food is on the table even if they don't always eat it.

My wife has joined me trying some herbs too. Top girl! In January each year the whole family does a 30-day parasite cleanse. We consider it a service for our bodies, just like you service your car yearly.

Wives and kids go hand in hand and I must say my wife was awe-some in handling me when I was oh so sick, listening to me, trusting me, and then implementing the diet changes I asked for our family. Total reinvention of shopping habits and cooking style was required to accommodate my newfound dietary knowledge. I work 10 hours-plus a day and the easiest thing in the world would have been to ignore my health-freak requests. I was most troublesome when I was at my worst.

My 10-year-old daughter has bravely done a couple of kid's herbal cleanses with me too. Top girl! She was not ill or sick, but was re-warded with being happier and a more contended kid. Her diet also became less fussy and the range of different foods she ate increased. All of which was completely invisible to her. Which is pretty cool consider-ing all it took was a few cheap herbs taken over 30 days and zero side effects. She was happy to play a part in my health quest, happy to help her health and overjoyed with the Playmobil Zoo she got at the end. Bribery never fails with kids!

My son arrived in the midst of my health and diet renaissance and I guess the little chap has benefited the most. He is three years old now, has had zero vaccinations and was exclusively breast fed with not one drop of that wicked baby formula milk.

One of the first things I did was to read up and research baby formula feed. I must say it made me feel the most disgusted and ashamed to be human I can ever remember feeling. The things these companies do to sell a product is gross in the extreme. I could maybe, if I squint out the corner of my eye, think it's not so bad to force on grown adults. But to newborn babies; mate, that's a bloody disgrace. Those people/companies need to get their priorities right, get a life, grow up, act their age and go away somewhere far far away from me. I would advise everyone on earth to avoid baby formula. It takes time to research, but Google it and be sickened. (See link at the end of this chapter for more info.)

The decision not to vaccinate was a big one, but an easy one for me. Many of the alternative healthcare books I'd already read had sections on the dangers of vaccinating. The mercury forums are awash with young mothers chelating their autistic kids too, some of whom I know personally.

I like to get low down and dirty with these types of important issues, so I bought a couple of books that dealt specifically with vaccinations and educated myself even more. Once you learn about a subject, the decision-making process becomes infinitely easier. Once you understand how the body works and what is expected of you to keep it working, the idea of injecting babies with weird medicines makes no sense whatsoever. And especially if those weird medicines contain known mega-poisons. With knowledge you can see the lies and bull$hit shining brightly like a full moon on a clear night.

Who do you believe? Huge corporations that flog the jabs and pocket millions of dollars? The naive doctors who blindly peddle them? Or the mothers who watched their beautiful children turn autistic after getting vaccinated? Don't believe mercury is in the vaccinations? Then why do autistic kids who chelate mercury get better?

What are the figures now? They seem to change for the worse every year. One in a thousand kids is autistic? One in a hundred? One in ten? No one knows for sure, but it's a lot and it's a very serious issue. From my point of view there is no need to take the risk of vaccinating against uncommon, non-lethal diseases when there is a massive chance that the vaccination could harm my son.

I am not a number. I am not a statistic. I am not some random passer-by. I don't give a $hit about herd immunity. This is me and my son, right here and right now. If I screw up, it's his life on the line. I'm in charge of him.

I have educated myself and I choose not to trust twats that treat me as a statistic.

Just like everyone else my age, I have been injected with all vaccinations, inoculations and travel shots known to man. I since learnt that most of those jabs contained mercury. I now know mercury is a vicious poison that is mostly responsible for my health crash. So yeah, the decision not to vaccinate my beautiful new son was as easy as falling off a log. No way in a million years.

But it was not so easy for my wife. She is not a health freak. She has not read countless books about the dangers of thimerosal in vaccinations. She does not know any mothers chelating their kids. All she knew was that 95 percent of the western population get vaccinated, and here I was demanding that our new kid on the block should not be.

This was all happening as I was starting to be normal-ish after being super-sized-sick for two years. It is difficult to believe sick people, even if they are loved ones. It's counter-intuitive. I know she had a tough time believing the information in front of her. Who to believe? Mad husband? Mad doctors? Mad governments?

Anyway, she chose well, trusted well and now has one super-cool, super-happy, super-healthy son. He sets the standards for good behaviour, good sleeping and good health. He has slept through the night, every night, since he was four months old. In his three years alive he has had some runny noses, mild chickenpox and that's it. No other major health issues whatsoever.

When his teeth arrived we had none of the usual crying and up-at-night-ness that is habitually associated with teething. All he had were rosy cheeks. Every teething day was just a normal happy day for him.

When he started on solids he ate virtually everything we put in front of him and he only ate whole foods, zero junk, zero baby food pots and no refined sugar. In fact the first food he ever refused was a pot of organic baby food. Why? It's pasteurised and taste it yourself: bland. I'm sure it will change when he gets older, the bad stuff is completely unavoidable, but I know he's had a fine start to life.

Weston A. Price would be proud, especially since his words have so greatly influenced me. In fact, his words have proved true. He predicted that kids on his healthy diet would be like this: happy, contented, calm, strong, healthy kids. If you saw the little chap you would see one of the happiest lads around. He cries when he is hungry, tired and with the odd bump, but that's about it. No colic, no up at night, no mystery crying, and never had nappy rash.

I must say I put it all down to the changes in our lifestyle we made. The clean house, clean diet and particularly the decision not to vaccinate. I must also sing the praises of my fantastic wife for listening to, and somehow believing her sick and now better husband. It would have been the easiest thing in the world to show me the door. I am lucky to have such a patient and understanding lady.

Further reading for baby formula feed: Google 'Replacing mother imitating human breast milk in the laboratory' by the Cornucopia Institute. (Free download)

Further reading for vaccinations:

The Truth about Vaccines: Making the Right Decision for Your Child by Richard Halvorsen

Vaccination Is Not Immunization by Tim O'Shea

64. Breakfast at Sunshine's

My diet is unrecognisable from what it was before all this started. Today I take great care and attention to make my food as life-giving as possible. Most of my diet is from Weston A. Price and Sally Fallon's influence on me. They speak with powerful voices, instilled with the almost-forgotten wisdom from our collective forefathers.

Their diet is the one that made the most sense and that I immediately grasped and understood. Reading Weston Price's masterpiece *Nutrition and Physical Degeneration* collated all my dietary knowledge and merged it into my daily life. It worked pretty well too; my good health is a testament to its effectiveness.

I follow their diet recommendations as well as possible, but I don't walk around with their book under my arm quoting passages to random waiters. A little compromise is inevitable because I live and work in the real world. I do the best I can given the business lifestyle I lead.

Life is full and I have little time to faff about. My diet takes modest pre-planning, but little actual time. Brown rice takes 45 minutes to cook, not 15 like white rice. Pre-soaking it takes 30 seconds, provided I remember I will be eating rice that evening. Some organisation is required, but little else once the basic concepts are understood.

Breakfast: Sometimes I start the day with homemade bread. The wheat/rye or spelt is organic and is freshly ground using an electric stone mill I have at home. Home-milling enables me to get the full benefit of all the goodness in the grains. Nothing is taken out, so nothing is lost. Importantly no nutrients are lost to oxidation either because it's done there and then. There is not enough time for anything to go rancid either.

This freshly-milled flour is then soaked overnight in kefir (a type of homemade yogurt). Whole grains contain phytic acid which combines with some minerals, especially calcium, magnesium, copper, iron and zinc and prevents absorption in the digestive tract. You don't really want that.

Soaking, or fermenting the grain beforehand will neutralise this phytic acid. This in turn increases vitamin content and makes all the nutrients in the grain more available to your body for easy absorption and digestion. To mill the grain takes two minutes: weigh out the wheat, pour into mill and press the ON button. Et voila, freshly-milled whole grain flour.

I use a bread maker because with the best will in the world, I have a full-on job and no time for hand-made bread. I did try, but no time in my busy life. But for bread-maker bread, it's an eight-minute job before I go to bed a couple of times a week. In the morning the mouth-watering smell of hot fresh bread floats around the house.

The butter I spread on is made from raw milk, delivered weekly along with raw milk. This is eaten with raw cheese, or honey, or home-made nut butter, or organic ham, or eggs or a combo of whatever I have hanging around. It's a fine way to start the day.

Muesli

If I don't have bread for breakfast, maybe I will have homemade muesli. The oats are freshly ground in the same stone mill the evening before and soaked overnight in kefir, again to neutralise the phytic acid. Again this pre-soaking makes all the goodness in the oats bio-available to my body. It is how our grandmothers used to prepare oats/porridge but has been forgotten in the sands of time in our world of instant satisfaction. All the rest of the usual muesli ingredients are organic; dates, figs, raisins, nuts, seeds and I always cut up some fresh fruit with that too. All mixed up with raw milk or kefir. No need for a mid-morning snack after this fit-for-a-king breakfast.

Other breakfast meals

If not bread and cheese or muesli, then breakfast could be brown rice, or eggs, or leftovers from the night before. When I feel the need for a mega vitamin hit I will have a liquid-only breakfast. Maybe a pint of raw milk, or maybe kefir, or maybe a fruit smoothie made with kefir, or maybe freshly-juiced veggies or fruits, or soup, or a combo.

Pre-health-crash I would have devoured a bacon sandwich three hours after I'd got up. Anything earlier made me gag. Now I need an early and a big breakfast every day. I need the energy and it sets me up a treat for the day's action.

Nuts

We eat a lot of nuts and seeds; cashew, almond, brazil, walnut, pumpkin seeds. The nut butter is greatly loved by the kids so there is often some around. The nuts and seeds are soaked for 4 to 12 hours in salted water, and then dehydrated in the oven on super-low heat for 48 hours. I buy in bulk, soak in bulk, dehydrate in bulk. It is piss easy and it just a matter of being organised. Takes five minutes of my time in total over two and a half days.

Why soak the nuts and seeds? A nut is a nut when it's just sitting there on the side. There are things inside that nut that stop it growing into a nut tree. Those things, called enzyme inhibitors, also stop you digesting the nut. This is why it is recommended that you don't eat too many nuts and seeds at any one time. You are not physically able to digest too many nuts at once because of the enzyme inhibitors inside them.

Soaking the nut makes the nut think it's time to grow. Those enzyme inhibitors are neutralised and the nut goes into grow mode. Grow mode is supremely good for you; it's full of life and energy. All the vitamins and minerals are now freely available for your body to use. Also you can eat as many nuts as you like without getting a stomach ache. Again, well worth the hassle. Five minutes' work for enough nuts and seeds to last a month. It's just a matter of being organised. And yes, of course they taste better too.

Electric mill: I have a 'Pico grain mill'
Quick intro to soaking info and explanation:
http://www.passionatehomemaking.com/2008/04/whole-grains-grinding-soaking.html
For in-depth soaking info: *Nourishing Traditions* by Sally Fallon

65. Raw Milk

I am a stickler for unpasteurised dairy products and I only consume raw dairy. My milk, cheese and yogurt are always made from straight-out-the-cow raw milk. I get my raw milk delivered weekly via mail-order, which makes for an easy life. It comes from healthy pasture-fed cows that live in fields, not factories. When my 80-year-old father-in-law first tasted the milk he was like:

"Wow! This is how milk used to taste when I was a kid in the war."
It does taste amazing.
Unpasteurised cheese I get in farmers markets, specialist cheese

shops, but even supermarkets have a few nowadays if you check the labels. I'm a bit of a cheese connoisseur these days: Reblochon, Gruyere, Lincolnshire Poacher, Flower Marie, Lancashire Bomb. Ummmm, I love a good cheese; makes my mouth water just typing these words. I guess my cheese fetish is my calcium deficiency shining and sparkling at me. Yes, I try to read all the little signs and signals my body gives me.

And yes, there is a world of difference between supermarket-bought yellow rubber and elegant handmade gooey works of art, lovingly made from straight-out-the-cow milk. Tastes about eight million times better and is equally that much healthier for you.

I also make kefir with the raw milk. This is a fermented milk drink, almost exactly like a yogurt but with oodles more beneficial bacteria. It's a simple two-minute job to make: pour milk into Kilner jar, add kefir grains, close lid, leave somewhere warm-ish, three or four days later strain out the kefir grains and Bob's your uncle, one awesome probiotic drink that is unbelievably good for me. This is a real probiotic drink fit for a king; none of that yak-$hit. Tastes wonderful too. I like mine super-strong, so I leave it fermenting until it fizzes when it touches my tongue. Power food.

There is a mass of confusing information and old wives' tales surrounding milk. I'm not going to bother preaching to you about the benefits of unpasteurised raw milk. Why? Because whatever I say will be wasted on the majority of people. Your mind is already made up by whatever else has gone on in your life. All those tests you heard about are done on pasteurised milk, not raw milk. All of them.

If you want to know for yourself about milk, I can recommend a book by Ron Schmid called *The Untold Story of Raw Milk*. If you read that you will then be in a position to make up your own mind, rather than just hearing it second-hand from me.

But I will leave you with a few thoughts to ponder.

You know when you reach for the milk from the fridge, you automatically have a quick sniff, just to make sure it doesn't stink. Sometimes you jerk your head back because the smell is disgusting. Ew, nasty! That is the smell of rotten, putrid milk. No way would you drink that gagmungus puke.

Well, raw milk does not putrefy, nor does it rot. Raw milk goes sour when it's been hanging around for too long. It's now fermented milk. And this sour milk smells like, well, sour cream. It is not an unpleasant smell. It is on the way to becoming cheese.

If you leave it a little longer, the milk will separate into white cream cheese called curds, and a clear liquid called whey. Yes, the same curds and whey that Little Miss Muffet ate sitting on her tuffet. And no, they would not invent a nursery rhyme for kids that encouraged them to eat putrid milk!

Incidentally it's almost impossible to get pasteurised milk to go sour because the pasteurisation process has killed all the beneficial bacteria in it, that's why it lasts longer, and why it rots. This may not sound like a big deal, but in the land of blind, the one-eyed health freak is king: we should be eating whole, fresh, unprocessed, natural foods. Raw dairy is one such food.

And make no mistake; raw milk and pasteurised milk are very different beasts. People who have dairy intolerances are usually totally fine with raw milk. Not always, but usually. Strange, eh! There must be a reason for this. Why would people with a dairy intolerance be fine with raw milk that's straight out of the cow? Odd, eh!

Pasteurisation changes the milk. The heat from the pasteurisation process kills any evil pathogens that might be lurking in the milk, but it also kills any goodness in the milk too. That's why our body produces mucus when we drink pasteurised milk. Pasteurisation has changed the milk from a lovely, healthy, life-giving drink, to a mucus-producing, lifeless drink that clogs up your insides.

Eaten or drunk once or twice is no problem whatsoever. Your supercool body is more than capable of handling such a miniscule amount of poor-quality food. No problem at all. But of course people drink milk all the time, usually daily. Pasteurised milk and its refined products are saturated throughout our diets and in the processed foods people eat. When eaten in large quantities daily, the consequences build up over the course of time and eventually cause digestive troubles. You are what you eat and if your digestive tract is awash in anything harmful that

frequently, then people are bound to have problems. Dairy allergies/
intolerances are some of the most frequent allergies people report.

Obviously it's a bit more complicated than my super-brief summary
and you should never believe anything anyone says from just reading a
brief summary. I can highly recommend that milk book; a truly amazing story. Wildly more enjoyable than you could ever imagine a story
about milk could be. It will also give you a clear picture about modern
farming practices and what the big corporations have to do in order to
earn their living. Education is key!

Further reading: *The Untold Story of Raw Milk* by Ron Schmid
Raw milk deliveries in the UK: www.hookandson.co.uk

66. "There's no such thing as a free lunch."
Milton Friedman
"Lunch is for wimps." Gordon Gekko, 1987

Lunch is usually salad, but I do a lot of business lunches and I eat as
healthily as possible in the restaurants I go to. I always go to good
restaurants that use quality ingredients, or maybe I should say less bad
ingredients than cheap restaurants. But my diet does not slip when
I go out. I always choose the healthy option: salad, lamb, veggies or
whatever is within my boundaries. And the healthy option excludes
any added trash like croutons, or house dressing, or lardons, or fried
stuff, or whatever sugary gimmick is added. It's no big deal and no one
notices anything odd, because there is nothing odd to notice: I order
off the same menu as everyone else.

Drink

I drink about two litres of water each day. Seventy five percent of my
body is water; it's good for me, agrees with me, oils my wheels and helps
with the removal of waste.

I have two to four herbal teas spread around the day too. I vary the tea as much as possible and have six to ten different types on the go at any one time: green, jasmine, tranquillity, ginkgo, cinnamon, fennel, camomile, peppermint, and the list goes on.

I greatly enjoy glasses of raw milk, raw milk kefir, ginger kefir as well as freshly-juiced fruits and veggies: usually heavy on the veggies and light on the fruit. Fruit only in the mornings does not totally agree with me and my adrenal glands.

That's about all I drink, except when I hit the booze. Yes I do drink, but I drink very much in moderation now. I rarely drink at home. Sometimes a month goes by that's completely dry. It was not planned as dry; it just turned out dry because my life does not revolve around drink anymore. A far cry from my twenty-somethings when booze was an everyday part of life.

I have two drinking styles now. First is the gentle, calm, controlled and irregular style, with just one or two glasses, once or twice a week. It's a pleasure to savour and enjoy a fine ale or some wine, but I treat it as a special occasion. I am taking time out to have a beer and I appreciate it as a treat. I have drunk more than enough in my life already and the urge to get spasticated frequently is long gone. Been there, done that, got many t-shirts.

But I do occasionally get smashed as well. My business involves a lot of entertaining, lunch frequently turns into dinner, and then on to a club. And honestly, I enjoy getting smashed. I'm good at it, I miss it, so I do occasionally let my hair down, unleash the dogs of war and get blasted like the good old dayz. Maybe, three to five times a year. But again, a far cry from my early years when I was out five nights a week, puffing through 40 fags a day.

When these infrequent heavy sessions happen, my second drinking style is slow, steady, controlled boozing. I pace myself like a long-distance runner: keeping track of my progress, having pit stops with glasses of water, and not bolting or rushing anything. I have plenty of colleagues and friends who turbo-drink like traditional city boys do. And afterwards the only thing that happens is I have a hangover.

Just that, just a hangover. Which is pretty cool considering how much grief I used to get from one sip of beer. I can live with the occasional hangover.

It's not hard to restrict myself to such infrequent drinking. Remember I was 100 percent teetotal for two years, and the four years prior to that, my drinking was sporadic, frustrating and painful. This drinking style is the minimum I can live with to maintain my sanity. There is a time and a place for zero booze, but when we come out the other-side, we need our treats. Life would be pretty dull otherwise.

Rice

We only have brown rice in the house. I sometimes remember to pre-soak it before cooking to make it more digestible. Soaking rice is less important than soaking grains or nuts, but I find it tastes better when pre-soaked. White rice has been refined and a great deal of the goodness taken out in the refining process. When I was sick, white rice clogged me up something horrid, but brown rice was usually fine, (except when I was intolerant to everything).

And don't give me any of that hard-rice $hit. No, don't even think it!

If you think you need your wrice all soft and fwuffy because your teeffy-weeffy can't chew the slightly harder wrice prwopewy, then you need to grow up and get a life. Slightly harder rice is no big deal, OK? Grown adults needing super-soft rice? Please! So many people say that, it's unreal. If you think it tastes hard, you need to cook it longer: village!

Meat

I eat meat. I eat meat often, but not every day. I eat the fat on the meat too. I did have a period of not eating meat, but I always feel better when I include meat in my diet, so I use my senses and eat what my body tells me is good. Meat agrees with me. But I don't eat any old meat. I am very selective.

When I'm out in restaurants, and I eat out a lot, I basically only eat lamb. Lamb, as a general rule cannot be factory farmed. You cannot keep sheep locked up in factories/barns and force-fed soya feed or grains or any old crap. As a general rule, sheep are pasture fed so that's what I eat in restaurants. I believe New Zealand lamb is always exclusively pasture fed due to their long spring, summer and autumn seasons in which grass grows all the time.

What's the big deal with pasture fed? Sheep have been designed by nature/God to have a diet of grass and other pasture plants. Grass is what they should eat in order to be healthy. Sheep cannot live and reproduce on a diet of anything else, so that is how they are kept even in today's commercialised world. In other words, they still live as nature/God intended them and as such they are healthy, happy sheep. Because they eat their natural diet, they get much less sick than other farmed animals and don't need nearly so many medicines. Medicines that might get wedged in their bodies, and which I might eat when I eat them.

Other animals are not so lucky. Other animals can get by on foods that they were not designed to eat, much like we humans can. Cows for example can be kept in a barn/factory/warehouse and fed a variety of different goodies. Some of those things, like grain, makes them lovely and fat too, which is excellent for big fat steaks, and big fat profits. Big fat cows are as healthy as big fat people!

The not-so-healthy cows require lots of vaccinations, inoculations, antibiotics, steroids and God knows what else to keep them alive, just like the average fat human.

When you eat fat steaks, from fat cows, that were raised in a factory, that never saw the light of day, that were fed on the cheapest of feeds, that were pumped full of magic beans, that only lived half their normal life span, you are unfortunately eating meat from unhealthy animals laced with weird medicines. Unsurprisingly that's not very good for you.

Imagine for a second you are a cannibal. You have the choice of eating a very fit and healthy Tarzan and Jane. They lived in the jungle their whole lives and never ate any junk food, nor got exposed to any pollution, nor weird medicines. They are just supremely healthy human beings. Or you can eat Mr. and Mrs. MacFat. They are triple the size of normal humans and ate crap food their whole lives. They get sick frequently and so have been pumped full of magic beans.

Who would you eat?

Exactly! You would choose the healthy option and it is the same in the world of animals. I choose to consume happy animals that eat and live how nature intended. It makes for much better tasting and healthier foods. Quality is vital.

Other meat

We have other meats at home too. Everything is organic and of the highest quality I can find; chicken, sausages, liver and occasionally game and pork, but I'm big on lamb. We have organic meat boxes delivered monthly from little farms in the countryside. Farms that focus on quality, not quantity. That 'organic' badge is the best chance I have of getting clean meat. They send a variety of types and cuts depending on the season. I freeze what we don't need. Again, it makes for an easy life.

It's not just ideology either, not just down to the educated choices I make. The meat tastes so much better too. Better than non-organic meat, but also better even than the organic meat from the supermarkets. When I first tried the stuff from the little farms I was startled to discover not all organic meats are created equal. Once you realise there are other options, once you test those options, once you discover they do taste better, then it's pretty easy to stick to the program.

Is it more expensive? No, the meat from the countryside is a fraction cheaper than the organic supermarket food. Why? I guess because we just pay the farmers and not shareholders.

Is it more expensive than regular non-organic meat? Yes, of course it is! Cheap animals, mass farmed, fed on floor sweepings is always gonna be cheaper. That's the definition of cheap.

Soya

I don't eat much beef. I think it's an irrational fear, but I worry even the organic cows are soya-fed, and soya sends shivers down my spine. Soya is the Devil's spunk as far as I am concerned. GM modified, covered in chemicals, cheap as chips, high in indigestible phytic acid, quick to spoil and easy to turn rancid. A toxic disaster that was never designed to be consumed in large quantities by anyone or anything. There are reams of papers and stories of the harm this is stuff does. Whole books dedicated to spreading the word to avoid this nightmare of a food and the company that flogs it. Neither animals nor humans should eat soya unless it's been fermented in traditional Chinese ways; natto, miso or tempeh.

Soya was one of the first foods to be genetically modified and they have effectively turned it into a poison. I used to have a nightshade allergy and eating tomatoes would give me strange weak-light-headed-scratchy-under-the-skin symptoms. I was eating those freshly steamed edamame beans in Japanese restaurants every week and I was confused as to why I got my nightshade allergy symptoms when eating them. I discovered edamame beans are fresh soya beans in the pod. Now I know why I got those reactions: the soya plant has been crossed with a tomato plant, amongst other things.

Today's genetically modified soya is now totally resistant to all the mega-toxic chemicals they spray on the plants. All bugs die in this toxic mist so the plant can grow big and strong, which in turn generates big and strong profits. We eat the modified soya beans along with all the toxic chemicals left stuck in the plant. Or we eat the animals that have been fed on soya and their meat passes the toxins on to us.

Genetically modifying any plants is looking for serious trouble in the grand scheme of things, but I object deeply to eating the toxic chemicals invisibly impregnated in the plants and meat that I eat.

Some baby formula food is made of this toxic nightmare. A dairy alternative no less! The first couple of years of some poor kid's life and filled with soya at every meal. Out of the frying pan and into the fire. Nightmare. Run a mile from that crap.

If you don't believe me, Google it or find a book on Amazon. If you can't be bothered to spend 30 minutes having a read, play it safe and don't give your kids that rubbish. They will thank you for it when they are older. OK, they will not; but you will sleep better knowing they are healthier.

Stock

For sauces and soups we always use homemade stock. Made using organic bones from pasture-fed animals, a few veggies and simmered for as long as possible. Usually minimum 10 hours, but sometimes it gets a full 24 hours simmering away to draw out the nutrients from all the bones and gizzards.

As every chef knows, the quality of the stock defines the taste of their food. Chefs go to great lengths to make quality stock because food smothered in a fine sauce, made with their fine stock, tastes amazing.

Why does liquid made out of old bones taste so wonderful? Because it is so good for you: packed full of minerals, particularly calcium, magnesium and potassium. The slow simmering draws them out and makes them easily digestible.

We have a sophisticated and inbuilt process to determine if our food is edible or not. We look, smell and then taste before we swallow our food. We use our eyes and brain to look, to ensure it looks OK and that it has not been soiled, refined or changed. We use our nose to make sure it smells good. Taste is the final frontier. Taste is very important because once you swallow, there is no turning back. If it's bad, you will get sick. That's why we have a strong sense of taste that can differentiate between such a wide selection of flavours. Our taste buds inform us as to the quality of the food we are about to eat. The better it tastes, the better it is for us. A good stock elevates food to a new level of taste and a new level of healthiness.

I usually make a batch and freeze it in little pots in the freezer. That way we can use it anytime we need it. Again, all it takes is being organised. Ten minutes of your time to make enough to last a month or two. Our soups and sauces now taste like posh restaurant food: my wife's spag bol tastes divine.

Our food tastes great

We have organic fruit and veg food boxes delivered weekly. Once these deliveries are set up, no special effort is required, the food just arrives. Just about everything we buy in the supermarket is organic too.

I have a veggie patch in the garden as well. This provides the family with organic potatoes, carrots, parsnips, runner beans, lettuce, onions, garlic, beets, sorrel, spinach, strawberries, blackberries, raspberries, tayberries, black currants, red currants, gooseberries, apples and pears.

The herb garden supplies us with ample herbs throughout the year too: sage, rosemary, marjoram, oregano, chives, curry, bay, thyme, camomile, peppermint, and spearmint. I have so much extra, I cut, dry and store for use in the winter months.

It's only a little plot, but it's been great fun learning how to be green-fingered. The kids love it too. Each year I make fewer mistakes and have bigger crops. Everything is growing and I eagerly await the new pear, cherry and fig trees to start giving. Last year we got one perfect nectarine off our little patio tree. We chopped it up into four bits and all had a taste; wonderful. Home grown parsnips, left in the ground and pulled on Christmas morning in time for lunch. Dreamy!

The home-made food we eat, using quality ingredients tastes amazing. When we eat normal non-organic food we can all taste the difference; it's bland and flat. There is no going back now, not for any of the family.

Overall summary of my diet style

If you research some of the different diets out there, really get involved and check out some of the gurus in this field, you will hear some funky points of view:

Eat only whole, fresh, unprocessed, natural foods.
Eat only what God made.
Eat only what you recognise.
Eat only foods that will spoil, but eat them before they do.

I read these words many times when I was investigating my diet and I always thought what a load of old cobblers: way too hardcore, way too sandal-like for a city bloke like me. But I am sorry to report I am basically there now. This is how I view the world. What have I become? I will have to watch myself and make sure I don't wear sandals to work instead of me brogues!

It really does seem to be the only way. There is so much rubbish out there, so much refining, so many chemicals, so many hidden nasties, so much poor preparation. If I don't know what I'm eating, or what's in it, I keep things simple and just don't eat it. There are always other options.

I must say it took a lot of reading to get this health-freaky about food. But after I had unsafe amalgam removal and virtually every food did something bad to me, I had little choice but to educate myself in an effort to understand what was wrong.

This diet is the consequence of all that pain and suffering. I am fully aware it is considered extreme. But I don't care what other people think. It's not my fault they don't understand nutrition. I'm not just blindly following some celebrity diet. I have read, researched and tested everything on myself. When I was sick, any deviation to poor quality food physically hurt me. I learnt the hard way. It took a while, but I eventually learnt from my mistakes.

OK, you have seen the kinds of food I do eat, but I think it's about time you found out what I don't!

Further reading: *Nourishing Traditions* by Sally Fallon, but to fully comprehend nutrition, Weston A. Price's book is essential reading: *Nutrition and Physical Degeneration*.

Organic meat deliveries in the UK: The Well Hung Meat Company
Organic veggie boxes in the UK: Able and Cole

67. Choose life

"What did you do to the microwave oven?"

"Who me? Nothing. Why?"

"It's not working any more. You cut the cable didn't you?"

"Me? Cut the cable? No way! That's absurd! Why would I do that?"

"Because you specifically told me of the research you discovered that showed microwaved food loses all its nutritional value, and that we should not use it. That's why!"

"I can't believe you think I would do such a thing without first consulting you!"

"Don't bull$hit me, Sunshine!"

"Do you think I crept down in the dead of night, unscrewed the front of the kitchen units, cut the cables, then put everything back together and then crept back into bed with you? Come on!"

"That's probably exactly what you did!"

"Not guilty here! No way! But let's look on the bright side; everyone is safer and healthier now the nuke-machine is broken. You know how floppy, flaccid and lifeless nuked food looks and tastes anyway. Baby food warmed up in there is a serious health hazard too. It only takes a little longer to use the hob. I don't think we should replace it. I'm just thinking of the children's health here."

"I know you too well. I know you sabotaged the microwave."

"I have no idea what you are talking about. I am completely innocent of all charges, m'lady."

The first time my beautiful wife will know the truth is when she reads this. She did smell a rat instantly, but I hope she laughs rather than shouts.

Yes, it was me. Yes, I sabotaged the microwave oven. Guilty as charged. The only thing it got regularly used for was warming up baby food. I couldn't bear the thought of the little chap eating nuked food every day. I am willing to live with the consequences of protecting my family, whatever they may be.

I like to set a good example in the things I do, the way I lead my life. My wife and family were not sick so they are much less enthusiastic about the quality of the food they consume. Healthy food is important, but just not as full-on as it is for me.

Cutting the microwave cable was just one example of the lengths I go to, to ensure my diet is as healthy as possible, but that's the tip of the iceberg.

I drink no sodas, no lemonades, no cokes, no diet soda, no zero drinks, no Gatorade, no energy drinks, no regular tea and no coffee. No boxed or bottled fruit juices, with or without sugar. No pasteurised milk, no UHT milk, no fortified milk, and no food with dried or skimmed milk in it.

I eat no Cornflakes, no Bran Flakes, no Cheerios, no Special K, no Coco Pops, no Weetabix, no shop-bought muesli, oat crunches or energy bars. No white bread, no cheap brown bread, no margarine, jam, jelly nor marmalade.

I eat no 'diet' foods, no 'low fat' foods and no ready-made meals. No deep-fried anythings: fries, chicken, onion rings, or the traditional English meal of fish 'n' chips. I consume no McDonald's, no Burger King, no KFCs, no cheap Chinese or Indian food, no doner kebabs, no shop-bought bacon or sausage sarnies, no sausage rolls, no hash browns, no samosas, nor any Cornish pasties.

For condiments I have no ketchup, no Daddies sauce, nor HP Sauce, no brown sauce, no BBQ sauce, no Texas sauce, no Reggae Reggae sauce, nor any mayonnaise. I don't eat food made with pre-made blocks of powdered stock cubes either.

I eat no biscuits, cakes, tarts, nor cookies. No chocolate bars, Mars Bars, Twixes, Kit Kats, Dime Bars, chocolate fingers. No wine gums, no mints, no chewing gum; nope, none of that crap.

I read every label of every product I buy. I consume no chemicals, no MSG, no refined sugar, no glucose, no maltose, no sucrose, no fructose. If it has long unpronounceable ingredients with Xs and Ys in it, it's just not for me.

Today I could, if I wished, eat any of the above no-foods. I would get zero side effects or reactions and life would go on as per normal. My cool body is more than capable of handling a little bit of junk. The difference now is, I choose not to eat any of that junk. I choose the healthy option; I choose life.

Just because I am better does not mean I forgot the lessons I learnt when I was sick. Back then if I did eat any of those no-foods, I felt the effects afterwards and those effects lasted seven to ten days. This showed me first-hand what they can do to a body on the edge. Just because I'm better does not mean I want to eat things that I know are harmful. Sure, I was mega-sick back then, but those foods are still harmful to me whether I'm sick or not. The only difference now is my body is strong enough to handle them.

I choose to learn from my mistakes.

I choose to remember the lessons my body gave me.

I choose life.

Making these choices is a bit more complicated and expensive, to say nothing of educating oneself which is certainly time consuming; but we are what we eat. Every ounce, every drop, goes into making me what I am. I know what happens when you put diesel in a petrol car.

After all I've been through, I deserve quality food to keep me fit and healthy. In the words of Hippocrates: 'Let food be thy medicine and medicine be thy food.'

68. Deprived? Cheated?

When I use the word diet, I don't mean some temporary change in how I eat. There is no turning back. When I use the word diet I mean this is the food I eat. And I do not feel cheated by this diet. I do not miss the old junk. I do not crave any of it. I don't feel deprived or constricted. I don't mope about, grumpily hankering after lost foods. In fact, when I do think about it, I feel lucky to know, happy to live the dream, proud to have the knowledge to avoid things that are so harmful.

I know some of you may be shocked, or stunned, or amazed at these wild confessions. Maybe some don't believe, or maybe you don't think it's even possible to avoid what most people eat every single day?

But it really is no big deal and I don't feel deprived, ever. Why would I? It's not like I am blindly restricting myself from eating won-der-foods. I have seen and felt everything for myself. I have read up and researched everything myself. I am not blindly taking orders from any doctors or dieticians or family or friends or neighbours or anyone. These are the educated choices I have made. Education is key! I choose not to eat that crap.

Back in my late twenties, before all this mercury trouble started, I wanted to give up smoking. I found that simple task exceedingly tricky. Denying myself something, anything, even damaging cigarette smoke, was frustratingly difficult and I repeatedly caved in. I didn't have enough mental strength to do what I wanted to do.

Then, at the beginning of the third year of trying to give up, I got very cross and angry with myself. There I was getting all bitter and twisted, depressed at my inability to give up something so harmful, and I just snapped. I remember the moment clearly. I yelled at my mind:

"This is just bull$hit! I can't let this fiasco ruin my life. I'm miser-able when I smoke because I want to give up, and I'm miserable when I give up because I want to smoke. This is totally mental. This can't go on! That's it. No more. Finished. The end. I've had enough of this mental torture. No more."

And that was that. It was like a switch being thrown in my mind. Once I had mentally decided enough was enough, that was it. I went from someone who was trying to give up smoking, to someone who no longer smoked. It's a fine line, but a big line.

This is how I mentally manage my mind with the food I eat. I learn what is bad, I understand why it is bad, and automatically the switch is flicked and Boom! No cravings, desires, lust or guilt. That food is simply off the menu. Education is essential in this process. With knowledge we have understanding, and with understanding we have the power to do as we wish. If I don't understand why something is bad for me, it's impossible give up. But if I do understand, then it's as easy as hugging my children, or being nice to the boss just before pay review.

I view those junk foods as a poison. All of them. I see them as things that would damage or hurt me. Maybe not immediately, but their slow insipid sucking-away and draining the life is all around for everyone to see.

I have a ten-minute experiment for you. Go to your local coffee shop, buy a drink and choose a seat where you can watch the world go by. Take ten minutes out to just sit and observe the people going about their business. Count the wonderfully healthy people you see. Don't count the sick people because there are too many. Count the really healthy, radiant, beautiful people.

No bald heads, no swollen ankles, no crooked backs or faces, no stoops, no twists, no worry lines or grimaces, none too fat and none too skinny. Count the gorgeous people who should be in the movies, count the people who you would sleep with!

You will be surprised at the lack of healthy people once you look around yourself. Once you become aware of the lack of truly healthy people, you will suddenly see the vast array of bizarre, deformed and amazingly ugly people who saturate our world. It's a wonder so many limp on.

When you have done that, remember the following: 'We are what we eat. Every ounce, every drop, goes into making me what I am. I know what happens when you put diesel in a petrol car.'

It's a good experiment that. If you have never people-watched for healthy people before, it's well worth a chuckle.

I am very happy and feel privileged to have a diet that tastes oh so much better, that protects and keeps me fit and healthy. It is no problem to stick to it...

...except of course when I cheat. Do I cheat? Of course I cheat! Everyone cheats! I'm a city-boy trader! That's what I do for a living!

Yeah, I cheat sometimes, how can I not? I have some pretty extreme dietary requirements. I'm not a guru living off the land in a hut. I live and work in a great big city of eight million people and my lifestyle choices are impossible to stick with 100 percent of the time. But my cheats are very different to the common man in the street's cheats!

I will tell you my cheats, but first let's put this in perspective. I never cheat at home. At home I live the dream in terms of my diet. Everything is as you have read. I have minimum two meals a day that can be maximum healthy: breakfast and dinner. Here at home I eat my quality ingredients, wonderfully prepared uber-healthy meals. I love them, enjoy them, I am proud to eat such tasty and life-giving foods. Yum.

But do I eat out a lot. Minimum five meals a week are in restaurants at lunchtime and this is where my ideals are inevitably compromised. I can't control the quality of the food there. I can't eat organic food there. I don't know how they prepared the food either.

Did they coat my lamb chop in canola oil? In sunflower oil? Did they marinade the chop with a packet of dried chemicals? Was the soup or sauce made from factory-made stock cubes that had MSG in it? Did the soup have a dash of pasteurised cream in it? Did they pre-soak the rice, lentils or chickpeas? Of course not. Was the lettuce, cucumber, tomato, celery organic? Of course not.

These are the types of concessions I must make. The only thing I can do is make the best choice I can, given the options I have. That's why I like to choose the restaurants myself and why I only go to good restaurants. They make an effort, whereas other restaurants are simply in it for the money.

I never eat fried or fast food. Ever. Do I ever scoff down a massive wedge of chocolate cake? Never. Do I ever have a Big Mac or Whopper? Never. Do I ever just pig out? Never. I always choose meals that are as close to my ideals as possible.

"Come on," I hear you cry. "You must have some treats? You can't go through life without treats!"

Oh course I have treats: my homemade chocolate tastes divine. My wife makes the most stunning apple cake with all Sunshine-suitable ingredients. Ditto her apple crumble. Oh it's lovely; I take such big bites it gets all stuck up in my teeth and gums; yummmm. The raw cheese I class as a wonderful snack too. My crispy nuts and seeds are amazing. If my sweet tooth kicks in I have some dried apricots or figs or dates or prunes. These are my treats and they suit me fine. I always have something available at home.

"But come on," I hear you whine, "You must cheat properly sometimes?"

Ok I admit it; I do occasionally have proper cheats. I occasionally have some ice cream. I love ice cream. But, it must be proper posh ice cream. None of that cheap chemical fluorescent auto-soft goop. Haagen-Dazs and Ben & Jerry's are not posh enough either. Good restaurants make ultra-smooth vanilla ice cream made with some real ingredients and occasionally I can't resist. But always with a platter of fresh fruit. And I only have one scoop. OK, sometimes two, but never three. Never three. Three would be just wild.

How often do I have my proper cheats? In the winter months probably never, but in the summer when it's hot maybe once or twice a month. But then again maybe not at all; depends what's going on. I mean, I don't have a cheat plan!

When we holiday in France I do let my guard down even more. It's so beautiful and relaxing down there. Maybe I would have a couple of scoops a day six or seven times in a two-week holiday. That's pretty wild. I enjoy it, savour it, marvel in the taste sensation, but I'm not a slave to it. It's a once-in-a-while treat, not a daily sin.

While I am confessing, I will also admit to having the odd slice of apple pie. Again got to be gourmet and only once or twice a year. But yeah, that's about it really. I can't think of any other proper cheats I indulge in. They keep me sane.

Notice I only cheat when I'm away from home. At home there is no need to have proper cheats because I always have some extra-special healthy treats on hand. I much prefer my healthy home treats anyway. I get double the pleasure: healthy and a treat.

Nope, I don't miss the old diet one iota, but my daughter does!

69. Why did I get so sick?

Why do I think I got so sick? Well first and foremost the mercury was my root cause. I've had my fair share of contamination sources too. This is what I have pieced together and remembered from my past:

My mother had a mouthful of amalgams her whole life, so I took a load in the womb. Ouch!

Grandfather Forsyth was a dentist and I played in his dental practice as a kid. Boom!

I had all the usual childhood and adult vaccinations, travel inoculations and plenty of flu shots. Most of which I have since discovered contained mercury. Ka-Pow!

I played with mercury in school chemistry class, rolling the little silver balls around a great silver tray. Ka-Bam!

When I was 14 years old, I broke a thermometer. This is a big, bold and bad standout exposure. I was at boarding school and I fancied a day off. I lay in bed faking illness. The matron took my temperature whilst I was lying in bed. When she turned her back, I dipped the end of the thermometer in my cuppa tea.

Ho hum, I got some big sighs coming on here. Makes me feel such a fool. Only an Englishman could get poisoned in such an imbecilic way. My lips are pursed, my face is red.

The thermometer exploded instantly when it hit my boiling hot cuppa tea. Luckily I noticed and didn't drink it, phew! I just poured it down the sink and got on with life. I didn't think of it again until 27 years later reading Cutler's mercury book. There was no clean-up operation. No changing of sheets. No opening of windows. I just lay in bed all day, all week, all year, wallowing in a toxic nightmerde, breathing in the flames of my demise. Ba-Da-Boom!

Was I sick at school because of this? The overriding memory I have of school was of being cold all the time. Winter, summer, day and night: I remember being perpetually cold. I wore long johns every day, winter, summer because I was eternally chilly. I was a frightfully skinny kid too. I guess my thyroid and adrenals took a massive hit from that. Biff!

I also assume that's why my kidneys got so bad. Cutler said kidneys are usually OK in mercury toxic people, unless they had a big one-off exposure. (As opposed to amalgams leaking which is a little-and-often exposure.) That big thermometer hit smacked my kidneys good and proper. Ba-Doom!

I had amalgams in my mouth for at least 25 years of my life. Ow!

I had one amalgam that was so big it was in direct contact with my gums. This is bad news and accelerates body contamination as the mercury leaks directly into the blood stream via the gums. This brute used to get perpetually infected and inflamed. Periodically a dentist would kindly drill and refill with fresh amalgam. I don't have my dental records and I can't remember for sure, but this happened at least five times. No safety. No protection. Five drillings. Five mega mercury dumps. Man, that makes me sigh great big sighs. Ka-Boom!

My red tattoo had mercury in it. Bosh!

Before I knew, part of my healthy lifestyle was eating Japanese food. I ate raw tuna two or three times a week for two years. Tuna are the fish known to have some of the largest concentrations of mercury in their bodies. They are near the top of their food chains and they live long lives accumulating many poisons picked up from our polluted oceans. Power stations bear a large responsibility for the mercury, but there are many other industries that share the blame. Mercury poisoning from fish consumption is becoming much more recognised now. Bash!

I had a jaw problem and I chewed and ground my teeth together hard for a good three years with amalgams in, releasing even more mercury vapour in the process. Crunch!

I had one amalgam removed with no safety precautions. That one tipped me over the edge. Bim-Bam-Boom!

I had seven amalgams removed with some safety protection; rubber dam and whatnot. My only essential contamination event. The toxin tap needed turning off. Nevertheless another Wham!

Individually each contamination event is survivable. Each is small enough to carry on with life unnoticed. Collectively they built up my toxic load. All this mercury polluted my body, contaminated all my organs, including my brain. It broke everything inside me, like a handful of sand clogging up the wheels and cogs in a clock. No wonder I can only handle a low chelator dose. No wonder it's taking so bloody long to chelate all this bloody mercury out.

But mercury wasn't the only factor in my downfall. I also took lots of antibiotics over the course of my life too. They certainly didn't help. Everyone took them; that's what was given to everyone when they had a cold, or the flu, or a tummy bug, or acne, or anything really. A cure-all magic-bullet perfect for our world of ignorant sick people. It's getting bad press now, but the damage is done. I will never take them again. There are many other better ways I have discovered, not least having a good diet in the first place.

But I can't just point the finger. I must also hold my hands up high in the air and totally admit that my lifestyle was much to do with what happened to me too. I had a rotten lifestyle. Exciting for sure, but nevertheless rather short-sighted. I drank heavily in my twenties and took many excellent mind-bending recreational drugs in my time. Oops, sorry Mum. Kids: Just say NO.

I had some fantastic fun, truly legendary times to remember with a massive grin on my face, but those good times were rewarded with double-triple-quadruple-one-hundred-fold worse times when my health crashed and burned and life almost dissolved.

Make no mistake kids: the drugs hurt me massively over the longer term. Just say NO. There are other cool things to do rather than get wasted. There is always a price to pay, always. You are reading of the price I paid. And yes, I am talking to you both!

I often wonder why I got into drugs in the first place because I was always against them when I was younger. Was it because it was the only way I could dull the pain? Was it because it was the only way I could come alive? Because I come ALIVE when I take uppers! Party animal style! Once bitten, need more! Full of magic beans!

Who knows? Anyway, all that's behind me now. Clean as a whistle now. I have way too much respect for my body now. To subject it to that kind of punishment again would be, yeah, would be unthinkable. Of course my diet was a big factor in my health too. I used to prefer Whoppers over Big Macs because Burger King didn't put salad in their burgers. Today I shake my head in shame at my stupidity. I didn't eat vegetables or salad until my mid-twenties.

The really sad thing is I am far from alone. Great swathes of our society remain totally nutrition ignorant. You may or may not approve of my diet. Maybe vegetarianism, or vegan, or raw, or specific carbohydrate diet, or Atkins, or whatever floats your boat; but at least I have studied and made my choices. Better than education via commercials.

So mercury, lifestyle and diet did me in. With a better, healthier way of life I may have avoided all this hassle. But I have had so many mercury exposures, from so many different sources; I think it would have hit me at some point or another, whatever I did.

Would I have had the balls to do what I had to do, when I was 64? Maybe? Maybe not?

On the tough days, I like to console myself with the fact that at least I had fun getting so gloriously screwed up, so many people just had crap lives. So many kids just woke up one day and everything was buggered.

I had to change everything about the way I live my life to get better. That's OK, change is cool, life is good again and I am happy again, but for a long time I didn't even know there was an alternative way to get better other than seeing my doctor, which is pretty stupid of me, and pretty stupid of our society. Hopefully my story will help others help themselves.

Further reading about fish and mercury poisoning: *Diagnosis: Mercury: Money, Politics and Poison* by Jane Hightower

70. "The path of the righteous man is beset on all sides by the iniquities of the selfish and the tyranny of evil men. Blessed is he who, in the name of charity and good will, shepherds the weak through the valley of darkness, for he is truly his brother's keeper and the finder of lost children. And I will strike down upon thee with great vengeance and furious anger those who would attempt to poison and destroy My brothers. And you will know My name is the Lord when I lay My vengeance upon thee. BAM, BAM, BAM, BAM..."
Jules, Pulp Fiction, 1994

My story is a success story, but it is also the story of my failure to look after myself in my early years. It is also the story of failure of the system to look after one of its own. I was just a common man in the street. My society, the culture I live in, allowed one of its population to almost die: repeatedly poisoned and the resulting illnesses repeatedly missed.

Make no mistake; I am to blame for my downfall. I realise that now. It is my body and my responsibility to look after myself. I should have known better. I should not have been so trusting.

I have now succeeded in regaining much of my health, but for the first 37 years of my life, I failed miserably. I delegated my health to someone else. I trusted our doctors.

Even though I admit responsibility for what happened, I can't help but point the finger at my accomplices. Just like when a senior politician gets caught with his pants around his ankles, they always drag a few buddies down with them. I'm gonna point my finger and blame someone else too.

I lay some blame at my doctors' doorstep. Not on purpose, not vindictively, or maliciously, nor spitefully: but ignorantly. Their collective ignorance, their got-the-wrong-end-of-the-stick-ness, their unaware-ness, their lack of knowledge, their inability to see clearly or have an open mind; they let me down on a grand scale.

These are the people on the front line of our health. They should be the canaries in the mine. They should be telling people of the current and coming problems. They have failed miserably.

The doctors I had telling me I was not even sick, the doctors I had telling me nothing could be done, the doctors I had laughing in my face at the cures I found: they are a disgrace. I am ashamed that our society could have such gaping holes in it.

Living the dream? Yeah, right. Maybe when you are 22 and living it up large; but not when you hit 37 and life's not worth living anymore.

I know it's down to my lifestyle and my dentistry, but I have had poor health my whole life. Certainly I have had adrenal and thyroid problems my whole life.

Why does it take me so long to build up the thyroid supplement doses? Because I had those problems my whole life. My body has never worked properly.

Why was I cold my whole life?

Why was I skinny and weak my whole life?

I used to think being colour blind was just one of those things. Now I find out it's because I'm mercury poisoned.

Why were my kidneys leaking blood half my life?

Why did the doctors not read the many signals I gave?

Not one doctor, not one, not once, ever, noticed. I can diagnose ad-renal and thyroid problems by asking a few simple questions to anyone I meet. It's not difficult at all.

How could they have missed it? All of them? Every single one? This was my life that got flushed down the pan here. I take it very seriously. I feel bitterly disappointed and massively let down by all the doctors I ever saw. Deep, hard, hurt.

And, how many other people have they missed?

Did they miss you?

For a long time I was very angry. I was going to prove them wrong. I was going to battle and fight and prove them all useless. I was going to burst into their offices and strike down with great vengeance and furious anger those who would attempt to poison and destroy me!

"Whoa man, chill-out dude."

You see the anger in my words? The bitterness? The rage? The fury? Once I started learning how to look after myself, once I had some success, I couldn't believe there were so many other options, so many different things to try.

This anger turned into a motivational tool. It worked for a while, enabled me to keep fighting and learning, but it made me bitter, resentful.

After I got better, all this anger remained. I didn't even realise it for a long time. I didn't do anything silly, but dark thoughts plagued my mind...

...until my friend Lauren saw this anger casting a shadow over me.

Why was I so angry? Could I not see it harming me? Was this really the way to view so many people? So many good people trying so hard to help so many?

And of course she was right. The bitterness was gnawing away inside me. Doesn't do the soul any good to have such dark thoughts festering away. I am grateful to my friends for showing me simple truths. Better to forgive.

I choose not to trust the doctors and it doesn't get me down anymore. Life is much better without hate in it. If I tell my story, hopefully others will be better able to help themselves.

There is nothing I can do to change today's doctor's ways, and I'm not gonna waste any more time and energy on them. I am just some bloke who was sick. I have no letters after my name. No one knows me outside my little world. There is no way for me to change the hundreds and thousands of doctor's views, ways and methods.

That is far outside my capabilities. That is not my skill. I would need to be a famous scientist, doctor, politician or film star in order to change such entrenched ways of life. I am none of these things.

But I don't need to change the world. I didn't need to change the world in order to heal myself. All I needed to do was change *my* world.

And that's what I urge everyone else to do. Change your world by educating yourself.

You don't need to explain yourself to anyone, except yourself.

You don't need to educate anyone, except yourself, in order to take actions to help yourself.

Focus inwards. Focus all your energy on learning about your situation and what can make you better.

Look, it's tough enough educating yourself, let alone trying to educate people who think they know everything already. Forget the doctors, forget everyone but yourself. Change yourself. If you look, all the answers are out there.

71. Doctor, doctor, when I press with my finger here... it hurts, and here... it hurts, and here... and here... What do you think is wrong with me? You have a broken finger!

These are some of the wise words I received from the doctors over the years:

"You need to exercise more." – I just told the doc I was working out five times a week.

"You need to exercise less." – I just told the doc I was working out five times a week.

"You are too stressed. You should chill-out more" – I was smoking three joints a day.

"It's the dust mites." – I was having trouble sleeping and my sinuses were permanently blocked.

"There's nothing we can do." – Chronic bad neck.

"There's nothing you can do." – Chronic bad shoulders.

"You must learn to live with the pain." – Chronic bad back.

"That's life." – Chronic bad back.

"Some people are just unlucky." – Heartburn 24 hours a day.

"Everyone gets dry skin when they get older, you must use moisturiser." – Crazy dry skin all over my legs.

"Then don't wash up, you have the perfect excuse, hahaha!" – After I complained that washing the dishes made my hands swell painfully up and itch like crazy for days on end.

"You need bladder re-training." – That's a beauty, that one. I complained of having to get up three times each night to have a pee. I mean please, bladder re-training is how they teach you how to hold on! I kid you not!

"There is nothing wrong with you." – After 24 blood tests came back 'in-range' and I had just listed out all my troubles to the doc.

"Go home and enjoy your good health." – As above.

"That's mumbo-jumbo." – After I showed my hair test to a posh Harley Street Doctor who specialised in mercury detox. I paid £250 ($400) an hour for the honour of receiving that pearl of wisdom.

"You should wash your hair less vigorously." – This is my personal favourite. I had permanent dandruff, great scabs of white flakes encrusted my skull and I was told to wash my scalp less vigorously. I mean please! I am sorry to report that I even followed that bull$hit advice for months too. I very gently massaged my hair with my fingertips each time I washed me hair! What a cock!

"Here, take these magic beans…" – Oh man! Stop!

What a bunch of bloody idiots! Took me 36 years to stop listening. The sad thing is, all the above quotes are real. Every single one of them. All wrong. All wrong. Such a shame.

Don't misunderstand me, personally doctors are fine. I go on holiday with friends who are doctors; they are all lovely people trying hard to help others have a better life. That's a wonderful profession to have. Helping others! How cool is that!

It's the training, advice and drugs that I believe are wrong. I believe healing is an art form, a gift, maybe even a natural ability, not something taught by companies that profit gigantically from the drugs they flog.

For the record:

Being allergic to dust mites means something is wrong with me that needs sorting out. The solution to the problem is not to avoid dust mites, which is impossible. The answer to the allergic problem is to clean out my insides and a diet upgrade.

Dry skin means something is wrong with me and it need's sorting out. The solution to the problem is not to add moisturiser to my skin. Dry skin could mean something in my diet disagrees with me, which in turn means I need to clean out my insides. Dry skin almost certainly means I am dehydrated. I should drink more water, but why am I dehydrated in the first place? It could easily be a signal that my adrenal glands are not working correctly. Maybe it's my kidneys? Maybe both? And why are they not working correctly? Maybe it's my diet? Maybe I'm mercury toxic? If my adrenal glands are not working, how is my thyroid?

Getting up in the night to pee means something is wrong with me that needs sorting out. The solution to the problem is not bladder re-training. Getting up in the night is a clear signal that something is wrong with my kidneys. You can't get a clearer message about kidneys than that. Maybe it's diet? Maybe it's dehydration? Why are the kidneys damaged?

If my lab tests all say I'm healthy but I tell you I feel unwell, it means something needs sorting out. The solution to the problem is not to tell me that I'm imagining my ill health.

Allergic to washing-up liquid means I have multiple chemical sensitivities, which in turn means liver problems.

Permanent dandruff means I have diet and dehydration problems.

Chronic digestive problems mean I have a congested digestive tract that needs cleaning out. Most likely a congested liver too.

Chronic back pain means I have digestive problems, food allergies, parasites, kidney stones, and just maybe mercury poisoning.

Everything means something. Every little symptom, no matter how small means something, and it's up to us to figure out what it means. In the cold light of day, now I know what some of these signals mean, I do not find it remotely funny that my doctors never once got it right.

Sad really.

It used to really get me down. All these missed opportunities to minimise my suffering. Maybe now you understand why I felt so let down. I had everything wrong and they missed it all.

• • •

Whilst I trash traditional western medicine, I must say I had some extraordinarily good care and help from the muscle tester dude, with one unfortunate exception. He is a natural practitioner and he was amazing. He opened my eyes to a world I'd never even heard of. He led me gingerly out of the darkness and into the light, just one step at a time. He knew too much, too soon, would scare me away.

I looked long and hard for someone like him and I am lucky I eventually found him. He was my ideas man, I bounced ideas off him every time we met. He slowly educated me, breaking me into the holistic world as gently as possible.

This was typical of him: before I lay down on the treatment table I always emptied my pockets of their clutter: mobile phone, handkerchief, wallet, coins and whatnot. One day this treasure trove included a pack of gum. He leaned over and picked up the pack. He just read the ingredients list. He didn't say a word, not one word. He glanced at me in slow-mo and raised an eyebrow. And that was enough. That's all it took for me to realise I didn't need that bunch of synthetic sweeteners and chemicals in my already damaged body. Sometimes we need a little nudge in order to see things more clearly.

He is a good man and I could not have got better without him. But even though he was amazingly helpful, sadly I still got hurt by his advice. I got one amalgam removed on his say-so. He did not warn me I needed a specialist dentist or I might get massively worse. He didn't know that amalgam removal with no protection could cause such serious problems. That's when I first learned: ignorance sure hurts like hell. But he knows now and will not let it happen again.

It is important to find someone you can trust, but it's easier said than done. I urge caution and cross-checking all advice when it comes to mercury issues. Any doubts, just ask on the mercury forums. Someone will shout the roof down if there is a potential problem.

72. Textbook mercury poisoning

After hearing of all the things I had to do to get better, people often ask if everything was actually necessary. Did I really have to do everything I did?

Certainly some things were more essential and powerful than others, but for me there could be no short cuts or half measures; I was just too sick. Almost everything in my body was screwed: liver, gallbladder, kidneys, adrenals, thyroids, lungs, digestive tract, blood, skin, eyes, ears, and my brain was all jumbled up too. Everything I did needed doing at some point.

I suppose I could have done half the stuff I did, maybe only a couple of cleanses each, but then I would only be a quarter as well as I am now. I'm not satisfied with a quarter better.

What have I missed investigating in my body to far? Spleen? Pancreas? Not sure what they do, nor how to test them. I assume there are still other unknown parts of me that got screwed too, but importantly, my list of damaged organs is textbook mercury poisoning. The mercury leaks out of the amalgams, gets transported around the body in the bloodstream and poisons everything everything everything. That poison goes everywhere everywhere everywhere. No corners are left untouched as the mercury percolates all around the body. It's a full-body experience.

This is how mercury poisoning works. And if this is how mercury poisoning works, am I so different from other people? Am I from Mars, Venus or Betelgeuse?

When my heath first crashed I had no idea why I was sick. I was just sick. Ignorantly sick. If people who are mercury toxic have the same root cause problem as me, then it's fair to assume they will be similarly troubled with a multitude of troubles like me.

What about you? Right here and right now? Could all these things also affect you? Did you have a mouth full of mercury? Did you break a thermometer? Did you have vaccinations? Did you eat too much fish? Could your problems be as far-reaching as mine? Am I so different from you?

Sure, I may have had more problems, and you may have less severe problems than me, but are we really so different? Everything in me was screwed. Everything. I did not have one part that was not affected. It's not like I had a really bad liver and great kidneys. Everything was buggered up to one degree or another.

Or maybe you are not so far gone as I was, but if you are half as sick as me, then maybe all your organs are only half as poisoned as mine. But if mercury is involved they are still ALL compromised in some way or another.

And what if you are sicker than me? Do you think some parts of your body got missed by the mercury? Are you so special that your mercury poisoning didn't behave as typical textbook mercury poisoning behaves? Do you really think only part of you got damaged?

If this discussion disturbs you, if my aggressive manner startles or dismays you, if I asked some hard and difficult questions, upfront and rude, right in your face; I just did it to get you thinking.

We are all different and we all have differing issues to contend with, but mercury poisoning is mercury poisoning. The fundamental problems caused by mercury are the same: Leaked mercury poisons every part of the body.

I believe it's important for mercury toxic people to understand the basic problems mercury causes. With understanding we can act, and if we act, we can get better. The actions we take totally depend on our understanding of a problem. If we don't understand, we have no hope of acting correctly.

Hey, I got better and if I can, so can anyone. All the answers are out there somewhere. I found them.

Another reason I said what I said in such pushy way is because I come across person after person who assumes that they do not have problem X, Y and Z. I did all the standard tests, almost all came up 'in range' but I was still totally poisoned everywhere.

We must forget what conventional wisdom has made us and our doctors believe. An open mind is crucial. I only got better when I had run out of ideas, when I tried the mother-of-all-long-shots, and when I did things I was convinced I did not need. Only when I ignored what western medicine had drummed into my head, only then did I get better. Am I so different from everyone else? Was it just me that was misdiagnosed a million times?

And, I come across person after person who gets side-tracked. This is very common and totally understandable. We have so many things wrong it's easy to miss the connections, easy to get muddled with all the pieces of the jigsaw puzzle, easy to go off on a tangent and get lost down a cul-de-sac.

Always remember: Mercury is the root cause of the vast majority of our problems. If not directly, then indirectly so.

I had terrible problems with bacteria and parasites. The mercury smashed my adrenal and thyroid glands. This in turn robbed my body of the energy and strength to fight and defend itself against the bugs. I had to kill the bugs, support and repair my adrenal glands, support and repair my thyroid gland, and also chelate mercury. A long chain of problems and solutions all caused by the big M.

When you can see the big picture, when you understand the broader perspective of mercury poisoning, you can follow each problem back to the source: mercury. It is important not to get side-tracked, but to keep all your plates busily twirling around in your incredible plate-spinning show.

And I have not finished yet, the rant continues: I come across person after person who assumes that they have 'done that' and they 'don't need to do it again.'

I have 'done that' and 'done it again' and 'continue doing it' and I keep on benefiting from the repeated things I do. Be it many chelation rounds, or the multiple herbal cleanses, or even just dry skin brushing every day for years. Whatever; the repetition of the things that worked is what got me better.

We need to appreciate that it may take many months of actions to clean, strengthen and heal parts of our body that have been sick for decades.

It's strange to me; it seems so simple; just keep on trying, keep on reading and researching, keep on repeating the things that work. But I know not everyone is like me. Not everyone can continue pushing. The overwhelming inclination is to let others take control, to get sidetracked, and to assume two weeks of action can solve 20 years of neglect and wrong-doing.

I guess I was like that too for 36 years. And I only changed when I was forced at life-point.

It is clear to me that few people understand how, or believe they can get better from mercury poisoning. It's not like there are loads of shining examples of mercury recovery stories out there. Even my recovery is not complete. I am massively better, but I am still chelating. I guess that's why I wrote my book; to show that recovery is actually possible. It takes time and effort sure, but it is do-able.

One thing's absolutely for sure; only the toughest make it back from mercury poisoning. The mercury forums are stuffed full of the bravest people I have ever met. The odds are well and truly stacked against us. To stay away from traditional western medicine, to break away from the doctors we are taught from birth to trust, to have to DIY ourselves back to better health. To be poisoned in such a way that people think you must be mad as a hatter just to utter the words:

"I was poisoned by my fillings."

The looks people gave me when I said that.

"Everyone has metal fillings! You don't see everyone sick do you!"

Someone actually said that to me once. Can you believe it?

Imagine I'd said, "I have throat cancer," and they'd replied, "Throat cancer! Everyone has throats and you don't see everyone sick with throat cancer do you!"

There are a lot of blind, as well as stupid Muggles in our world.

If you are looking for short cuts, my advice is to get stuck into reading about the subjects that pique your interest. Taking responsibility for our own health is vital and that is achieved through education. I recommend reading whole books about the subjects that grab your attention. The internet is awesome, but very often the information is shallow. Ditto magazine articles. To understand things you need to get involved in the nitty-gritty, delving as deep as you dare. One-page articles about the perfect diet in Good Housekeeping is probably not the best source.

I read some pretty dry and lifeless books on my travels, but the books I mention here in my book are the books that sparkled and inspired me. I wouldn't recommend them if they were crap, although I freely admit some of them are pretty freaky at first.

If you a looking for magic bullets, then I am deeply sorry to report I found none. I kept hoping something would magically cure everything in one fell swoop. You read about so many magic pills and potions that supposedly cure people overnight, but I never found them. I tried them, but seems I was sold a dream.

73. To friends and relations

Hi there! Funny, eh? I bet you didn't figure out what I was doing when I was oh so bloody sick! You knew I was distracted, but I bet reading this is a bit of an eye-opener for you.

I just wanted to say something to the people who know me in the flesh. I guess some of you will have thought something like this when reading my story:

"Huh?! Why didn't he tell me about X?"

"Why didn't he warn me about Y?"

"He could have easily told me about X, Y or Z!"

"Why did he deny me such powerful, health-building and lifesaving knowledge?"

Do not deny it! I'm sure you thought something along those lines at least once whilst reading my tale.

Well, I was a little preoccupied sorting myself out, but the overriding reason was because you would not have believed me. I did try to tell some things to some people, and I just made a massive cock of myself every single time. Their eyes glazed over, faces went blank, followed by disbelief, incomprehension, denial, and on the odd occasion, rage.

It was so strange to speak to people of their problems, to tell them that I'd had those same problems, to explain how I'd solved that same problem, and to watch them do nothing. No-nada! They didn't even want to help themselves. All I'd done was expose my weaknesses for people to gossip over.

I quickly learned to keep my gob firmly shut. I still don't understand why people can't be bothered to help themselves, and especially so when it's laid out on a plate for them.

I am faced with moral dilemmas on a daily basis. Should I, or shouldn't I say something to help the people I am surrounded by when they have their health issues?

I know my experience and knowledge could help them, but I have learnt to say nothing. Sad, depressing, and heartbreaking I know, but this is the real world and this is how our world works. People find it grossly offensive when non-doctors offer them advice on health issues. The knowledge I have gained puts me firmly in the minority and I feel the outsider when I discuss health issues with Muggles who have no clue. It's way too much to take in, in one quick conversation. If people ask, I will say what I know in a very small, limited, step-by-step, child-like way. Too much, too soon and that's the end of that.

Part of the reason for writing my story is because of all the moral dilemmas I face every day of my life. If I tell the whole story, you may be able to understand, you might be able to believe, and you might be able to use some of my hard-earned knowledge.

I diagnosed, or was party to diagnosing everything I had wrong with me, and I had a lot of things wrong. I healed myself by educating myself and then by doing lots of different things. So yes, I can diagnose other people's problems and I obviously know how to heal them because I healed myself.

Don't get carried away, I'm not the all-seeing-eye or anything funky like that. But when you learn something, that knowledge stays inside, ready to be used again, crying out to be used again.

So yeah, I see sickness all around me. Sickness I had, sickness I healed, and sickness I can't do anything about it. You must know what I mean. You must have known how to help someone, but it was just too difficult to bring the subject up.

I tried, but was defeated by the mass of Muggle ignorance. I don't have the patience to tell grown adults how to tie up their own shoelaces either. Many times I led the horse to water, but the dumb beast didn't, couldn't, or wouldn't drink. There is only so much I can do. As I said, these moral dilemmas are one of the reasons I wrote this book.

Today I take the stance that everyone knew I was ultra-sick, if others get sick they might ask me how I got better. And now I have written my story, it is free to be used by those who wish to help themselves.

For people who ask, who can listen, who want to help themselves, my door is always open. I have all the time in the world for you. I'm eager to share, eager to help, eager to learn.

And before you say you would have believed me if I had explained it to you…Bull$hit!

74. Live for today, chelate for tomorrow

I think about my situation a lot. I have some unanswered questions.

Stardate: 18th May 2011. Chelation continues on a regular basis even though I am better. I have done 68 rounds in three and a half years. That's exactly 201 days of chelation. A couple of months ago I tried to raise my dose up from 5mg to 6.25mg ALA. I was rewarded with a jolly good kick in the balls for the trouble. Luckily I only had a couple of days of hassles, but still the lesson was crystal clear: stick at 5mg ALA for the time being.

Why can I only handle such low levels of chelators? I am not alone, but it is not the norm. Why am I a low doser?

What is supposed to happen is that as people chelate their mercury out, their tolerance to the chelators increases as they gradually raise their dose. Higher dosages clear mercury faster, the less mercury in your body, the stronger you are, and the easier you can handle chelation.

Cutler says once people are all better and get no reactions from chelation, they should chelate for another six months at high dosages to completely clear the body of mercury. Everyone is different and will take their own special time, but seems odd I'm still on such a low dose after so many rounds.

Maybe it's because I'm allergic to mercury? Maybe pulling mercury around my body in even small amounts really disagrees with me? But then why am I better? I guess it would be vaguely interesting to do a MELISA test to see if I am allergic, but I can't really be arsed to spend money on something that makes no real difference. Whatever the result of the test, my situation will remain unchanged. I already know I only tolerate a low dose and I already chelate in a low-dose style.

Maybe the removal of mucoid plaque is the reason for my low dosage tolerance? Maybe I'm clean inside and the chelators can be assimilated so much better now the gunk is gone? The removal of the rubbery slime definitely had an effect on absorption because I put on 10kg (22 lbs) in weight over two months after I got the first load out.

Maybe I am just super-mercury-toxic? Maybe I just have a bigger load than normal and it's going to take me longer? But if I am super-toxic, why am I better?

Maybe it's because I have not had a dumping phase? Maybe the dumping phase is an essential part of getting a huge load out? Maybe I still have a dumping phase to come?

Maybe I am so outrageously mercury toxic, so allergic, that I will be stuck on a low dosage forever? Maybe the only way to keep the mercury at bay will be perpetual-chelation-at-low-dose for the rest of my life? I think that's wildly unlikely, but you never know.

Maybe I'm just a pussy? Maybe I should endure the side-effects from higher dosages and stop being a wimp? But that doesn't feel right; I think I have a fairly high tolerance to pain, misery and suffering. I've had enough practice!

Maybe I should speed my chelation? Maybe I should high dose to turbo mercury removal? Maybe endure six tough months as I crank it up and power the mercury out? Oh yes, baby! One-speed: GO! I know people who tolerate 200mg ALA per dose, maybe I could too, if I tried?

The answer to that one is an easy big-fat-NO. There is no need to speed, rush, push, power or mega-dose my chelation. I don't need to: I am already better.

The answers to these questions are not particularly important. They are just questions that float and flap around me. It doesn't actually matter that I can only handle a low dose, nor how long I will be chelating. I don't really even need to know why I am better even when I have mercury still in me. All that matters is that I am better. Right here and right now I am better. That's the most important thing.

Today I live my life as I do. I work. I play. I herb. I chelate. I am better. If anything tricky crops up, I handle it. I have enough time and it fits into each day. No special effort is needed anymore. Just like learning to drive a car is difficult and you need to take time to have lessons, but once you have learnt and gained experience, driving your car takes no effort. You jump in your car, you drive.

I jump in my car each day, I drive. I do the things required each day to drive, like using the brake, accelerator, mirror, signal, and manoeuvre. All that happens without any significant effort on my part. I have learnt how to drive, just exactly the same way as I have learnt how to look after myself. And I don't really need to know the answers to these questions because I am getting on with life again.

But I still can't stop asking myself the question: why am I better when I still have mercury in me? And I must assume I have quite a lot because whenever I attempt higher doses I get a good kickin'.

I know I am better because of all the things I have done: the chelation, the herbs, the adrenals, the thyroid, the supplements, the lifestyle, the diet, the education, the yoga, the Alexander Technique, the meditation. I guess all of this lowered my toxic load sufficiently so that I can enjoy a normal and happy life again.

But I don't totally comprehend why I am better, but yet I'm still full of mercury.

I take one day at a time because that's all I can do. I still have mercury in me, so I will continue chelating until it's all gone. Chelation is like a pension. It's an investment. An investment in my future.

I live for today, and chelate for tomorrow.

75. So long and thanks for all the fish

That's about all for now. That's what's happened the last four years of my life. It's been hard, difficult, fun and exciting, and I still have a ways to go too. Just because I finished my book does not mean I finished my chelation. I still have a lot of chelation ahead of me, and there will undoubtedly be potholes along the way. Dips are inevitable in this game: chelation is hard and will definitely cause me problems in the coming years. But I got this far and I am confident in my ability to battle and find solutions wherever I need them.

For the record I reckon I will have to do about 200 chelation rounds in total to get rid of all my mercury. Why 200? That's a wild educated guess. I know I have a lot of mercury in me and it's only coming out slow. As of May 2011 I have done 68 rounds in total over four years. I wish I could have chelated more, but life is full and chelation is hard, so that's all I've managed.

132 rounds to go.

That's cool: I will do them tomorrow.

• • •

It's worth just listing out all the problems I have solved so far:

Dairy allergy – gone
Wheat allergy – gone
Gluten allergy - gone
Soya allergy – gone
Nightshade allergy – gone
Passive smoking allergy – gone
All processed food allergy – gone
Sulphur food intolerance – gone
Fruit intolerance – gone
Sugar problem/hypoglycaemia – gone
Chronic heartburn – gone.
Constipation – gone
Bloating – gone
Dry skin – gone
Sleeping badly – gone
Libido – back to normal
Multiple chemical sensitivities – gone
Chronic back problems and pain for 10 years – gone
Muscle weakness – gone
Short term memory problems – gone
Brain fog – gone
Depression – gone
Tinnitus – gone
Anger – gone
Hypothyroidism – gone
Adrenal fatigue – gone
Chronic fatigue – gone
Fear of spiders – gone
Grumpy – mostly gone!

All in all my life is totally back on track now. I no longer need to focus so intensely on my health either, and I am no longer in constant pain. The brain fog lifted long ago and I am back to being a normal bloke again.

I would say my current health status is that of a normal 42-year-old city bloke, which is not saying that much; the difference is I know what's wrong and I know how to put it right. The revolving system of chelation and cleansing is easy and I don't have to think too much about them now. I am 42 years old and I plan on having a long happy life.

I will end where I started because never in a million years did I think I would have this much fun regaining my health:

"All truth passes through three stages. First, it is ridiculed. Second, it is violently opposed. Third it is accepted as being self-evident."

That's all folks!

Sunshine
28 May 2011

Part III

Some final bits'n'bobs

76. Send cash now!

Just a quick word to all the companies and authors I have recommended in this book. Please feel free to send me loads of cash. Cash is king and I deserve huge wads after plugging your wares. You know there are no free lunches! I scratch your back, you scratch mine! Remember I paid full price for your products, I got no doctor's discount and I'm telling you not to feel shy or embarrassed about sending me money. Often is good, but one-off cash payments work just fine too. I don't want discounts, I'm better now, so just send the cash.

On a serious note, I get nothing from anyone for recommending any of the companies, products, books or protocols mentioned in here. If my book sells loads and those companies sell more products; great. I'll be happy because lots more people will be getting better.

I get bugger all monetary gain out of this book. No way will it pay for the huge time it took to write. Four years' work!

The mercury toxic world is small and it is extremely unlikely to get big any time soon, but this book was never about the money. I get enough money from my job in the city. This book is all about how anyone can get better if they put their mind to it.

I bought most of my basic supplements from:
http://www.cytoplan.co.uk

The rest of my supplements from online supplement supermarkets:
UK: www.nutricentre.com
USA: www.iherb.com

Adrenal glandular:
ACE: 50mg size *Adrenal Cortex* from Thorne Research
ACE: 250mg size *Adrenal Cortex* from Nutricology

Both made from Adrenal Cortex (Bovine)
(Note: I was fine switching between the two brands. Five capsules of the Thorne Research did the same as one capsule from Nutricology.)

Thyroid glandular: *Nutri Thyroid*
Armour for thyroid support: I used *Armour Thyroid (generic) Thyroid* from Greater Pharma, purchased from:
http://www.1drugstore-online.com

I got my herbs from:
Humaworm: www.Humaworm.com
Andreas Moritz liver and kidney herbs from:
www.presentmoment.com
UK herbs: www.shs100.com

Unfortunately in April 2011, the European medical authorities banned some of the ingredients in Humaworm. This applies to all the countries in the EU, including me and everyone else in England.

This was done because some of the herbs have not been tested according to some mega-expensive-made-up-rules-and-regulations-that-ignore-common-sense. It costs between £80,000 and £120,000 per herb to run these herb trials and get a licence. ($120,000 and $200,000). Humaworm has 24 herbs in it.

A few of the most common herbs are exempt or already licensed, but most need these expensive tests. You cannot patent these herbs, which in turn means anyone can grow them and sell them, which in turn means they are cheap, which in turn means you cannot make oodles of cash from selling them. The herbal companies cannot spend this amount of money on each herb because there is simply not enough money to be made. So it's extremely unlikely that these amazing herbs will ever be tested. So they have basically been banned.

This of course has nothing to do with the fact they work just fine thank you very much. Everyone knows this is just Big Pharma crushing its competition. They've done a good job too. It's a long-term project, but they have done sterling work for their shareholders: well done boys, just don't start with your incredible excuses about protecting the masses, snake oil and whatnot.

I have used these herbs.

They have cured me.

I know they work.

You can't pull the wool over my eyes.

Now I must resort to smuggling my herbs in. Wild, eh! Who would have thought it? Smuggling herbs to help my own health. Herbs that have been used since the dawn of time. Proven to work by all the people down through history. As of April 2011 not a single product used in traditional Chinese medicine or Ayurvedic medicine had been licensed. The arrogance of the people banning these herbs is astonishing. We live in a screwed-up time. Future generations will look back and laugh at our stupidity.

My opinion is these herbs work gloriously, but my opinion is valueless in the eyes of these authorities. Just because they healed me is of no consequence to them. My voice, my experience, my pain, my suffering, my success has no value.

It's all terribly sad really and I could go on for pages and pages, but there's nothing I can do about it: the herbs that cured me have been banned. If you live in the EU you are denied the choice to buy them.

If you are looking for a herbal formula to try out, just get Googling. If you look, you will find. There are plenty of herbal companies providing herbs to every corner of the world. There are always loopholes, always little people selling little things. The authorities can't catch them. Look and you will find.

You want companies that tell you exactly which herbs are in their formulas. Forget all the companies that don't tell you and keep it a secret. If you can't find the exact ingredients, don't buy it. You also want herbs that are as fresh as possible. Herbs go stale if they sit on a shelf for six months. If you find fresh, herb-only formulas, they should rock 'n' roll.

I have recently started using the herbs from Specialist Herbal Supplies at www.shs100.com. They don't sell a parasite cleanse, but they have everything else and more. Based here in the UK and so far, so good.

77. Books that sparkled and inspired me

"Read first the best books. The important thing for you is not how much you know, but the quality of what you know."
Desiderius Erasmus 1466-1536

I read a heck of a lot of alternative health books. I had no medical education so I don't understand all those official medical text books written in gobbledygook. No idea why they write those books/reports in language that is so completely unintelligible to the common man. It's so strange that companies spend millions on research, yet write the results in mumbo jumbo. It's pointless and makes me think they don't want me to understand. There is no need to write so that normal people can't understand. I read some most excellent books that clearly explained medical issues.

Yes, luckily for me there are loads of cool people that translated traditional medical gibberish into fantastically understandable works of art. Below I list out the magnificent books that enabled me to understand and to heal myself. They taught me what was expected of me to make my body work again.

I would like to thank all the authors of these books. Thank you for all the time and effort you took in writing your books. I learnt a great deal from them all. You saved my life.

Listed in order of value, worth, greatness and importance:

1) *Amalgam Illness* by Andrew Cutler
For mercury troubles there is no equal. Tricky to understand at first, especially if symptoms are driving you wild, but top of the list and essential reading. The protocol is so simple it could be written on two sides of A4 paper. But what the book does do and is so awesome at, is

explaining what's happened to you, which parts of you need investigating, what to do about the various problems and ultimately a path/route to get better.

2) *Timeless Secrets of Health & Rejuvenation* by Andreas Moritz
OK, now this is the alternative-health nuclear-warhead of a book. The big bomb that will launch you into the alterative world of holistic healthcare. Very extensive, detailed, full-on, it covers a multitude of topics. I read this near the beginning of my journey and it blew my mind. Every page I learnt something new: so much knowledge and information given for the price of a simple book. This guy is a wizard (ha!) at explaining what is wrong with your body, what is expected of you to make it work correctly and the many different things to try to help you get better.

He is a guru for liver flushing, which incidentally Cutler (and little me) says are too heavy duty for us mercury toxic. But his book is filled with masses of information, ideas and explanations. Lots to take in, lots to learn.

When I first read it, I was not capable of understanding many of the things he explains because I was a holistic-virgin at the time. But I read it again later when I knew what I was doing and it is a mega book.

I must warn you it is a little freaky in places. I didn't agree with some things either; like not eating meat and liver flushing. And his emotional stuff is way, way beyond me. But I should not put you off: major book. Read it and make your own mind up about what he says. A giant leap in understanding your body and what is expected of you to make it work correctly. It's number two on my list for a reason.

3) *Nutrition and Physical Degeneration* by Weston A. Price
Already talked about this book, but this is the missing link in your dietary understandings. Heavy duty, old skool and too long, but an amazing book. Make sure you read the last three chapters that are the diet recommendations!

4) *Nourishing Traditions* by Sally Fallon
Great in explaining how to cook and implement Weston A. Price's ideas in your life.

5) *Hair Test Interpretation* by Andrew Cutler
Ah man, I guess this looks like an Andy Cutler love-fest. OK, I will lend out my copy to anyone who wants it, but it's a loan, I want it back, need it back, email me if you want to borrow it.

The reason I put this in here is because I learnt a gigantic amount about myself from this book. Adrenals, thyroid, blood sugar, copper, mercury and a host of supplements to consider taking too.

I don't know of any other test you can take that yields so much information. Information that I could research and understand for myself. Takes five or six hours to read with your hair test in your hand and you get a list of issues to investigate. Priceless.

6) Adrenals and Thyroid
I found this a very difficult subject to figure out, so I am going to group these books together, but the standout book is called *Your Thyroid and How to Keep it Healthy* by Barry Durrant-Peatfield. You may have to read it twice but it's the best of the batch. This book also tells you how to actually treat yourself, on your own, with no medical supervision. His supplement recommendations are very similar to Cutler's and I have found no equal in treating metabolic health.

Adrenal Fatigue, The 21st Century Stress Syndrome by James Wilson is very good, and clearly explains adrenal problems. Strangely lacking in thyroid info, but a very good book nevertheless. Clear and easy to understand.

www.drrind.com
Dr Rind's website is well worth reading top to bottom. His explanation of the temperature chart to diagnose and track adrenal and thyroid issues is awesome.

Hypothyroidism Type 2 by Mark Starr
Good at explaining how you got ill. I didn't agree with his treatment, but an interesting book nevertheless and it does talk about mercury and toxins in our environment.

7) Bowel care
Cleanse & Purify Thyself: Book 1 by Rich Anderson
Dr. Jensen's Guide to Better Bowel Care by Dr. Bernard Jensen
These two guys make your digestive tract an interesting and fun place to be. If you want to understand why your digestive tract is not doing the right thing, these two books will explain what's happened and what's expected of you to put it right. Remember good health starts in the bowels!

8) *The Untold Story of Milk* by Ron Schmid
This book is a beauty. Way more interesting that a book about milk should be. If you want to understand how our modern commercial food and farming world works, this will give you a clear understanding. If you've heard about raw milk and want to investigate it first before you try, this is the book.

9) *Water & Salt* by Hendel and Ferreira
A book about the importance of water quality and the incredible value of salt in our body and diet.

10) *Live Without Pain* by Simon King (AKA the Muscle Tester Dude)
I can highly recommend the Muscle Tester Dude's book which I found fascinating. Ever wondered why some people get miraculously better after amalgam removal, like the next day the majority of their symptoms disappear? This book goes a long way in explaining how and why that happens. It's not a book about mercury chelation, he doesn't know about chelation, it's a book about identifying the causes of chronic pain and removing the root problem, of which mercury is just one. The best parts are where he explains how and why our body/muscles react to toxins/poisons and specifically to mercury.

I read a lot and I've never seen anyone else come close to explaining exactly how our bodies react to mercury, and why simply removing mercury is enough for some people to get better. It also implies why we are still ill even after amalgam removal: because we have too much mercury in our body and we must safely chelate it out.

Anyone with amalgams, muscle weakness, gold crowns, or jewellery will find this book interesting. He also explains how muscle testing works.

11) *Getting The Mercury Out: A Recovery Memoir* by Aine Ni Cheallaigh Another mercury recovery story, this time from a lady in New York State. She also chelated using the Cutler protocol.

I found myself laughing and taking deep sighs in equal measure as Aine's deeply personal story unfolded. It reminds us all that mercury poisoning is a truly horrific ordeal to endure. She talks in detail about the hardship and suffering she went through when her body and mind crumbled, but also of the joy of recovering what she had lost when she was well again after her chelation regime started working and life returned to normal again.

I know Aine pretty well; she helped me greatly on this book. If you want to know how someone of the fairer sex managed it, this is a good read.

A few other books well worth reading:

Natural Cures 'They' Don't Want You To Know About by Kevin Trudeau.

Hypo-thyroidism: The Unsuspected Illness by Broda Barnes and Lawrence Galton.

Earthing: The Most Important Health Discovery Ever? by Ober, Sinatra, Zucker.

*Here are all the other books, links and research places that
I mention in the main body of the story:*

It's All in Your Head: The Link Between Mercury Amalgams and Illness by Hal Huggins.

Google 'Colour vision and contrast sensitivity losses of mercury intoxicated industry workers in Brazil'.

The Chemical Maze Shopping Companion by Bill Statham.

Pottenger's Cats: A Study in Nutrition by Francis Pottenger.

Natural Nutrition for Cats by Kymythy R. Schultze.

Juice Fasting & Detoxification by Steve Meyerowitz.
If you are going to juice fast, it's well worth getting this little book. Tells you what to expect, how to do it and importantly how to break the fast. If you break the fast eating pizza and chips, you will make yourself sick again! You have been warned!

Parasites and full body health: *The Cure For All Diseases* by Hulda Clark – Old skool writing from a little old lady, but she knows her stuff. The queen of parasites!

Loads of hair test details, info and instructions here:
http://home.earthlink.net/~moriam/HOW_TO_hair_test.html

Lab for hair test: www.directlabs.com and the correct hair test is: 'Hair Elements'

Sulphur exclusion test: Google 'Sulphur exclusion test Cutler'.

Google: 'Analogue cordless phone'. I got mine from a company called Orchid. This website is helpful too: http://www.emfields.org/index.asp

EMF research: *The Powerwatch Handbook* by Alasdair & Jean Philips.

Organic mattress: www.abacaorganic.co.uk

Detox baths: http://www.massagetherapy.com/articles/index.php/article_id/309/Water-Wealth-

Castor oil: *The Oil That Heals* by William A. McGarey.

Clock with multiple alarms: 'Neverlate Executive' by American Innovative.

Vibrating wrist watch: Vibralite8.

Compounded chelators from : www.livingnetwork.co.za/products/
The guy that runs this show, Dean, he is mercury toxic, chelates using the Cutler protocol, and has an amazing mercury helpful website. http://livingnetwork.co.za

Heart: *Put Your Heart in Your Mouth* by Dr Campbell-McBride.

Sinus trouble: Google and YouTube 'Neti Pot' for more instructions. Oh yeah, you want a Rhino Horn shaped one, or a NoseBuddy: they work best.

Healing protocol from Curezone: http://curezone.com/diseases/health.asp

Baby formula: Google 'Replacing mother imitating human breast milk in the laboratory' by the Cornucopia Institute. (Free download)

Vaccinations: *The Truth about Vaccines: Making the Right Decision for Your Child* by Richard Halvorsen.
Vaccination Is Not Immunization by Tim O'Shea.

Grain mill: I have a 'Pico grain mill'.

Soaking info and explanation:
http://www.passionatehomemaking.com/2008/04/whole-grains-grinding-soaking.html

Soaking info: *Nourishing Traditions* by Sally Fallon.

Raw milk deliveries in the UK: www.hookandson.co.uk

Organic meat deliveries in the UK: The Well Hung Meat Company.

Organic veggie boxes in the UK: Able and Cole.

Fish and mercury poisoning: *Diagnosis: Mercury: Money, Politics and Poison* by Jane Hightower.

78. Mercury Attack Check-List

1. Chill out and remain calm. Relax.

2. Be on my own. Avoid everyone.

3. Be ready for two days of troubles.

4. Digestive problems always happen. Drink plenty of apple cider vinegar even before the heartburn comes, because you know it will come!

5. Detox bath—any type but make it hot hot hot and follow with a one-minute freezing cold shower. Should clear a lot of hanging around mercury.

6. Bowel cleanse of some type—mercury dumps into the bowels and having a clearout is a great idea. Psyllium or P&B shakes, anything easy and simple.

7. Make sure all supplements are taken.

8. Increase dose of vitamin C to bowel tolerance. Divided doses, four times a day at mealtimes and before bed. This is very important and will help big-time-Charlie, so do it ASAP.

9. Dry skin brushing. It will tell your body you love it and you will help get that mercury out as quickly as possible. Before a detox bath is great too: wakes up the skin. Help your body help itself.

10 Oil massage after the dry skin brushing.

11 Oil pulling. Lots of it. I did 3 x 20 minutes back-to-back once and it helped a lot.

12 Meridian Massage. Always seems to make me feel better and only takes seven minutes.

13. Self Reiki. Set aside an hour or two , and make 100 percent sure of no interruptions.

14. Don't Worry. This is only short-term hassle. It will pass. It always passes. In a couple of days you will feel good again and you will have learnt a bit more about yourself from whatever experiment just backfired.

79. Summary of what I did

1. Diet clean up and food education
2. Bowel cleansing
3. Parasite cleanse (which can be done at the same time as the bowel cleanse)
4. Dental clean up (amalgams, root canals, nickel crowns, cavitations)
5. Kidney cleansing
6. Liver cleansing

http://curezone.com/diseases/health.asp

Mercury chelation using the Cutler protocol
Detox baths
Castor oil packs
Adrenals–understanding and treating
Thyroids–understanding and treating

Morning routine (15-20 minutes total)
Dry skin brushing–daily
Oil massages–daily
Oil pulling–daily
Contrast showers–daily
These morning routines are all explained in the book *Timeless Secrets of Health & Rejuvenation* by Andreas Moritz

Tackle each topic individually. Focus on just one topic at a time, dive in and see if you can figure it out. You will know when you understand because you will start making choices and deciding to do things. My rule was to only try something when I understood it. And I mean hand-on-my-heart understood it, not squinting out the corner of my eye and hoping for the best!

80. About this book

Phew! Finally finished. That was a project and a half. Where are all the ghostwriters when you need them! Now I have the utmost respect for all authors. Holy cow, it takes a long time to write a book. Five years, mine took me. Hundreds and hundreds of hours of work. I was not chained to a desk slaving away, I wrote it in those in-between moments in life and I loved every minute of it. An hour or two in the evening after the kids had gone to bed. I did a lot on the train commuting back and forth to the office.

The main outline was done during the second year of chelation, in 2008. The next three years were spent refining and editing everything. I am not a writer, or I wasn't at the beginning anyway. I guess I am now, but in the beginning this was written by a mercury toxic health freak who didn't have the faintest idea of how to write a story. It was all over the place and I still can't spell to save my life. Prior to my troubles I showed zero knowledge, ability or will to write anything.

Everything was re-written at least three times as I learnt and refined my writing style. I know to the reader it just seems like the words spill out and magically work well. Now I know, writing takes a heck of a lot of effort.

I did struggle with the order of things and getting events down in a way that you could understand and connect with. I did a heck of a lot of different things in a very short space of time; making it all fit and flow nicely was pretty tricky.

The vast majority of the order is correct. The only mis-match, editorial gimmick I employed was the cat experiment, the juice fast, the first parasite cleanse and the colonic. If you remember this was the major turning point when I started healing.

This group of things actually happened one month before I had the final quadrant of amalgams removed. What I mean is, I started getting better just prior to amalgam free. Which is no big deal and the story works just fine like you just read it.

Except it is a big deal to me. It's my story and I object to having to fanny around with the time line in order to make the story smoother and more understandable for you. One of the many reasons I wrote this is to give me some finality. An ending for me. I had such a terrible time. It really was as bad you just read about. I thought it would be cool to write it all up, to help others in the same boat, but also to draw a line underneath my health-crash. So, this book is just as much for me, as for you. To heal me. So I can move on and get on with life.

So, I want the story straight. That's all. The cat experiment, the juice fast, the first parasite cleanse and the colonic all happened just prior to amalgam removal. That's how I knew all the herbs and cleanses worked so well: because I started healing before I was completely amalgam free.

• • •

I would also like to say how much I enjoyed myself writing this. It really is very therapeutic getting the words out. It's not a skill I knew I had. Gives a real sense of joy to unleash the words, and I thought I kept the swearing down to wildly low levels. If you didn't like the minuscule amount of swearing I did use: tough!

• • •

In my story I did not touch on the politics of mercury at all. I'm not involved in any agency, fund, charity, website or political movement trying to rid the world of mercury. I had way too much on my own plate to have any time to dedicate to those worthy causes. I needed all my energy just to help myself. This is how most people are. Just trying to get on with life as smoothly as possible.

However there is a close community within the mercury world, within the mercury forums where people band together and help each other out. I was very involved with my generation of mercury toxic folks on the forums. Helping out where I could, passing on some of the understanding I'd learnt in order to help people. I was just repaying the help I received when I first arrived and was ignorant.

I guess my book is the culmination of those years helping myself, and helping others. I would urge everyone involved in mercury to make a little effort to spread the word and to help others, especially those struggling with their health. You don't need a trumpet, and often a whisper is better anyway, but warning people, protecting people and of course educating people is so important. In fact, it is the only way our world is gonna change.

Individually it is very difficult to change the world, but collectively the mercury bandwagon is gaining a little momentum. Twenty years ago I would have had little hope of curing myself. The diagnosis and education process was nothing like today's information super-highways with knowledge available just a couple of clicks away.

Already in 2012 mercury fillings are no longer the automatic filling material in rotten teeth. Mercury is also being removed from some vaccinations too. You can buy books all about mercury poisoning and how to help your health. And now there are people like me writing their story of how they regained their health.

But us little people, the people who got hurt, we don't have huge budgets to market our wares. My budget for marketing this book is about $100, plus any time I can spare on the mercury forums. The only other method I have in getting my story out is on the Amazon.com book reviews pages. Seriously, this is a low-budget, long-tail operation.

The only way the mercury toxic world can spread the word, growing our numbers of educated people, is to talk about the pain we went through, and what works in getting us better again. So spread the word, recommend the books to people, make reviews and recommendations on places like Amazon.com and Barnes and Noble.

I healed myself by reading loads of health books. I got loads of book recommendations along my travels and I urge you to do the same and recommend a book or two. You see someone who's sick, tap them on the shoulder and tell them which book to read. It can be your good deed for the day.

Dedication

Dedicated to all those who have the balls to get better, but haven't quite made it yet.

81. Thanks

I should say thanks to a few people, but the largest, biggest, most gigantic thank you goes to me, myself and I. If it wasn't for me, I would not have got myself better. Thanks mate, you are The Man!

Kate for standing by me, for putting up with me when it was so tough. Thanks, babes. You complete me. Losing everything we have was a major driving force for me to keep battling on. I love you truly, madly and deeply.

Lily for being the best daughter a Dad could have.

Felix for being my number one son.

Simon King, aka The muscle tester dude: Top man. Thank you for holding the torch up for me to see where I was going.

Katie Furness, my osteopath. Thanks for going the extra mile. You know you started all this off! You started it off with your muscle testing experiments on me. I guess I would have found my way eventually, but you are responsible for enabling me to take that first step. Respect. Thank you.

Editing Respect

Áine Ní Cheallaigh: I couldn't have written this without you. Your kindness, help, understanding and encouragement were superb. A massive thank you.

Leanne: For reminding me that not everyone swears as much as city boys do.

Lauren Rick: For reminding me to calm down, and for the energy.

Kelly Kingman: for coming up with the title of this book.

Monique, SteH, Nora: Thank you for your feedback in reading the early chapters. The encouragement you gave me enabled me to keep on plugging away until, voila, a finished book appeared.

Mercury-Toxic Respect
Rebecca (Bex) for the warm welcome and for introducing me to Cutler's book—thanks a mill, Sosick for the friendship, Linda T, Jinx, TK, Linda, Jackie, Sunflower, Angelbaby26, Carlin W, Diana (DR), Dawn, Dean at LivingNetwork, Mike D, Nicola B, Peter M, Skies-the-Limit, Stuart H, Stuart S, Tina, Vicki D, Misscallie, Petshopgirl6, Topbroker (Michael), Dudley, Denise D, Donna T, Gabriella, Gladioli, Heather D, Henrik K, Jessica, KD Ironside, Kristin, Lisa L, Liz B, Mister Lion, Melissa H, Michelle, PGM, Russ Tanner, Wanda, Moria, Steven C, and everyone who ever posted on Yahoo Frequent Dose Chelation: your problems, solutions and wisdom helped me, and helped everyone. Respect.

Mates Respect
Respect goes out to: Mum, Dad, Myles, Will, Lee, Jessy & Caroline, Jes & Anna, Nick & Gill, Stu F, Foz, Jon S, Andy A, Ben B, Caroline, Apollonia, Trevor & Margaret, Fledgling, David T, John W, Tom P, Dan Y, Dan H, James T, Charlie B, Steve C, Nigel R, Graham B, Simon F, Simen E, Adam T, Soren S, Andreas C, Dave C, Marc K, Steve K, Christian MDP, Chris S, Glenn H, CH, Radu.

Random Respect
Andy Cutler, Andreas Moritz, Yogi, Master, Satguru Sri Sharavana Baba, RG @ Humaworm, The Gallery, Danny Tenaglia, AC/DC, Michael Jackson, Frankie Goes to Hollywood, Danny Howells, Laurent Garnier, Leftfield, Steve Lawler, JBO, Hybrid, David Holmes, Fat Boy Slim, The Chemical Brothers, Daft Punk, Crystal Meth, BT, Renaissance, Reactivate, Pete Tong, Real Ibiza, Massive Attack, Back to Mine, Nick Warren, Nightmares on Wax, Air, Underworld, The KLF, The Orb, Groove Armanda, Carl Cox, Peace Division, Green Velvet, Deadmau5, Dave Seaman, Nirvana, Happy Mondays, Jimi Hendrix, Radiohead, Oasis, Pink Floyd, Red Hot Chilli Peppers, Global Underground, Timo Maas, Moby, System 7 and all the DJs that played on the BBC's Essential Mix; I listened to a load of your tunes while writing this.

My Alexander teachers: Fumiaki, Paul and Milton.

Clive Barker, Stephen King, Phillip Pullman, Neal Stephenson, Iain M Banks, William Boyd, Alastair Reynolds, Neal Asher, Peter F Hamilton, Stephen Baxter, Orson Scott Card, Robert Sawyer, Isaac Asimov, Arthur C Clarke, Greg Egan, Carl Sagan, David Mitchell.

If you find yourself in these lists, it's either because I like you or I learnt from you, or both. Respect.

And yeah, I know I added too many people in here, but when am I ever going to get the chance to show the respect due to all the amazing people who influenced my life in such cool and wonderful ways? Respect to everyone!

Oh yeah, one more thing

I would like to state on record that I reserve the right to change my mind. I am not The President, Head of State, Prime Minister, King, Queen, chief, politician, doctor, nurse, scientist, or dietitian and my livelihood does not depend on these words. There are multiple points of view on every single subject in the known universe and I'm not gonna be hemmed in just because I wrote this book. If something changes, if I learn something new, I will change my mind as I see fit. My words stand still, but my life education will continue every moment I'm alive.

Epilogue:
'It's A Long Way To The Top (If You Wanna Rock 'n' Roll)'
AC/DC

Ah!

Oh no!

Oh man, what a 'mare.

I didn't want to write an epilogue. No way. Not at all. I wanted my book to have a happy ending.

Damn.

I got sick again.

How gutted am I? What a disappointment. It's not like I let my guard down. I kept on and on. I didn't stop anything. I kept on chelating and I kept on using the herbs because I knew that some mercury toxic people relapse after a couple of good years.

Even though I kept detoxing, I still got sick again.

Gutted. Totally gutted. This is exactly why I kept on battling, so I would not have any more health crashes. I wanted to avoid the bad old dayz. And yet, here I was, again. Nightmare.

I have thought long and hard about including this epilogue, but I have been open all along on my journey and it would be wrong to hide the facts, even if they are painful and disappointing. But I will sneak it in at the very every end of the book, so hopefully some of you will miss it!

During the time it took to edit and finish this book, I got sick again.

• • •

It was five years since my mercury health-crash. I had rebuilt my health and my life. Everything was cool and I was all better. I was enjoying myself, work was easy, and my workouts frequent. Life was good. I even started working on a long-term goal of mine: learning how to play golf.

There was no sign of any problems so I decided to get some decent chelation rounds under my belt with some weekly chelation; three days on, four days off. In May and June 2011 I did seven rounds in eight weeks, all according to protocol. No big deal. But after the seventh round I was left feeling drained and tired. My workouts stopped and something was not right. I stopped the intensive chelation program to assess the situation.

I was lacking energy, my temperatures fell and became erratic from day to day indicating adrenal fatigue. So I restarted adrenal support, starting low and built up the dose until the temps levelled out. They took a couple of months to go back to normal.

Next I restarted thyroid support to raise my temps. After three months of daily monitoring and gradually increasing the dose, nothing had happened. I was puzzled because I should have been feeling better, and my temps should have been rising. Something, somewhere was wrong.

I hit the books, re-reading the appropriate parts. It was in fact while re-reading my own story that I spotted a mistake. I found I was dosing the thyroid supplements incorrectly. I was dosing the Armour only in the mornings. Theoretically I should have been dosing morning and evening to give my body an even spread throughout the day.

So I corrected it and started dosing morning and evening. Just in case, I lowered my dose from three and a half grains of Armour per day, down to three grains. One and a half in the morning and one and a half in the evening. Seemed like no big deal, but immediately all hell broke loose.

Within a day of correcting the thyroid dosage I had some kind of major overload episode. I couldn't put a name to it, but I had a massive reaction. Suddenly I had super-bad hypoglycaemia. The jitteriness kicked off big time and I had to eat six meals a day in an attempt to calm things down. I was mega tired and my pulse was going bananas. Blood pressure shot up to 155/85 and I could feel my heart hammering away all the time. My head got all foggy and in the clouds and I was scared out of my pants. Whoa!

I stopped all adrenal and thyroid support to assess the situation. It took about a month to return to an even keel, but something was definitely still buggered up. I tried various lower adrenal dosages, and again with lower thyroid support, but each time I got the same weird reactions, although only mildly because I was on lower dosages.

I tried various set of herbs, candida, kidney and bowel. They helped a bit, but not overall. I still seemed to have dwindling health. Next I tried a parasite cleanse but it was too hard and I had to stop taking the pills after 22 days. The side effects were driving me wild and making life completely unbearable.

Next I had a telephone meeting with Dr. Peatfield. He said what was happening was very unusual and he had never heard of such strange reactions to the adrenal and thyroid support. The correction of the Armour dose should not have given me such a wild reaction. It's not a big mistake. We were both perplexed and didn't understand what was going on.

It was decided I would go off all adrenal and thyroid support for two weeks, let my body adjust down to an unsupported clean state, then restart each to see what would happen. If my body was rejecting the Armour I might need to go on to synthetic T3-only support. This does happen sometimes.

I waited a couple of weeks and tried the adrenal support at an ultra-low dosage for two days. That did not agree at all. So I waited another two weeks to again clear my system and then tried the thyroid support. Again at an ultra-low dosage, just a quarter of a grain, and, and, and - Boom! The $hit-hit-the-fan big-time-Charlie.

The same thing happened as when I corrected the Armour dosage, except this was 50 times worse, 50 times more powerful, 50 times more painful and 100 times more scary.

Super-bad hypoglycaemia kicked in hard. I had to eat food every hour, on the hour. I even had to wake in the night to eat. If I didn't the jittery-freak was even wilder. My digestion went down the pan and food intolerances resurfaced. I had a total and massive lack of energy. I got tired, out of breath and dizzy just walking up stairs. My temperatures plunged and I was perpetually cold all over again. In contrast my feet became burning hot, almost on fire. I had a total loss of libido. Blood pressure and pulse rate sky rocketed. I was house-bound.

On top of all this lot I started having panic attacks. Everything was flaring up at the same time, my heart was going haywire, I had no idea why this was happening and the fear hit me right between the eyes.

This is it.

I am going to die.

I have never had panic attacks before. I consider myself an extremely confident and self-assured person. Panicking is not in my nature. Not at all. But no doubt about it, I was scared out of my tiny mind and convinced I was going to die. For the first time in my life the tears flowed freely.

What a total and utter nightmare.

Unsurprisingly I hit the panic button. I had no idea why this was happening. Everything was going berserk and help was needed instantly.

I rushed to see my regular NHS doctor. He had no idea what was going on either, but because my heart was running at a million miles an hour, he sent me see a cardiologist. I had an armload of blood tests, ECGs and was put on a 24-hour heart monitor.

The cardiologist diagnosed an irregular heartbeat called Lone Atrial Fibrillation, or LAF for short. The Lone part means Atrial Fibrillation without heart disease. It means an irregular heartbeat without a known cause. A subject I knew nothing about. He prescribed warfarin to thin the blood and beta blockers to calm the heart. Warfarin is rat poison. Beta blockers have many side effects. Yes, my idea of hell.

The panic attacks continued, my heart raced, life was scary and horrible. My wife attended all my doctor's appointments, to drive me there, but more importantly to give me much-needed moral support. Life was tough all over again.

I had an emergency meeting with Dr. Peatfield to discuss the situation. Did I have a heart problem? Or adrenal or thyroid problems? He didn't know, but he said I was in serious trouble and I needed to calm my heart down ASAP.

I thought long and hard about the warfarin and beta blockers. In the end I decided to take them because I was operating in the dark. I had zero understanding of this new LAF diagnosis and I felt completely out of control. The doctors didn't explain anything: the only option they offered was drugs. I could not just sit around wishing these problems away. This was an emergency. I needed to calm things down now. I was too sick and educating myself would take too long. Because I didn't understand what was going on, I actually had no other choices. So yeah, I took the damn things, but I also took the herbal heart pills Mukta Vati as well. They halved the amount of beta blockers I needed to take.

The drugs calmed things down to a degree, but something was still seriously wrong. It felt as bad as when I had unsafe amalgam removal five years ago, although the brain fog was replaced with rampant fear.

The cardiologist briefly explained that my heart was beating incorrectly. Instead of a beat, followed by a pause, followed by a beat, my heart was missing out the pause. The electrical circuits in my heart had malfunctioned and my heart was in effect doing lots of mini beats when it should be paused. It was 'persistent' too. There are different variants of LAF. Some people have an episode for an hour, or a day, and then the heart returns to normal. Mine didn't revert to normal; it was persistently stuck on bonkers.

I did ask, but the cardiologist told me nothing deep about my situation. He gave no possible reasons why this was happening, no lifestyle changes that I might make, no diet changes, no nothing except take his drugs. Drugs that I detested. Educating me was not an option for him.

So for my next specialist subject I embarked on teaching myself all about Lone Atrial Fibrillation. I found an LAF forum and started asking questions. I quickly realised my questions were falling on deaf ears. The forum was about moral support, not education. So I just got my head down and did some serious Googling. Eventually I found a load of book recommendations. I was off work so I spent all my limited energy learning about my newfound heart condition.

Whilst I was educating myself the cardiologist explained the next phase of his plans for me. If my heart did not kick back to normal soon, he would electrocute me with his defibrillators. DDDZZZIIITTTT! What fun, eh!

A specific jolt of electricity would be delivered to my heart, at precisely the right moment, and this would shock my heart back into a regular beat. It is a standard medical procedure with minimal chance of a problem, but still, I decided I'd better get on reading and learning about my options!

There is a 50 percent chance of the irregular heart beat returning within 12 months of the treatment. In other words, it's just a band-aid. It does nothing to solve, cure or mend the root cause, whatever that may be.

I powered through the first book which was written by someone like me. Someone who'd been sick, who'd educated himself and then wrote up the story of how he'd mostly cured himself. The next book was a lot more technical but gave a good contrast to the first. It quickly became obvious that there is no known cause and no known cure, just a multitude of mini options and lifestyle choices to make. Most of which I had already taken.

The first and obvious thing was the thyroid support I'd taken that had kicked me into LAF in the first place. The books talked about too many hormones and hyper-thyroidism being a causing factor. That was obviously part of my puzzle, but I had only taken minimal amounts of the stuff, and I had not had any for over a month and I was still supersized ill.

The most standout and suspicious problem was that all LAF victims had major nutritional deficiencies. The books detailed long lists of vitamins and minerals that would likely be out of kilter or massively lacking. Each book went into considerable detail about it, what to do and how much it would help.

Why would my body have nutritional deficiencies?

I considered my diet fantastic.

Why was my diet lacking?

The obvious cause of my nutritional shortage was because I am still mercury toxic. My last three hair tests all showed deranged mineral transport which indicates my body's inability to move the minerals to the right places. The heart books all said most LAF people had amalgam fillings too, so here's mercury showing its face again. Mercury was obviously a big reason, but I've been mercury toxic long-time-lah! Why was this problem rearing its ugly head now?

No. It must be something else too. But what?

It must be my diet. I must be doing something wrong, and it must be something I eat a lot of. I zeroed in on the oats I was eating for breakfast five times a week. My lovely homemade muesli. I knew that if I didn't prepare the oats correctly, the phytic acid would prevent absorption and cause major nutritional deficiencies. But I was preparing them correctly, wasn't I?

Each batch was pre-soaked in my raw kefir for at least 12 hours, and sometimes three or four days. This should have neutralised the phytic acid and made them super healthy.

Muscle testing the oats gave a strong negative signal. What? Why?

I got my books out and re-read the soaking information and instructions. The only minor difference was the temperature. I was using kefir from the fridge, and water at room temperature. The instructions said to use a warm soaking medium. Oh man! What? Such a small thing can't be a big deal? Can it?

I stopped eating the oats and within 24 hours I started getting better for the first time since the mega overload of problems tumbled on my head. It was blindingly obvious the oats had caused all of this fuss. The lifting of my symptoms directly after stopping eating them clearly backed up my muscle testing experiments.

Just when I needed him the muscle tester dude was in town. I prepared the oats in the normal way with cold water and kefir, and a second batch soaked with the same ingredients but warmed up instead. I took them to him and we tested them on me. His testing confirmed my body rejected the poorly prepared oats. My body didn't exactly welcome the correctly prepared oats, but the two reactions were very different. One was a violent rejection. The other was a mild shake of the head. They tasted different too and had a completely different texture; softer on the tongue. Obviously I stopped eating oats in any form.

Turns out, the heat of the soaking medium is required to kick-start the neutralisation process in the oats. Just like when you make bread, you have to use warm water to activate the yeast. Without the heat the yeast does not activate and the bread will not rise. And same with the oats: the oats needed the heat to start the neutralisation process.

There's a fine line between success and failure.

Phew, I seemed to have figured out the cause of the problem. Now I had righted the wrong, now I could get on with the getting better. Finding the root of the problem is the number one priority. You can't get better if you don't stop the wrong. It's like having a stone in your shoe. There are many potential reasons for limping, but if you want to walk normally again; you gotta understand and then remove that stone. I wondered how long this would take? Hopefully not too long.

I had been eating the incorrectly prepared oats for about three years. This had damaged my digestion, my absorption and that in turn had effected every part of my body. The result was a slow dwindling of my health. Other factors, like having deranged mineral transport will not have helped. That is why mercury poisoning is so hard: it amplifies and multiplies any other problems.

• • •

The heart problems started in June 2011 and came to a head in February 2012. It's now eight months since then, in September 2012, and I have been gradually getting better. But it's been a slow, laborious task. I have had some very miserable months as I attempted to work out how to mend three years of wrongs. I have turned the corner now, but the first seven months were absolutely desolate and wretched.

Obviously I hit the herbs, as is my way, but at first everything caused too many problems and I did not get better. Each morning I awoke with a painful lower back. I know this is a kidney signal, but the kidney herbs caused way too many side effects even for me to manage. I tried liver herbs too, but they made life unbearable and had to be stopped as well. I also tried bowel cleaning herbs at the same time as both those sets of herbs, to try and speed waste removal, but again it was just too strong for me and had to be stopped.

My heart didn't automatically flip back to normal. I found no other natural way to do it, so I had the electric shock treatment. Defibrillators powered up and blasted me back to a regular beat. How mental is that! Pretty unpleasant and scary it was too, but it worked and I have had no other heart issues since then.

I went to see as many different people as possible to see if anyone had a magic cure or solution. Acupuncture was recommended. I had appointments weekly and that helped a little. But after a while I was feeling even worse after the appointments. The lady would treat my liver or kidneys and I'd have a week of horrid and powerful detox reactions to cope with. Not fun. The acupuncturist was dumbfounded.

I had distance Reiki from an Indian guru, but I felt wildly frazzled afterwards.

I had Brennan healing which gave good initial results, but the subsequent appointments resulted in me feeling considerably worse as too much detoxing was happening.

I saw a Chinese herbal man and he tailor-made some herbs to calm my heart and system down. They were way too strong and drove my parasites wild with desire. Made my heartburn and digestive troubles flip into la-la land. I was scared out of my wits because it gave me major chest pains. I thought I was having a massive LAF episode and was about to die, again. Took six weeks to figure out the herbs did not suit. Not helpful. Not fun.

I was tested by a Vega machine man. Vega machines are electronic versions of muscle tester dudes, or something like that. The results pointed out the exact mineral deficiencies I had, so that I could target them with specific supplements. That was actually quite helpful and I loaded up with 15 different supplements to re-mineralise myself.

Also saw a traditional thyroid man as recommended by my cardiologist. That was a massive waste of time, money and energy. Guy refused to treat me and my symptoms and would only look at my lab results. Would not even give an opinion if I did or did not have adrenal or thyroid issues. Completely pointless.

I am extremely grateful for the irregular heartbeat diagnosis, but the cardiologist now considers me cured because my heart is now doing the right thing. He has no experience or understanding of how to clean up the mess this has caused, so there is no point in seeing him again. I don't want his drugs either. I stopped taking the drugs two months after the electric shock treatment.

I did have one standout success in the hands of a lovely healing lady. I have been meditating five or six times a week for three years now and I am pretty into the whole energy side of healing. I'd met Alison a few times when she was channelling and I called her into action to help. Her hands-on healing was awesome. Totally relaxed me down and turned my heart down from Richter scale 10, to a nice tranquil 3. I almost hugged her after that first appointment. I saw her weekly for a couple of months after that. She gave much needed relief and I could not have got through those toughest months without her. But after a while I plateaued out, so I stopped seeing her.

As you can see, nothing really hit the spot. The fear and panic attacks were gone, but I was feeling pretty ropey all the time. The hypoglycaemia was still horrendous. I has serious multiple chemical intolerances and was reacting to all the chemicals I came in contact with: a sure sign of a congested liver. Parasites, yeasts and Candida returned with a vengeance. My hot feet hurt like hell all the time. I lost 5kg (11 pounds) over six months because my digestion was screwed. I still had full-on nausea every morning. I slipped into uber-healthy diet mode, cut out wheat and dairy for a while, but I felt better eating them so I re-introduced them after a couple of months.

From the acupuncture, herbs, healers and symptoms I knew my bowels were blocked, my kidneys and liver were severely congested again, and my parasites were back, but attempting to detox any of them was proving way too much for my poor frazzled body.

After a while I realised I was on my own again. These helpers and healers didn't really understand what was going on in my body. Nor did I, but it was obvious I was wasting my time and money with them now I was over the worst of the initial LAF attack. Their treatments were causing too many side effects.

That's when I realised I needed to go back to basics, right back to square one. That's when I fully realised just how bad I was, and just how long this was gonna take.

How long's it gonna take?

How long's a piece of string?

I rearranged my mental mind map for another hard slog up another bloody ladder.

Anyway, back to basics. I decided to tackle each part of my body in the correct order of healing, one at a time and slowly, slowly. Giving plenty of time to clean each part separately, without trying to do other things at the same time. Starting with the easiest parts and working up through my body to the harder, more difficult things to clean. Calm, controlled and focused. Just as I should have done at the very beginning.

1) Bowel cleaning
2) Parasite cleaning
3) Liver cleaning
4) Kidney cleaning

I started with a six month psyllium and herbal bowel cleanse. I knew I could do this at the same time as other herbal formulas, but to start with I needed to do them on their own. To give myself a turbo start I also went back to the lady with the pearl necklace and had six colonics in two weeks. I was way past being squeamish: good health was massively more important now.

The colonics were not much fun, I felt very nauseous, but it reduced the hypoglycaemia by 75 percent which was a godsend. Morning nausea also reduced by 50 percent too. You know you hit the nail on the head when you get results like that! Time, money and energy well spent.

I knew then that I was correct. I just had to go back to basics. Use what I'd already learnt on my travels. Heal each part of my body one at a time and slowly get better.

I had to stop aiming to solve everything overnight, stop trying to clean all the difficult parts of me at the same time, and stop relying on other people to heal me.

I took my health firmly back into my own hands.

I had to use my hard-earned knowledge to clear the digestive tract, kill the bugs, and once that's done I could tackle the things causing the aching body, fatigue, chemical sensitivities and the hot feet: the liver and the kidneys. It is frustrating to have to go slow, but my body was unable to detox any faster.

• • •

Five weeks into the bowel cleaning operation, BMs returned to semi-normality. So next up was time for a parasite purge. A good friend smuggled in an emergency Humaworm parasite and Candida cleanse. Yeah, I have a cool set of international smugglers and dealers!

I did the parasite herbs first and that was one of the hardest cleanses I have ever done. Side effects and roughness lasted the full month. I had major painful shoulders for the whole time too: a sure sign of a congested liver. Life was difficult, depressing and I just wanted to jack the job, admit defeat and go lick my wounds somewhere calm and quiet. But I resisted the urge and just got on with the job at hand. I didn't feel much better afterwards either. It just felt like a long hard grind.

Next it was the turn of the candida herbs. I had a super furry tongue each morning, which is a clear candida signal. If the previous set of herbs was one of the hardest ever, then these candida herbs took the award for the toughest ever. Yes, even more difficult that the first set when I had the logjam,

Side effects kicked me firmly and repeated in the balls for the full 30 days. I had to reduce the dosage repeatedly in an attempt to manage the boatload of hassles that bombarded me daily.

I was dizzy, mega tired and I needed to swear even more frequently than usual. Physically I was a wreck, mentally I was in agony. Jim Carrey paid me frequent visits as the jittery cha-cha-chas returned with a vengeance. Everything was 50 times harder and more tiring than normal. Life was just miserable and I was as grumpy as hell.

Interestingly, in amongst all this hardship I had the funkiest dreams on earth. Almost every night I was having the most awesome lucid dreams imaginable. Not sure exactly what that means, but it can only be a good thing. Most of the dreams were about 'change'. Curious, eh!

When you are in the midst of all this mega detoxing, it always feels like the end of the world. Always feels like everything is screwed and there is no point in continuing. But, I've done this all before, so I hoped, really hoped like mad, that all this pain and suffering would eventually pay dividends and afterwards I'd be a little better.

And happy dayz, that's exactly what happened. After I finished the candida herbs the sky cleared, the sun came out and a warm happy friendly smile appeared on my face again. At last I'd turned the corner. I'd got that big turning point that everyone hopes for. The point of tipping from miserable declining health, to bashing through and regaining health again. This time it was the candida herbs that did it. It was like night and day, again. One moment I was miserable and suffering, the next I was out the other side, happy, healthy and healing again.

Hooray!

Hallelujah!

Phew!

Oh yes baby!

Who's the Daddy!

And you see, we still get a happy ending to the book!

Sure, I still have a ways to go, but I have unquestionably broken the camel's back. Very quickly, life returned to mostly normal again. All the physical pains faded into the background. I started gaining weight again. I was happy again. All thoughts of jacking the job retreated as my normality returned. I started thinking about beer again, always a sign that I'm feeling fine.

My dodgy hot left foot was now 90 percent better. Ear infection gone. Hypoglyceamia 95 percent gone. Tiredness reduced by 50 percent. Super furry tongue is 60 percent better. Sinus still blocked making yoga impossible and meditation weak, but less blocked. So all in all we are on the up!

This is obviously an unfinished task. I still can't work out or do anything too physical. I have still to address and unclog the liver and kidneys. And then I will have to do everything again, especially the candida herbs. But hey, that's cool, I will do that tomorrow.

During all this mess I have obviously had to take a break from chelation. I've had one year off so far. Yup, not ideal, but no way on earth could I have chelated at the same time as all these problems. No way José. I will restart once I have cleaned the liver and kidneys, so probably in four or five months' time.

After killing the bad bacteria in the gut, it's always good to build up the good afterwards. So I have started a month of probiotics to rebuild my inner wildlife. It's a yin-yang thing.

Three and a half months into the bowel cleaning operation everything is working correctly again. I stopped the psyllium after three months and now I'm just taking the herbs that stimulate the digestive tract.

I have just started the Essiac formula. These are the anti-cancer herbs. If they can cure cancer, just think how powerful they must be! Today, 10th September 2012 I am 10 days in. I am currently at two thirds of the minimum dose. Anything higher gives me wild pounding headaches. But I know, I know deep inside me, that these are the right things to take. Already my BMs have gone dark, so I know my liver and gallbladder are being detoxed. I know these will take time, minimum two months and probably four. Then will I switch to liver herbs for some months, then kidney herbs after that. Then restart chelation. But hey, the toughest part has been and gone.

I made it again.

Easy when you know how!

"The future is not set. There is no fate but what we make for ourselves."
John Connor, Terminator II: Judgement Day

So, what did I learn from all this mess?

I learnt how important attention to detail is. One silly little mistake in preparing the oats led to all this hassle. It is disappointing to have made the mistake, but I know it was amplified greatly by being mercury toxic. Such is life. I am not perfect. $hit happens.

I learnt that my Mukta Vati miracle cure for my raised blood pressure had in fact been just a band-aid. It had just masked the real problem. In curing myself I had just hidden the problem. Once the Mutka Vati had 'cured' my high blood pressure, I motored on through life, with the causative factor still doing its damage, until Boom! It led to a massive problem that's gonna take ages to tidy up. That's why I am suspicious of miracle cures. I knew there was something fishy about it. Oh well, you live and you learn.

I experienced something really strange when I was at my sickest with the LAF. I explained to people that I had a dodgy heart, I was in hospital, seeing doctors, taking drugs, and wow, I got a whole load of sympathy. Seriously, it was weird. I've had some mega serious problems these last ten years and never got much sympathy from anyone. But now I got it in spades! Everyone was super kind, thoughtful and caring. My parents came down to help. Friends called up to make sure I was okay. Work colleagues expressed sympathy! It almost felt like I was milking it. Odd, eh!

I put it down to understanding. People understand what a dodgy heartbeat means. They understand it is a serious problem, just like having cancer or a brain tumour. Muggles don't understand mercury poisoning, parasites, adrenal or thyroid fatigue or many of the problems I endured. And if people don't understand, they can't empathise. Deep, eh!

It was odd learning about a new health topic: Lone Atrial Fibrillation. I found the doctors and the way they handled my problems totally unchanged. There was no attempt to get to the root cause of the problem. No attempt to educate me so I could help myself. And their treatments did nothing to actually solve the problem. All the drugs did was manage the situation.

It reinforced my need to continue chelation. I need to get the mercury out because problems will perpetually plague me if I don't.

Why did my parasites take over again? Well because my immune system was down, again. When the immune system is not strong enough to defend itself, the predators sweep in and take over. (okay, I didn't learn anything new on that one, more a sharp reminder!)

Was else did I learn? Well, maybe when I'm feeling fine I should enjoy it even more!

Big sigh…and that really is the end now. That's more than enough. I'm getting better and I'm definitely on the mend after that crisis. There will be good days and bad days; I will handle them as they come.

Thanks for reading my story. Goodbye, take good care of yourself. I wish you well on your journey. I hope my experiences help you help yourself.

Sunshine
10th September 2012

You can email me if you want to say hello, or maybe tell me some of your journey. Or even better, tell me of the success you've had. I always love that. We live in an amazing world and hearing of people's marvellous triumphs always makes me laugh and smile.

Email: sunshinep1969@gmail.com

I also have a blog with details of all my chelation rounds, herbal cleanses and anything else funky that I discover: www.mercurydiaries.com

Further reading about heart problems:
Lone Atrial Fibrillation ebook by Hans R Larsen
The High Blood Pressure Solution by R. Moore
The Sinatra Solution: Metabolic Cardiology by S. Sinatra
The Magnesium Factor by Seelig & Rosanoff

CPSIA information can be obtained at www.ICGtesting.com
Printed in the USA
LVOW101924061112

306130LV00002B/4/P